"WE CAN THANK *Masterpiece Theatre's producers for delivering that rarity in modern promotion: products that they promised with their ambitious title. For a quarter of a century, their offerings, with remarkably few exceptions, truly have been masterpieces of the modern theater.*"

Walter Cronkite

"MASTERPIECE THEATRE *is the only program that makes us put down our books and turn on the television. We wouldn't miss a single one!*"

Joanne Woodward and
Paul Newman

"TELEVISION OFTEN BRINGS *the guilty escapism of reading a tabloid, but turning on Masterpiece Theatre is like a great novel—it opens passages to the self and the world.*"

Gloria Steinem

"MASTERPIECE THEATRE *is entitled to a masterfully organized celebration of its anniversary. It has brought so many hours of pleasure, so marvelously presented and introduced. I am confident that in the 21st Century it will be recognized as a vital part of our cultural heritage.*"

William F. Buckley, Jr.

"MASTERPIECE THEATRE *shows are equal to the best serious Hollywood dramas and, in most cases, are far better. Every library should retain as many of the available productions as possible so that young people will have an opportunity to view the best, now and in the future.*"

Ed Koch

"MASTERPIECE THEATRE *is in the top five of all the shows I enjoy or have ever enjoyed on television, and I'm not even sure what the other four are! The pageantry, the drama, the passion, the story line are beyond compare ... shall we say master pieces?*"

Helen Gurley Brown

A
CELEBRATION OF
25 YEARS
OF OUTSTANDING
TELEVISION

Masterpiece

Theatre

❧

TERRENCE O'FLAHERTY

Interviews by *Ron Miller*

Edited by *Karen Sharpe*

Reminiscences by *Alistair Cooke*

Foreword by *Russell Baker*

KQED BOOKS

SAN FRANCISCO

Vice President for Publishing & New Ventures: Mark K. Powelson

Publisher: Pamela Byers
Project Editor: Karen Sharpe
Researcher: Ellen Baskin
Research Consultant: Nathan Hasson
Editorial Assistance: Amy Einsohn, Kim Haglund, Mu'frida Bell, Trisha Feuerstein, Andrea Buffa, Romesh Ratnesar, Alex Lyon
Book design: Marianne Ackerman, Patricia Koren, Laurie Smith, Gordon Smith

KQED President & CEO: Mary G. F. Bitterman

Photographs in this book are used by the kind permission of the copyright holders, as follows: British Broadcasting Corporation (front cover, four bottom photos, pages II top left, bottom left, III, 18-35, 47-55, 62-81, 92-96, 123-127, 138-141, 148-157, 164-167, 174-180, 186-201, 204-205, 208-211, 213 bottom, 214 left, 215-217, 219 left, 220, 221 top, 222, 224-225, back cover top, middle); *TV Times* (36-39, 40 top, bottom, 41 top, 42 right, 43 top right, bottom left, 44-45, 83 top, 84 bottom, 85 bottom, 86 top, 89 top, middle, 91, 97-101, 112-122, 206 left, 207, 212, 219 right); Granada Television (II bottom right, 128-137, 142, 168-173, 213 top, 218, back cover bottom); London Weekend Television (front cover top, 40 middle, 41 middle, bottom, 42 left, 43 top left, lower right, 82, 83 bottom, 84 top, middle, 85 top, 86 bottom, 87-88, 89 bottom, 90, 214 right); Channel 4 (II upper right, 158-163); Henry Crawford (108-111); Central Television (223 top); London Management (206 right); WGBH (2, 10, 221 bottom); Frank Conner (223 bottom); Christopher Sarson (6); John Hawkesworth (56); Andrew Davies (102).

Posters are used courtesy of Mobil Corporation and: Chermayeff and Geismar (pages VI, 202, 232, 245), The Pushpin Group (4, 240), and Paul Davis (14).

We thank the following publishers for permission to reprint excerpts: Atheneum Publishers for excerpts from *Portrait of a Marriage* by Nigel Nicolson, *Chicago Sun-Times* for a review of *Edward and Mrs. Simpson*, *Connoisseur* for a review of *Bleak House*, *Mirabella* for a review of *Traffik*, *New York Magazine* for a review of *Middlemarch*.

The *Masterpiece Theatre* name is copyright by WGBH-TV and used by permission.

Educational and non-profit groups wishing to order this book at attractive quantity discounts may contact KQED Books & Tapes, 2601 Mariposa St., San Francisco, CA 94110.

Library of Congress Cataloguing-in-Publication Data
O'Flaherty, Terrence
        Masterpiece theatre : a celebration of 25 years of outstanding television / Terrence O'Flaherty ; interviews by Ron Miller ; edited by Karen Sharpe ; with reminiscences by Alistair Cooke and a foreword by Russell Baker.
                p.   cm.
        ISBN 0-912333-74-X (pbk.)
        1. Masterpiece theatre (Television program)   I. Sharpe, Karen.
        II. Title.
        PN1992.77.M293046   1995
        791.45'72—dc20   95-38710
                                                CIP

ISBN 0-912333-74-X

Manufactured in the United States of America
10 9 8 7 6 5 4 3 2 1

Photographs on the title page are from: (left side, clockwise from upper left) *Anna Karenina, Traffik, Jeeves and Wooster,* and *Shoulder to Shoulder*; (right side) *Elizabeth R.*

Distributed to the trade by Publishers Group West

IN MEMORIAM

MICHAEL ALDRIDGE

HARRY ANDREWS

DAME PEGGY ASHCROFT

ANGELA BADDELEY

STANLEY BAKER

RALPH BATES

JOAN BENHAM

JILL BENNETT

COLIN BLAKELY

JEREMY BRETT

GEORGIA BROWN

CYRIL CUSACK

FABIA DRAKE

DENHOLM ELLIOTT

DAME EDITH EVANS

MICHAEL HORDERN

GORDON JACKSON

DAVID LANGTON

RAY MCANALLY

CATHLEEN NESBITT

SIR LAURENCE OLIVIER

DONALD PLEASENCE

ERIC PORTER

ALASTAIR SIM

GWEN WATFORD

JOAN WILSON, *Executive Producer*
Masterpiece Theatre, WGBH Boston, 1973-1985
DALI CAHILL, *Associate Producer*
Masterpiece Theatre, 1977-1991

---

*I would like to dedicate this book to
Philo T. Farnsworth who produced the world's first
all-electronic television picture in San Francisco on
September 7, 1927, an achievement equal to Edison's
phonograph and Bell's telephone, and which forever
transformed the way we live and eventually provided
the stage for Masterpiece Theatre's enchanted
playhouse in the sky.*

Terrence O'Flaherty

For Darla

Ron Miller

*For David Gancher, for his excellent advice
and support*

Karen Sharpe

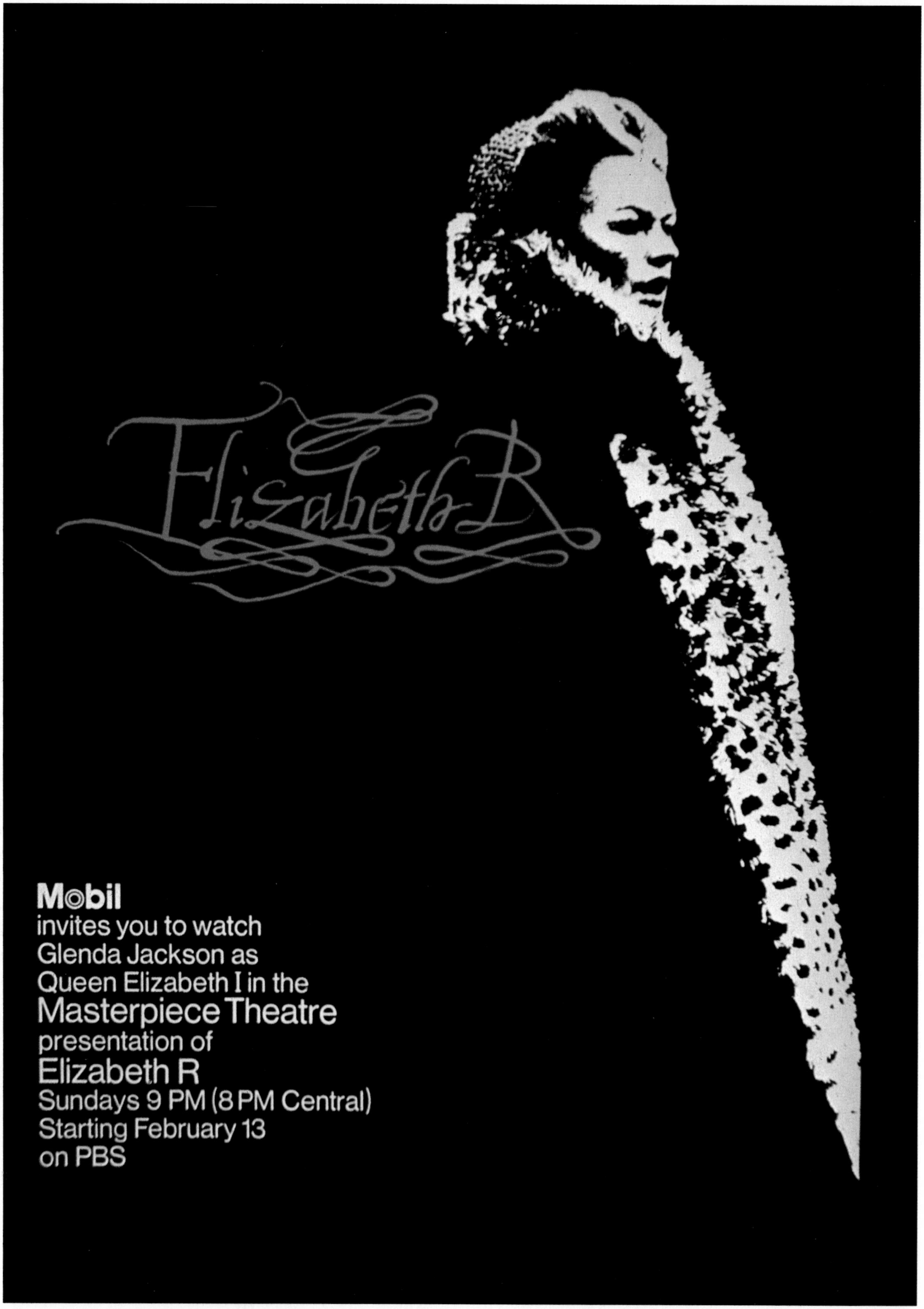

Elizabeth R

M⊙bil
invites you to watch
Glenda Jackson as
Queen Elizabeth I in the
Masterpiece Theatre
presentation of
Elizabeth R
Sundays 9 PM (8 PM Central)
Starting February 13
on PBS

Acknowledgments

A BOOK OF THIS SIZE and complexity could only have been done with the tireless help and generous support of many individuals and organizations, for which we are most grateful. To all of you who made this book possible, a big round of applause and heartfelt thanks.

Beginning at the beginning, we are very grateful to Mark Powelson for dreaming of a Masterpiece Theatre book in the first place, and to Pamela Byers for assuring that his dream could become a reality. Our warm thanks to WGBH for encouragement, connections, and access to their archives: most especially to Rebecca Eaton, Karen Johnson, Mary Cahill Farella, and Virginia Jackson. Nathan Hasson, who worked for ten years in the Masterpiece Theatre office, served as our eminently informed consultant, answering questions from the frivolous to the frantic and reviewing the manuscript during its many iterations.

Across the Atlantic, our friends at the television production companies in Britain were incredibly forthcoming in helping us find and allowing us to use the many exquisite photographs that appear in this book. At the BBC we wish to thank Laura Clarke, Bobbie Mitchell, and Nicola Smith for making arrangements for and duping some 750 transparencies. At *TV Times* (part of IPC Magazines), Peter Genower and Jo Laycock were most generous in opening up their photo files to us. Our thanks, too, to Elaine Collins and Kathryn de Belle at Granada, Shane Chapman at London Weekend Television, and Louise Fawkner-Corbett at Channel 4. From down under, Henry Crawford very kindly sent us the only existing photographs of *A Town Like Alice*. Also, we extend our thanks to Rachel Lynch at Ashgate Publishing for allowing us to use portions of *Serials on British Television* (by Ellen Baskin) in compiling the filmographies. And thanks, too, to the many British and American publishers who kindly granted us permission to use excerpts from their newspapers and magazines.

In New York, Ellen Frey generously gave us access to some 30 boxes of Masterpiece Theatre files at Michael Shepley PR, while Aisha Sharpe had the thankless task of copying those files. A special thanks to Frank Goodman, who not only filled in informational gaps, but produced much of the materials in those files when he headed the public relations effort for Mobil. For use of the gorgeous posters, we are grateful to Mobil Corporation and Chermayeff and Geismar, The Pushpin Group, and Paul Davis.

On the home front, our wonderful writers Terrence O'Flaherty, Ron Miller, and Ellen Baskin shared their knowledge of and love for Masterpiece Theatre in a way that made this book a true celebration, while Amy Einsohn, Kim Haglund, Mu'frida Bell, Andrea Buffa, Romesh Ratnesar, and Trisha Feuerstein helped assure correct use of language and factual accuracy, and the design team—Marianne Ackerman, Pat Koren, Laurie Smith, and Gordon Smith—did wonders with the mass of material we gave them.

And lastly, but surely foremostly, we extend our eternal gratitude to all the producers, directors, writers, actors, and behind-the-scenes personnel who created the magnificent productions that prompted us to publish this celebratory book. And to Mobil Corporation for making this superb series possible.

—Karen Sharpe

Thanks to Our Supporters

Henry P. Becton, Jr.
President and General Manager
WGBH, Boston

IT'S HARD TO BELIEVE it's been 25 years since we first brought Alistair Cooke into our studios to introduce PBS viewers nationwide to a new series we hoped would become a weekly television theater. He was sufficiently dubious about the success of this venture to keep his "day job" and sign only a one-year contract. He needn't have worried.

Masterfully hosted first by Alistair and since 1993 by Russell Baker, Masterpiece Theatre has entertained millions with the best British drama available anywhere on television. We celebrate this important birthday by showcasing our finest works, and by honoring public broadcasting's greatest corporate friend: Mobil Corporation, the series' sole funder for a quarter of a century.

Mobil agreed to fund Masterpiece Theatre in the belief that as a corporation helps preserve and enhance society's best values, it creates a more beneficial environment for all. That philosophy still fuels Mobil's commitment today. We couldn't be more pleased than to have the series linked with a company that values excellence and respects the intelligence of the American people.

In an age of disposable television, how do we keep a show like Masterpiece Theatre fresh? Start with gifted producers: Christopher Sarson, who originated the series; Joan Wilson, who succeeded him; and Rebecca Eaton, who's been at the helm since 1985. Add great material and talent from our partners in England. Keep the series in tune with the times by mixing in some contemporary stories and American authors with the British masters, and by presenting some miniseries over consecutive days rather than weeks. And have the good fortune to team up with the nation's most committed and generous funder of public broadcasting.

It takes a long time to develop drama projects and it takes a long time to make them the way we feel they deserve to be made—with intelligence and integrity. Mobil has given us the freedom to pursue the very best productions and the very best partners. Our thanks to Mobil for its generous support, and our thanks to you, our fans, for tuning in for 25 years of great drama. Onward to the next 25...

A Word from WGBH

Rebecca Eaton
Executive Producer
Masterpiece Theatre

LIKE MOST OF YOU, I first met Alistair Cooke while sitting on the couch in my living room. I was in my bathrobe. He, I believe, was wearing a suit from Savile Row.

I was a fan of Masterpiece Theatre for years before it was my extreme good fortune to become its executive producer in 1985. Like you, I scheduled my Sundays around sitting on the couch at 9 p.m. I was there when Sarah had her baby during the Bellamy's dinner party on *Upstairs, Downstairs.* I was there for the first note of the imperial theme music of every episode of *The Jewel in the Crown.*

Because the television landscape is now so crowded with choices, it's hard to remember that Masterpiece Theatre invented Sunday nights as *the* time to broadcast dramatic miniseries. It was a new idea in January 1971, pre-*Roots,* and viewers over the years have made the series "appointment" viewing.

So much has changed in the television industry over 25 years that Masterpiece Theatre's survival is quite remarkable. *I, Claudius* ran for 13 weeks, but today a "long-run" or "major" miniseries is merely three or four episodes. Much has changed at Masterpiece Theatre during that time also. Until we aired the taut, contemporary political thriller *A Very British Coup* in 1989 (one of my personal favorites), Masterpiece Theatre had rarely done material set any later than 1950. With that program, we dis-covered that viewers were happy to venture into the late 20th century occasionally. Today nearly half of our programming is contemporary.

But our mainstay and trademark is literature, first-class adaptations of good books. Through the talent and creativity of our British partners, who, after all, make these programs, Masterpiece Theatre has single-handedly served up the likes of Charles Dickens, Henry James, Thomas Hardy, Jane Austen, Joseph Conrad, George Eliot, and Edith Wharton to millions of American television viewers. This feat, perhaps more than any other, is the lasting cultural contribution that Masterpiece Theatre, under the auspices of WGBH and our loyal underwriter, Mobil Corporation, has made.

We live in an age of dwindling attention spans and disposable television. The noise level of all the "entertainment" options competing for our consideration is deafening. Don't you occasionally find yourself more tired and jangled after an hour of trying to find something to watch on TV than you were before you sat down? The challenge for Masterpiece Theatre is to maintain its standards of quality in this ear-splitting din, to continue to provide well-written, beautifully produced, provocative, and thoughtful programs that will transport you to another time and place and to a new awareness.

Masterpiece Theatre has had a great run over 25 years and we're extraordinarily lucky to have the opportunity to revitalize the icon we've become. Not many institutions get the chance.

Table of Contents

Foreword

by Russell Baker

JOINING THE MASTERPIECE Theatre company in its twenty-third year—the new boy on the block, as it were—I anticipated a few humbling experiences and, sure enough, humbling quickly came my way.

First off, innocent as a newborn, I knew the secret of being comfortable, charming, and irresistible on television. "Just be yourself." That was the way I thought of it. Just be myself. So that's what I did when filming the first show—just be myself.

Reader, should you ever have to go before a TV camera, take my advice: Do not, whatever the provocation, just be yourself.

That self of mine, when I saw it weeks later on the first Sunday night of the 1993 season, was a self in torment. It had hands that twisted and writhed like Lady Macbeth's while the rest of this miserable self looked as if it were being swallowed by an enormous chair.

Afterward, it was bad enough having close friends and utter strangers all over America write pleading with me to never again just be myself. Worse than that, the show being introduced—*Selected Exits*—starred Anthony Hopkins.

Anthony Hopkins! Is there a more magnificently calm, collected, under-control actor anywhere in the world than Anthony Hopkins? I had shared billing with this consummate professional, and had come across as the consummate amateur.

Well, I was a writer of course, not a performer, and so what if I was not Anthony Hopkins before the camera? I had my prose style to show off with. My field, after all, was literature, not the performing arts, and in the vast, fevered, hyperthyroid, chase-ridden, blood-soaked, bullet-riddled world of television where even the end of the world will have to wait until right after these messages, Masterpiece Theatre was the unique and enduring fortress of literature.

Alas, unique and enduring fortress it was all right, but it had endured uniquely by clinging stubbornly to its faith in writers like Shakespeare, Jane Austen, Balzac, Tolstoy, Dostoyevsky, Dickens, George Eliot, Henry James, E. M. Forster, Evelyn Waugh—

Well, in short, Masterpiece Theatre wanted the host to keep it short. Just quietly open the door for the guests, take their coats, see them comfortably settled, then disappear and let the stars perform. Some introductions had to be got through in a mere four or five sentences. It was rare to have as much as 250 words—slightly more than a single typed page double-spaced.

Books with 100,000 words I could write and 700-word newspaper columns I could write, but in these miniature introductions nothing was possible. Nothing! Was that all they wanted—this nothing? To say anything that was interesting in that cramped space would be like trying to stage a ballet in a telephone booth.

Ah yes, another thing: No long sentences. No long words. Shakespearean actors may be able to do them, but most of us cannot, not in front of a TV camera. Here, for instance, in this piece you are now reading there is scarcely a sentence that would not have to have most of the gas let out of it or be chopped down or completely rewritten in a speaking diction if it were meant to be read on television. Words of which a writer may be particularly fond have to be abandoned because they are particularly difficult to get the tongue around. A particularly good example is the word "particularly."

I recite all this with some pride. It is my slyly modest way of boasting about how much I've learned since that first rocky outing with Anthony Hopkins. Starting from a base of total ignorance and learning strange new work from the ground up is my idea of enjoying myself. It helps, of course, when the work is with something as elegant and as important to so many people as Masterpiece Theatre is. In a medium famously destructive to the printed word, Masterpiece Theatre has created and held a caring audience for 25 years. It strikes me as remarkable that a television show based on devotion to books should have succeeded through a quarter-century that has been notoriously hostile to bookishness.

Can it be that reports of the death of the book are grossly exaggerated? Vital people keep telling us books have reached the end of the road. Television, movies, talk radio, car telephones, computers, digital libraries, cyberfun galore—with so many gaudy delights competing for our favor in this busy, busy, busy age, books are said to be doomed. We are talking now about book books, the kind of books they used to tell you about in high school, not non-books, how-to books, cookbooks, self-help books, tabloid books, or comic books, but honest-to-goodness book books.

So how to explain the durability of Masterpiece Theatre? Part of the explanation has been Mobil's generosity in underwriting it from the beginning. Public television stations immediately discovered a substantial audience waiting for such a show, which must have amazed many an analyst of American culture. Words like "masterpiece" and "classics," after all, had become sneers in a world where commercial TV people sometimes told you apologetically that their job was just to "give the slobs what they want."

During my early tenure with Masterpiece Theatre I was surprised to discover how passionately viewers were devoted to it, cared about it, and worried about it. In talking about the feminist show *The Rector's Wife,* I made the mistake of saying there was an analogy between the heroine's fictional problems and Hillary Clinton's in real-life. Vociferous protests came in the mail from fans: How dare I contaminate their favorite show with such sly political poison? Though the programs are often packed with fictional politics, viewers, it seemed, felt that any reference to real-world politics violated some kind of high institutional devotion audiences feel toward the show.

The harshest critics? They are the people with a lifelong love for a classic like *Middlemarch* or *Martin Chuzzlewit.* Inevitably, they find the dramatization at best a disappointment, at worst an unforgiveable botch. They berate the scriptwriter, abuse the set designer, denounce the cinematographer, and scold the host.

Since the supply of masterpieces is finite, the show also dramatizes books that are not yet acclaimed masterpieces, and may never be. Now and then a book whose own author would blanch to hear it called a masterpiece gets itself dramatized into a triumphant show. Why? Because a brilliant television writer throws out almost everything but the title and basic idea and turns out a masterpiece of its own. It shows what miracles can be passed if you don't think of the audience as "the slobs."

In the Beginning

SUNDAY EVENING, January 10, 1971, was the end of a typical winter weekend all across America. Television viewers who were tuned to *The First Churchills* did not know that they were watching television history in the making: the beginning of a westward flow of British dramatic entertainment unmatched in quality and diversity in this country. That night PBS viewers witnessed the premiere offering of a new series called Masterpiece Theatre without realizing they were taking their seats in an imaginary playhouse that would scan the shelves of classic and contemporary literature to deliver a series of unforgettable and eminently entertaining television dramas.

Masterpiece Theatre came at a point in time when the quality of American commercial television entertainment was deteriorating and when programming was increasingly being directed at youngsters, often at the expense of their elders. Viewers who weren't interested in bimbos in peril or teenagers in heat were forced to join The Lost Audience, doomed to wander the television wasteland looking in vain for entertainment that didn't upset their intelligence, their tastes, or their stomach. Into this bleak landscape stepped a few visionaries at WGBH in Boston who set the stage for Masterpiece Theatre, a television playhouse devoted to dramatic adaptations of great fiction and significant biography.

The appeal of such dramas had already been demonstrated by the adulation of viewers who devotedly tuned in once a week to *The Forsyte Saga*, the first British serial drama aired in this country. That was in 1969, the year *Sesame Street* premiered over the fledgling Public Broadcasting System (PBS), which had, in turn, been stimulated by the Carnegie Commission's indictment of American television as a "vast wasteland." As WGBH and other early educational stations were forming themselves into PBS, WGBH was beginning the work of creating Masterpiece Theatre.

This new series took off with an overwhelmingly rich profusion of offerings—eleven in the first season alone (*The Six Wives of Henry VIII*, *Elizabeth R*, *The Possessed*, *Pere Goriot*, and *The Last of the Mohicans* among them). Thanks in part to the popularity of those productions, PBS gained tremendous support and has continued to serve as a venue for the outstanding programming crossing these shores from Great Britain. Mobil has seen to it that these dramas always travel first class, and Alistair Cooke and Russell Baker have been our brilliant stewards, bringing a style and insight equal to the productions.

And the rest is history, a history that is still being made on Sunday evenings on television sets across the country.

Masterpiece Theatre's Founding Father

Christopher Sarson

JOHN CHRISTOPHER "CHRIS" SARSON was the founding father of Masterpiece Theatre and served as its first executive producer from 1970 to 1973, followed by the late Joan Wilson and her successor, Rebecca Eaton.

Born in London in 1935, Sarson graduated with honors from Trinity College, Cambridge, in 1960, and worked as a producer and director for Granada Television. In 1963 he came to America to work in public television, first at WETA-TV in Washington, D.C., then at WGBH-TV in Boston. He also created and produced the Emmy-winning PBS children's show, *Zoom,* and produced PBS' *Live from the Met* from 1977 to 1979 and Nickelodeon's *Kid's Writes* from 1982 to1983.

Based in Boulder, Colorado, he's now an independent producer of television programs including *Parenting Works,* a 13-episode PBS series scheduled for fall 1996.

Should we assume your classical English education at Cambridge University had something to do with the creation of Masterpiece Theatre?

Sarson I think it's one of those myths that probably ought to be propagated. Actually, I started reading classic novels much earlier. I remember reading my first Thomas Hardy novel at 13. I was absolutely bowled over by it, so I read another and another. It wasn't really Cambridge, but just my genuine love of good stories.

You went to Cambridge to study law and accounting. What made you switch to a career in television?

Sarson It was absolutely by accident. It was quite clear after the second year that I wasn't going to be a lawyer, accountant, or anything quite as good as that. I had been playing double bass in the theater orchestra to earn money, and music kind of took over. I had a bigamous grandfather who was a clarinetist in a local orchestra, so I suppose there's a streak of perversity in the family somewhere.

I ended up doing a lot of theatrical stuff. I wrote the music for a play, and people from London came up to review it. Someone from Granada Television came backstage and asked if I'd ever thought about doing music for television. I was going to be the music director at the Bristol Old Vic, but they were paying £25 a week and Granada was offering £35, so I went off to Manchester to be an intern there.

What effect did that training have on your subsequent career plans?

Sarson They made interns spend a week in every department, so we got an overview of the company. At the end, they asked us what we wanted to do. Most of us wanted to be directors. They gave us shows to direct that nobody watched. They started you off with religious programs. Later, I was the director of a Welsh-language program called *Good Afternoon.* Then you went on to children's programming and finally to adult soaps and that kind of stuff. When the opportunity to do arts programming came up, I just jumped at it.

Going from an internship at Granada to working in American public television seems like a giant leap. How did that happen?

Sarson I got married in 1963, and we came over on our honeymoon. We were planning to go around the world, and we had set out for America by boat, but my wife's seasickness turned out to be morning sickness. We had the baby, bought a house, and stayed in America.

I worked for a year in Washington for WETA, which then was operating out of a schoolhouse in Arlington, Virginia, then joined WGBH in Boston. WGBH in those days was in the basement of the Museum of Science.

What was the creative atmosphere like in those early days of public television at WGBH, before the PBS network was born?

Sarson I was a neophyte in the business, the country, and everything. I was still in the "omigosh" stage of wonderment. It was a vital, enormously exciting place to be. We were doing programming that had never been done before. People allowed you to do things in a way that was significantly different from stuffy old England.

For example, when I got to Boston, I was given the program *Performance.* It was a very staid program with people dressed in penguin suits playing in a string quartet. It was real boring. So, with a kind of English trepidation, I asked if we could turn it into something a bit more interesting. The program manager yawned and said, "Sure." So we turned it into a rehearsal, done all in shirt sleeves. We had a ball with it, the audience watched it, and the people who took part loved it. People were very ready for those ideas.

Was the concept for Masterpiece Theatre inspired by the tremendous popularity in America of the BBC's serial drama The Forsyte Saga, *and the failure of anyone else to follow it up?*

Sarson That's exactly right. It was quite clear they had whetted the audience's appetite with *The Forsyte Saga.* I was a kind of leader of a group that said "let's do serialized drama." There was no serialized drama—no *Roots,* not anything like that on television.

How did you bring the idea to life?

Sarson I went to [General Manager] Stan Calderwood with the idea. He was from Polaroid and was new at WGBH. Everybody was very suspicious of him because he was a commercial entity. But he just grasped the idea. Like any astute businessman, he wanted to make his mark. He reckoned Mobil would be the right company for something like this. Within a couple of weeks, he had put me in touch with Herb Schmertz, who was the public relations vice-president for Mobil.

How long did it take to get the project rolling?

Sarson This was a show that came together in about three to four days—all of the planning for the last 25 years. It was just plain luck. First, *The Forsyte Saga* was a 26-week series. It just went on and on and gave us time to produce a show. If it had only been a 13-week series, by the time the public appetite had been whetted, we would not have been able to muster the forces necessary to get Masterpiece Theatre on the air. As it was, we were able to follow *The Forsyte Saga* with the first episode of Masterpiece Theatre.

How similar was your original concept to the Masterpiece Theatre that finally went on the air?

Sarson It was very different from the way it panned out. In my innocence, I didn't want to be just importing programs. I wanted to produce our own programs in America. So the scheme we presented to Mobil was that we would continue whetting the audience's appetite for a three-year period, and over that three years we would muster our own forces so we could begin a series of weekly presentations of our own dramas. The huge disappointment to me is that it didn't turn to American serial dramas.

That first season, 1971–72, was packed with eleven different productions, including the wildly popular Elizabeth R *with Glenda Jackson and* The Six Wives of Henry VIII *with Keith Michell. How did you put together such an awesome opening lineup?*

Sarson There was no cassette-swapping between countries, so I had to spend two to three weeks in England looking for shows. We had a five-year backlog of shows in color that we could pick from, and we picked the cream of those. We concentrated on the BBC before we went to other companies because they had the best track record and inventory of material.

Alistair Cooke calls you "the young rogue of an Englishman" who talked him into hosting Masterpiece Theatre for more than 20 years. What was behind that legendary negotiation?

Sarson I'll tell you the real story. I felt the host should be English, but Cooke was even more ideal because he was "transatlantic"—an Englishman living in America. He had been the host of *Omnibus* and was filming the NBC show *America* at that time. When I called Cooke, he said no, because he didn't want his image from *Omnibus* to be tarnished before he was seen in the *America* series.

Then he came up to Boston and borrowed the WGBH crew to film there. So I went with the crew. After the shooting, we had drinks, and his daughter Susan was there. She listened to me pleading with him to be the host, but he said no again. That was at the beginning of November.

We interviewed dozens of people who just didn't measure up. So we began writing a visual introduction to the show because we didn't have a host. We had to go on the air in January. Just as we were going out to lunch, a phone call came, and it was Cooke. He said he'd spent Thanksgiving with his daughter and she had convinced him I was right, that it wouldn't do him any harm to be the host of Masterpiece Theatre. So we put together the first six shows rather quickly.

Some critics, including Alistair Cooke, thought the opening show, The First Churchills, *was something less than a masterpiece, even though it was popular and its star, Susan Hampshire, won an Emmy. Did you have reservations about it?*

Sarson I was very determined that this should be a success, but anyone who thought they should open the series with *The First Churchills* was really out of his mind. We were supposed to do serialized dramas of classic books, but *The First Churchills* was not a classic book. It wasn't even a terribly good script, wasn't very well shot, and the acting behind the wigs and masks was pretty lousy.

So why did we do it? Well, Susan Hampshire had just finished *The Forsyte Saga,* so everybody knew her. Then the name Churchill was in the title, and that was another reason they were going to watch.

One of your other long-standing contributions to Masterpiece Theatre was choosing the theme music. How did that come about?

Sarson In 1962 my future wife and I went to one of the Club Med villages in Italy. We were in these little straw huts and every morning we were summoned to breakfast by that theme. It was just magic. I found out it was "Symphonies and Fanfares for the King's Supper" by the French composer Mouret. I wanted to use it for Masterpiece Theatre, but there was no way I could bear to put a French piece of music on something that was supposed to be English. I went through all kinds of English composers and nothing worked. So, it became the theme. The nice little twist on that is that about five years ago someone from the *New York Times* went to a Club Med in Mexico and commented on what a classy joint it was because they used the music of Masterpiece Theatre to summon people to meals.

Speaking of long-standing contributions, isn't that your voice saying "Masterpiece Theatre is brought to you by a grant from Mobil Corporation"?

Sarson Yes, they still let me do that, which is rather nice.

Why did you leave WGBH after the first three years of Masterpiece Theatre?

Sarson It was the exhaustion of running two nationally successful shows, Masterpiece Theatre and *Zoom.* In those days, I was too greedy to give either of them up. It was also the fact that WGBH wouldn't give me a raise to what I thought was appropriate.

It was just the right time for my career. I'd been at WGBH for ten years. In spite of the fun I was having and the work I was doing, I had been very much restricted to the public television sector. I wanted to get out and flap my wings a bit. I've never regretted it.

When you look at Masterpiece Theatre today, are you a proud parent?

Sarson I left Masterpiece Theatre when it was three years old. I didn't look at my own kids when they were three and wonder what they'd be like at 25. But they actually turned out very well—and so has Masterpiece Theatre. ❦

Our Hospitable Host for 22 Years

Alistair Cooke

FOR 22 YEARS, Alistair Cooke was the face—some say the soul—of Masterpiece Theatre. A cultured and insouciant host, he was also warm, witty, and eternally hospitable—the ideal chap to find sitting in your family room, preferably in a Chippendale chair, cheerfully waiting to explain anything you might need to know to better enjoy the latest chapter of Masterpiece Theatre.

Born Alfred Alistair Cooke on November 20, 1908, in Manchester, England, he came to America in the early 1930s with a distinguished Cambridge education and pursued additional studies at both Yale and Harvard. Primed for a career as a writer and critic, Cooke was diverted into a broadcasting career, first as a film critic for the BBC. A U.S. citizen since 1941, Cooke worked as a U.S.-based BBC foreign correspondent from 1938 to 1942, then began—in March 1946—what is now the longest-running radio program of all time, his weekly *Letter from America,* which he still writes and broadcasts for the BBC.

Cooke agreed to become the first host for PBS's Masterpiece Theatre when it went on the air in 1971. Then 62, Cooke already was a world-renowned broadcaster, author, and lecturer whose earlier TV hosting jobs included *Omnibus,* the most celebrated cultural program of the early 1950s.

As the host of Masterpiece Theatre, he offered his pungent observations of the relevant social, economic, and cultural backgrounds well laced with his impish sense of humor. He skillfully created the illusion he was merely having a quiet conversation, sharing a bit of social, political, and cultural background to that night's episode.

In 1992 Cooke stunned millions of loyal fans by announcing he would step down as host of the series. Russell Baker took over as host early in the 1993–94 season. Cooke continues to write and record his radio broadcasts in New York City, but he agreed to a rare interview at his favorite "home away from home," the Alistair Cooke penthouse suite at the Huntington Hotel on San Francisco's Nob Hill, where he talked about his long association with Masterpiece Theatre.

Long before Masterpiece Theatre, you were an internationally respected broadcaster. How did it all begin?

Cooke I don't have any theories about destiny or fate, but I can focus on one newspaper headline that totally dictated the rest of my life. I was here from 1932 to 1934 on what was then known as a Commonwealth fellowship. At the end of the two years, of course, the world outside began to reverberate a little, saying, What about a job?

I was walking out in Boston on a very fine spring day when I saw this headline on a newspaper: "BBC Fires PM's Son." The PM was British Prime Minister Stanley Baldwin, and his son was Oliver Baldwin, who was the BBC's film critic. If he had not been the prime minister's son, I'm certain I wouldn't have read about it and wouldn't be here now. The last sentence of the article said, "Now the BBC is looking for another film critic."

I immediately went to Western Union and wrote out a cablegram to "the Director of Talks"—I presumed there must be such a character at the BBC—and asked if I would be considered as a prospect. By the grace of God, when the BBC director looked at this cablegram, at his elbow was Desmond McCarthy, the BBC's book critic, who said, "Wait a minute. I think this man did a series on Hollywood in this summer's *Observer.*"

They looked the articles over and decided I'd be worth interviewing. So I went over on the *Aquitania* and walked into the BBC. A very languid, authoritative type said, "Well, we have to have an example of what you sound like." I was 25 and full of gall, so I said, "Give me a typewriter and 15 minutes and I'll bang out something on the last film I saw." I did that, recorded it, and they sent it over to the director, who said, "Call those other people and dismiss them. The job's filled."

By the time you became the first host of Masterpiece Theatre in 1971, you had become an American citizen and built a career around your observations of our culture. For that reason, the series' first producer, Christopher Sarson, felt you were the ideal guide to lead the American audience through a series of British dramas. Yet you turned down his offer because you didn't want to pre-empt any interest in your upcoming television history of America. But isn't it true that you had always wanted to do something like the assignment Sarson had in mind?

Cooke Yes. I liked the idea of doing something like a three- or four-minute piece on the life of Balzac or Thomas Hardy or something, trying to get it so concise that you don't have a spare word. I had reached the age where I liked clarity and condensation. My attitude is, Make your point and sit down.

So how did your daughter Susan convince you to change your mind?

Cooke We were up in Connecticut for Thanksgiving sitting around before dinner and Susan said, "I can see your scruple about it, but the people who are going to see this on public television are going to watch *America* anyway, whereas a lot of people who are going to see *America* are not going to see this, so you're going to have two audiences. The ones who like you on Masterpiece Theatre are certainly going to watch *America*."

So I called Chris and asked if he was still looking for a host. As it turned out, he was.

How long did you expect to do it?

Cooke I think it was just for the first season and a little beyond—to the spring of 1973. At the time, that sounded like 2010 or something. It just grew from there.

There's a persistent rumor that you almost lost heart when you sat down and watched The First Churchills, *which was to be the debut of Masterpiece Theatre as well as your first hosting assignment.*

Cooke It was probably the worst series we've ever done. I remember laughing about the quirks and eccentricities in that series. All the men wore black wigs and many of them talked with their backs to you. You never knew if you were in Holland unless they had a tulip on the table. You never knew if it was William of Orange or his brother or his enemy. It was so badly put together. Most series had a run of 13 episodes, but this was so awful they gave up after 12. But somehow it got a decent reception and right away we went into fine stuff.

You've never been judgmental about the programs in your introductions. How did you manage to get through so many weeks of commentary on shows like The First Churchills *and* Poldark, *which you really didn't like?*

Cooke It was a little difficult. You just had to get into a frame of mind where you took the plot seriously. I must say, when it came to *Poldark,* there was really very little social or historical background because it was sheer adventure and could have been in any period. It was the hardest thing to memorize of any I did because I did my entire part in one day: 13 episodes. It was entirely plot. There was nothing else to say. The great danger there was you do three or four, then you start the fifth and you're right back in the old phonograph groove. Somehow I managed it.

While doing the last episode of *Poldark,* I remember the clock was getting down to 5 o'clock, which was the end of our studio time. I had one two-minute extro to do. It must have been about five minutes to 5. They were going to have to strike the sets and come back the next day. That was going to be double golden overtime, so I said to the floor manager, "Let's get this done." There was a clock with a second hand, and I was watching it as I said, "and that is the end of *Poldark*" with about four seconds left. I was so relieved.

Playing it back in the control room, the producer and I and the crew all fell on the floor laughing. It was so complicated that you couldn't possibly follow it, but the director said, "He seems to know what he's talking about."

By the way, didn't you invent the word "extro" to describe the wrap-up remarks you made at the close of each broadcast?

Cooke That's the only thing I've contributed to the language—the word "extro." At first, the crew called them intros and epilogues, but if they said "intro" for introductions, I said they should call the others "extros." They've called them extros ever since.

Your standard procedure was very unusual for a TV host: You would look at the tapes first, make notes, write your commentaries, memorize them, and tape them without using any kind of prompting device. Why do things that way?

Cooke I did it to make it more realistic as talk. I've always tried to imagine that I'm talking to one person in a room, sitting on a sofa. Ninety-nine percent of people in television use a TelePrompTer. But, by that time, I'd been doing radio for so long that I knew how to talk. It takes years to learn to be yourself—and I'm still learning.

Why did you insist on doing your own research?

Cooke I wouldn't trust a secretary to look up a date. I'll be the researcher. I'm too fussy to do otherwise.

How much involvement did you have with the settings, lighting, camera angles, and other technical details of your commentaries?

Cooke I spent 15 years protesting the lighting. Television took over the style of stage lighting—with ceiling lights. You had to have a helluva face with small features to withstand it. It took about 10 years or more to bring the lights down to face level. The switch to a second camera during the commentary was something I also resisted. When the director jumped from a medium shot to a long shot, a friend of ours said it looked like a stranger had come into the room, and he would scream, "Who's that guy on the sofa?" But they thought it gave the pieces variety, so they did it. Otherwise, I left everything else to them, although I did say, "Please don't bring the camera in through 16 pepper trees and then eventually come to me."

In the beginning with Chris Sarson, I just did the commentaries against a scrim. There was a chair, but no background, no setting. That suited me fine. It was with his successor, Joan Wilson, that they brought in a designer. For some reason, people think I always did the commentaries against a wall of books. I don't remember a single episode where I was sitting against a wall of books. But that's the impression. To the contrary, when we were doing D. H. Lawrence, we were sitting in a backyard of a coal-mining town, and so on.

Over the years, many comedians have done parodies of you. Did any leave a lasting impression on you?

Cooke Jackie Gleason did a character called Aristotle Cookie. I have one friend to this day who calls me Aristotle because of Jackie Gleason.

Many people would consider you the most well-read man in America. Did you always read every book that was dramatized by Masterpiece Theatre?

Cooke No, that wasn't possible. For instance, I didn't read all four books that they adapted for *The Jewel in the Crown,* but I read enough to get the feel. They did a marvelous job of adaptation.

Do you think a series called Masterpiece Theatre should do only recognized literary classics and not adventures, mysteries, or soap operas like Upstairs, Downstairs?

Cooke Over the years, the very word "masterpiece" began to lose all meaning to me. I loved *Upstairs, Downstairs.* When I first saw it, my reaction was, "I'll be amazed if this thing doesn't really hit the headlines. It's marvelous. It allows you to identify with the downstairs people while vicariously enjoying the life of the upstairs people." In contrast, I think much of Dickens is unfilmable.

How important do you think it was for American viewers to have someone to interpret British culture for them?

Cooke That to me was the job. I'd been doing it for years for the other side. You don't say "interstate commerce" to an English audience without saying what the phrase means. You don't mention the FBI and let them assume it's our national police force. So doing it for the American audience was quite easy. Now you wonder if they know what the sixth form is, what a prefect is, and so on. I'm probably hypersensitive to that. And that's the whole point of having a talking head, I think.

Did you ever see a program you really wanted to introduce, but couldn't because it wasn't acquired for Masterpiece Theatre?

Cooke The only time that happened, God was listening and changed the plan. It was *Edward and Mrs. Simpson.* I really wanted to do that because I had covered the abdication for NBC and knew it so well. Then Joan Wilson told me the bad news: It wasn't going to be on Masterpiece Theatre. I remember turning on my TV and there was Robert MacNeil introducing it. The first few episodes were so bad I began to be glad I hadn't done it, but the later episodes were excellent and really got into the constitutional questions. As it turned out, nobody watched it that time, and they wound up running it again on Masterpiece Theatre, so I got to introduce it after all.

Since you left Masterpiece Theatre, have you seen anything that you really wished you could have introduced?

Cooke I would have liked to have done *To Play the King,* that second Ian Richardson drama about the corrupt prime minister.

Has public reaction to you changed since you left Masterpiece Theatre?

Cooke This role of mine had a kind of prestige I had no idea about in the beginning. But the visual memory of the public is so short. If you're not there to reinforce it, it goes. Three people came up to me the last time I passed through the airport. From 1992 on back, there would have been 15 or 20. This time an older man told me I had a very familiar face and asked if I was a composer. ❧

Mobil Masterpiece Theatre presents

George Eliot's

MIDDLEMARCH

A town divided by love and hate - on the brink of social revolution

A six-part series begins Sunday, April 10 9PM on PBS

Starring: Juliet Aubrey, Robert Hardy, Douglas Hodge, Patrick Malahide and Rufus Sewell

Host: Russell Baker

Mobil

The 25 Seasons

FOR DECADES Americans had been fed a dramatic diet of abbreviated classics routinely shredded in Hollywood studios and delivered to neighborhood theaters as two-hour movies. The screenwriter's need to turn a sprawling 500-page book into a set of 25 or 30 scenes was understandable, but it meant that the audience might get *Moby Dick* without the whale, or crime without punishment, or only three of the six wives of Henry VIII. Masterpiece Theatre approached the problem by presenting the television miniseries that give the world's greatest story-tellers a broader canvas for their work. In doing so, Masterpiece Theatre has preserved the richness of the original works while at the same time offering a new way of enjoying them.

Many of the classics serialized on Masterpiece Theatre were originally written in installments and published in newspapers and magazines a chapter at a time over a period of many months. In this manner American readers of the last century read Thackeray, Eliot, Dickens, and others. During the serialization of *The Old Curiosity Shop* in this country, it is said that enthralled readers met ships from Britain at the docks in Boston and New York, shouting to passengers before the gangplank was lowered, "Did Little Nell die?" Today Masterpiece Theatre viewers also eagerly await news of the next episode—not on the docks, but in their own homes on Sunday evenings.

In the first 25 seasons Masterpiece Theatre has led us on a fantastic tour of Western literature, pausing at 19th-century landmarks such as *Pride and Prejudice, Madame Bovary,* and *Anna Karenina,* and visiting towns like Barchester, Middlemarch, Casterbridge, Thika, and Alice. We have been guided through the Tudors, the Stuarts, the Hanovers, the Windsors, the Victorians, the Edwardians, and the Suffragettes, with rural side trips into *Country Matters, The Little Farm,* and *How Green Was My Valley.*

We haven't missed a battle from the Napoleonic campaigns of Becky Sharp and Ross Poldark to both world wars to local skirmishes with the Mohicans, the Irish, and the Indians of the Raj. We danced the Charleston with Lydia, survived the twenties with Jeeves, and were dragged into the present with *House of Cards, To Play the King,* and *Traffik.* We've met Lillie Langtry, Sarah Bernhardt, and other sociable ladies of Edward VII's well-stocked drawing room as well as such historical and fictional eccentrics as Bertie Wooster, George Sand, Barbie Batchelor, and Vita Sackville-West. And we've heard all kinds of hearty regional British accents, some more intelligible than others.

These presentations of Masterpiece Theatre are, to put it simply and directly, the finest filmed entertainment of the twentieth century. Never in theatrical history has such a large audience seen such a splendid array of quality programming presented on a single stage.

The First Churchills (BBC)
January 10–March 28, 1971, 12 episodes

The Spoils of Poynton (BBC)
April 4–April 25, 1971, 4 episodes
Based on the novel by Henry James

The Possessed (BBC)
May 2–June 6, 1971, 6 episodes
Based on the novel by Fyodor Dostoyevsky

Pere Goriot (BBC)
June 13–July 4, 1971, 4 episodes
Based on the novel by Honoré de Balzac

Jude the Obscure (BBC) *
October 3–November 7, 1971, 6 episodes
Based on the novel by Thomas Hardy

The Gambler (BBC)
November 14–November 21, 1971, 2 episodes
Based on the novel by Fyodor Dostoyevsky

Resurrection (BBC)
November 28–December 19, 1971, 4 episodes
Based on the novel by Leo Tolstoy

Cold Comfort Farm (BBC)
December 26, 1971, 1 episode
Based on the novel by Stella Gibbons

The Six Wives of Henry VIII (BBC) *
January 1–February 6, 1972, 6 episodes

Elizabeth R (BBC) *
February 13–March 19, 1972, 6 episodes

The Last of the Mohicans (BBC)
March 26–May 14, 1972, 8 episodes
Based on the novel by James Fenimore Cooper

Vanity Fair (BBC)
October 1–October 29, 1972, 5 episodes
Based on the novel by William Makepeace
Thackeray

Cousin Bette (BBC)
November 5–December 3, 1972, 5 episodes
Based on the novel by Honoré de Balzac

The Moonstone (BBC)
December 10, 1972–January 7, 1973, 5 episodes
Based on the novel by Wilkie Collins

Tom Brown's Schooldays (BBC)
January 14–February 11, 1973, 5 episodes
Based on the novel by Thomas Hughes

Point Counterpoint (BBC)
February 18–March 18, 1973, 5 episodes
Based on the novel by Aldous Huxley

The Golden Bowl (BBC)
March 25–April 29, 1973, 6 episodes
Based on the novel by Henry James

Clouds of Witness (BBC)
October 7–November 4, 1973, 5 episodes
Based on the novel by Dorothy L. Sayers

The Man Who Was Hunting Himself (BBC)
November 11–November 26, 1973, 3 episodes

The Unpleasantness at the Bellona Club (BBC)
December 2–December 23, 1973, 4 episodes
Based on the novel by Dorothy L. Sayers

The Little Farm (Granada Television)
December 30, 1973, 1 episode
Based on the story by H. E. Bates

Upstairs, Downstairs, Series 1 (London Weekend
Television)*
January 6–March 31, 1974, 13 episodes
Series created by Jean Marsh and Eileen Atkins

The Edwardians (BBC)
July 7–July 28, 1974, 4 episodes

Murder Must Advertise (BBC)
October 6–October 27, 1974, 4 episodes
Based on the novel by Dorothy L. Sayers

Upstairs, Downstairs, Series 2 (London Weekend
Television)*
November 3, 1974–January 26, 1975, 13 episodes

Country Matters, Series 1 (Granada Television)
February 2–February 23, 1975, 4 episodes
Based on three stories by A. E. Coppard and one by
H. E. Bates

Vienna 1900 (BBC)
March 2–April 6, 1975, 6 episodes
Based on five stories by Arthur Schnitzler

The Nine Tailors (BBC)
April 13–May 4, 1975, 4 episodes
Based on the novel by Dorothy L. Sayers

Shoulder to Shoulder (BBC and Warner Bros.
Television)§
October 5–November 9, 1975, 6 episodes

Notorious Woman (BBC and Warner Bros.
Television)
November 16–December 28, 1975, 7 episodes

Upstairs, Downstairs, Series 3 (London Weekend
Television)
January 4–March 28, 1976, 13 episodes

Cakes and Ale (BBC)
April 4–April 18, 1976, 3 episodes
Based on the novel by W. Somerset Maugham

Sunset Song (BBC)
April 25–May 30, 1976, 6 episodes
Based on the novel by Lewis Grassic Gibbon

---

*Available on video §Video out of print
*Video cassettes of many Masterpiece Theatre programs are
available at public libraries and video rental stores. For
information about the availability of any program or about
purchasing videos, call VideoFinders, a service of public television station KCET, at 1-800-343-4727.*

Seasons 1–5

THE FIRST *Churchills*

12 EPISODES
January 10–March 28, 1971
Produced by *BBC*
Producer *Donald Wilson*
Original story by *Donald Wilson*
Writer *Donald Wilson*
Director *David Giles*

CAST
John Churchill *John Neville*
Sarah Jennings Churchill *Susan Hampshire*
Charles II *James Villiers*
James II *John Westbrook*
Queen Anne *Margaret Tyzack*
Sidney Godolphin *John Standing*
Duke of Monmouth *James Kerry*
Lord Shaftesbury *Frederick Peisley*
Barbara, Duchess of Cleveland *Moira Redmond*
Abigail Hill *Jill Balcon*
Emmy Award *1970–1971*
Best Actress *Susan Hampshire*

*S*EXUAL PROMISCUITY *has always been acceptable to American audiences if the actors are wearing historical costumes, and public television was quick to see the possibilities inherent in such an attitude. The initial Masterpiece Theatre offering,* THE FIRST CHURCHILLS, *begins in the bawdy court of Charles II, which historians have called the most immoral in English history. No other television series in PBS history was publicized with such enticing sexuality, and the viewers of "educational television" reacted with remarkable* enthusiasm to Britain's combination of contemporary enlightenment and historical copulation.

It was evident from the start that this was to be a class act by the BBC, but some difficulties surfaced immediately for American viewers. First, there were the accents, which soon prompted some to give Masterpiece Theatre the affectionate nickname of the "What-Did-He-Say? Series." The biggest stumbling block, though, was Americans' unfamiliarity with British history, particularly of a period that often confuses even the English. The scriptwriters were aware of this problem. The BBC preparatory script notes for the series make this cautionary observation: "Historical background seems so important. Otherwise the average viewer has no idea why all these courtiers are traipsing back and forth from one country or province to another."

This problem was solved for PBS viewers with grace and lucidity by British-born American journalist, Alistair Cooke, who served dutifully as the viewers' chaperon through this 12-part Churchill pajama party and most of the other dramas in the brilliant parade that was to follow.

*R*ags to Riches

The First Churchills is drawn from Sir Winston Churchill's *Marlborough,* a biography of his distinguished ancestor. In the series the whole panorama of 17th-century England is seen through the eyes of Sarah, her love for John and their family, and their love for England.

The Battle to Build Blenheim

For winning one of the most decisive battles of all time, the Battle of Blenheim, Queen Anne awarded John a grant of land and a palace to be built by the grateful people of England. Like many new home owners, the Marlboroughs experienced their share of difficulties. After seven years and £130,000, their digs were half-finished. The workers were owed £60,000, so they struck, they sued, and they rioted. The Treasury allotted more money. Then the Duke died, and, like any widow left with such a mess, Sarah ranted and raged and sued 400 people. The palace was finally completed 24 years after it was begun. Blenheim Palace still stands today. Not too long ago, in one of the ladies' cloakrooms, a beautiful woman from Brooklyn began having stomach pains that weren't caused by indigestion or dancing too exuberantly at the ball. Very shortly thereafter she gave birth to a strapping son—Sir Winston Churchill.

"Their love story is the most complete love story in English history. They had each other until he died, and then after his death, she spent the rest of her life writing articles and books to make it clear to the world what a great man he was." —Susan Hampshire

"It all looks lovely; the colours are sumptuous; it is rich in wit, lust, love, ambition, intrigue, 'history.' How can it fail?"
—Maurice Wiggin,
The Sunday Times

Contrasted with other court marriages made for territory, power, and politics, John and Sarah's is made for love and lasts nearly 50 years, through wars on the continent and intrigue at home.

John and Sarah's is a tale of rags to riches—the sort of story that Americans cherish but the English often overlook. They both compensate for their humble beginnings by attaching themselves to the right people.

"Americans like to say that the great thing about England is its order, its serenity, its unfailing habit of muddling into a decent compromise. Well, if this is so—and I vividly remember doubting it during the week of Edward VIII's abdication—it's a new thing. The United States has rarely had two decades of such turbulence and treachery as the 1670s and '80s in England. These plays about the First Churchills are, if anything, understated." —Alistair Cooke

The series takes place during the Restoration, a period of great events manipulated by great men wherever they happened to be—in battle or in bed, and John Churchill was adept in both. At the end of the first installment John meets Sarah, Princess Anne's saucy lady-in-waiting, who is not exactly a lady but she is waiting, for the right man. John, the most famous Englishman of his time, fits the bill. He is 26 and already a military genius. She is 16 and his match in wit, intelligence, vitality, and shrewdness. She is also vain, imperious, and argumentative. Put these traits all together, and you have a "torpedo in petticoats," as one contemporary called her.

John goes off to France, Holland, and Spain, winning battle after battle for England, while Sarah stays home touting his victories and becoming the intimate friend of Princess Anne, who later becomes Queen of England. As a reward for John's great military victories, the queen gives the attractive young couple the titles of Duke and Duchess of Marlborough—but no money. This causes Sarah to say to her husband, "I'm glad, my love, but Lord! Can we afford them?"

During Anne's reign the power of the duke and duchess is virtually unchecked, and virtue itself is not essential to political survival. Indeed it could be a deterrent, as this series demonstrates. When Sarah and the queen have a falling out because of politics,

Sarah loses her place to Abigail Hill, one of her poor relations and a spy at court for the enemies of the Churchills. John and Sarah are banished from court and battlefield to live abroad, where they are honored by Europeans who are amazed at England's ingratitude. The series ends on a touching note when George I, the new English king, reinstates the pair and invites them to live out their lives in England.

John Neville is excellent in the role of the first Churchill (and also manages to look comfortable in knee pants, which is half the battle). Susan Hampshire, who was already familiar to American viewers from the popular *The Forsyte Saga,* brought a spiritedness and depth of understanding to her portrayal, which helped her win her second Emmy award.

The first Churchills proved to be an interesting crowd to hang out with on Sunday evenings—"addicting" is how some referred to the experience. The size of the audience showed Mobil Corporation that its idea of an American playhouse for high-quality English television dramas was very welcome. Masterpiece Theatre was open and the curtain was just going up.

"This may be as good a place as any, to clear up something about 17th-century history that is so wild, so puzzling to us today: the way these people swapped thrones as often as they swapped wives. Most of the royal families of Europe in those days intermarried like mad—inbreeding occasionally to the point of idiocy. Quite often they knew as little about a country they acquired as a farmer in Vermont knows about a block of Brazilian stock he's offered." —Alistair Cooke

"Sarah is not likeable, except to her husband. She is domineering, politically brilliant, and probably the most important woman in England who hasn't been the Queen. She had a perfectly fiery temper." —Susan Hampshire

The Six Wives of
HENRY VIII

6 EPISODES
January 1–February 6, 1972
Produced by *BBC*
Producers *Mark Shivas and Ronald Travers*
Writers *Rosemary Anne Sisson, Nick McCarty,
Ian Thorne, Jean Morris, Beverley Cross, John Prebble*
Directors *John Glenister and Naomi Capon*
Based on an idea by *Maurice Cowan*

CAST
Henry VIII *Keith Michell*
Duke of Norfolk *Patrick Troughton*
Catherine of Aragon *Annette Crosbie*
Anne Boleyn *Dorothy Tutin*
Jane Seymour *Anne Stallybrass*
Anne of Cleves *Elvi Hale*
Catherine Howard *Angela Pleasence*
Catherine Parr *Rosalie Crutchley*
Emmy Award *1971–1972*
**Outstanding Continued Performance in a Leading Role
in a Dramatic Series** *Keith Michell*

T HE HOLY STATE *of matrimony has seldom faced a more exhausting challenge than that provided by boisterous Henry VIII in his desperate effort to perpetuate the Tudor dynasty with a male heir, an activity that involved six wives of such enthralling diversity they might have been plucked from the card files of fiction. Considering the perennial American fascination with women in jeopardy—from Little Eliza to Pearl White—the* BBC's THE SIX WIVES OF HENRY VIII *was an excellent choice for the first season of Masterpiece*

The alluring marital exercises of Henry VIII were shown in six episodes (one per wife), each written by a different playwright from a different point of view, yet based on historical sources.

Theatre, even though it had been shown previously on CBS. This time, though, the beheading of Anne Boleyn would not be in danger of interruption by a headache commercial.

When it came to producing a new Henry, the BBC had a formidable predecessor in Charles Laughton's swaggering portrait in *The Private Life of Henry VIII*, the first British import to be a runaway hit in America, and it had left an impression of the man on American audiences that was still fresh. Also, there was the Hans Holbein portrait commissioned by Henry, a splendid image of a man of power that fixes Henry firmly in the public mind as fat and forty. So the BBC writers showed us a new Henry, not as a womanizer but as England's first civilized king. He was an excellent athlete, proficient as a horseman, wrestler, and tennis player. He knew Latin, French, Greek, and Italian and was an apt student of mathematics, geometry, and astronomy. But above all he was a gifted musician, playing the lute (he had 26), the organ, and singing. Keith Michell in the title role fleshed out the six scripts with great style—more handsome than Laughton and more human as well—and viewers followed him from week to week and wife to wife with interest and affection.

"Keith Michell's Henry VIII is a splendid monster, a coarse childish tyrant with a will of steel. Wolfe Morris' Thomas Cromwell is a perfect villain, a real toad, and Bernard Hepton's Archbishop Cranmer was full of subtle contradictions, a redeemable if corrupt soul. But dominating the play, and rightly, was Dorothy Tutin's Anne. She made it quite clear why so many fell under her spell. Her wit, charm, and courage shone like the sun; but what a world!" —George Melly, The Observer

"There's something terribly endearing about Henry in a funny sort of way. One feels that all those women weren't just captivated by the fact that he was king—he must have had an aura."

—Dorothy Tutin, *Image*

"The makeup got more and more complicated. Toward the end it was a four-hour job. I'd come in about 7 and wouldn't start work until 11. At the end Henry was bald, and that meant wearing plastic all over my head, a plastic nose, things in my face, padding up to my neck. With nothing exposed to the air, it was murder!"

—Keith Michell

Filled with the pageantry, opulence, and court intrigue that reflects Henry's reign, the series not only showcases the individual wives but gives viewers a lively portrait of Henry from 18 years of age to his death at 56, possibly from matrimonial exhaustion.

ℐix Chances to Hit the Jackpot

Today, of course, we know that it is the sperm that determine the sex of a child. Considering that Henry had six chances to hit the jackpot, his score of two girls and one boy is not impressive. But his six tries gave six fine BBC actresses a good chance to romp through this lively period of English history and introduce themselves to American viewers who would recognize them in future roles in the great repertory theater company that Masterpiece Theatre was soon to become.

Michell managed to sneak behind the Holbein portrait to give us a peek at a younger Henry deeply in love with his first wife Catherine of Aragon (Annette Crosbie), his brother's widow and the daughter of Ferdinand and Isabella of Spain. She gives him an unwanted girl named Mary who lives to make everyone miserable. When he tries to divorce Catherine, he finds himself up against the

"I thought of Henry as a kind of cigar-smoking American millionaire, very rich and very powerful. The costumes were a big help—the great jackets with pearls and all that fur. They gave me a much larger appearance." —Keith Michell

brick wall of the Vatican because his wife's nephew is Charles V of Spain, head of the Holy Roman Empire, a kissing buddy of the Pope, and dead-set against divorce. So Henry does what every bright kid on the block would expect a real king to do: He sings arrivederci to Roma and invents his own religion, one that allows for divorce with just cause—and what better cause than to marry Anne Boleyn (Dorothy Tutin), the only one of his wives anyone can recall for sure without looking in the encyclopedia. She doesn't give Henry a son, but she does the next best thing and gives him a daughter who would become Elizabeth I—though this achievement is not enough to keep Anne from a tragic end on the gallows on a debatable charge of adultery and incest.

Henry finally gets a male heir from his next wife, Jane Seymour (Anne Stallybrass), but this fragile son, Edward VI, dies of tuberculosis at 15. After Jane there is Anne of Cleves (Elvi Hale), whom he divorces to marry Catherine Howard (Angela Pleasence), the 16-year-old niece of the Duke of Norfolk. She is appalled by Henry's age and ugliness, and when the groom cannot perform on his wedding night, her uncle insists that she must bear a son, whether Henry is the father or not. So Catherine dutifully seduces Thomas Culpepper (Ralph Bates), a young man about court. When the king learns of the potential deception, Catherine gets the ax along with Culpepper.

Henry is now over 40, turning mean, and getting lonely. Having run out of eligible women as well as sexual steam, he settles down with a twice-married divinity student, Catherine Parr (Rosalie Crutchley), who nurses and scolds him to the bitter end at 56 years of age—in an era when most men died at 35.

The Six Wives of Henry VIII served as a thoughtful introduction to *Elizabeth R,* leaving viewers eagerly awaiting the appearance of Henry's unwanted daughter, her lace collars and chalky makeup, and the series that became the biggest success of the first season of Masterpiece Theatre.

Creating the Rich Look

Costume designer John Bloomfield worked for nearly a year on the series. Three months were spent in basic research at the National Portrait Gallery, Windsor Castle, and various libraries, going through books and papers, and studying paintings and drawings—especially those by Holbein.

Apart from the sheer number of costumes involved—300, including 25 for Henry—the real challenge was to recreate the richness of court dress. This was done by using cheap heavy materials and working on them with paints and resins, using screen printing methods. Fabric patterns with an embossed effect were achieved by drawing on the basic material with fiber pens and then painting over.

Elizabeth R

6 EPISODES

February 13–March 19, 1972

Produced by *BBC*

Producer *Roderick Graham*

Writers *John Hale, Rosemary Anne Sisson,*
Julian Mitchell, Hugh Whitemore,
John Prebble, Ian Rodger

Directors *Claude Whatham, Herbert Wise,*
Richard Martin, Roderick Graham, Donald McWhinnie

CAST

Elizabeth I *Glenda Jackson*

Earl of Essex *Robin Ellis*

Earl of Leicester *Robert Hardy*

Mary Queen of Scots *Vivian Pickles*

Kay Ashley *Rachel Kempson*

Catherine Parr *Rosalie Crutchley*

Lord Burghley *Ronald Hines*

Philip II *Peter Jeffrey*

Edward VI *Jason Kemp*

Emmy Awards *1971–1972*

Outstanding Single Performance in a
Leading Role *Glenda Jackson*

Outstanding Continued Performance in a Leading Role
in a Dramatic Series *Glenda Jackson*

Outstanding New Series

Outstanding Dramatic Series

THE OFFICIAL IMAGE *of Queen Elizabeth I passed down to us by historians for centuries and more recently by moviemakers is of a pasty-faced woman with a splendid dressmaker and an indifferent sex life.* ELIZABETH R *came along just in time to expand this narrow vision of the virgin queen. The series gave Glenda Jackson nine hours to*

develop a character that Bette Davis, Flora Robson, and other silver-screen stars had barely two hours to create. Time was on Jackson's side, and she made the most of it with a stunning portrayal of the brocade-and-whalebone queen that is likely to replace all the others as the definitive image of this extraordinary sovereign.

A Lion's Cub

The daughter of Henry VIII and Anne Boleyn, Elizabeth comes to the throne as a young woman who had already survived ordeals that would have destroyed a weaker person. Her mother was beheaded and so was her stepmother, Catherine Howard. She had been declared illegitimate, accused of treason, and imprisoned in the Tower to await execution. Henry's will stated that the crown should pass to his other children, Edward and Mary, and their offspring. When Mary died with the blood of thousands of Protestants on her hands, the country welcomed her half-sister Elizabeth to the throne with great relief. Elizabeth was ready for the challenge, and the BBC scriptwriters gave her a splendid line in the

"Each writer saw Elizabeth in a different light. It's not just Bossy Betty all the way through. I had to find a personality that could be cruel and ruthless, yet sentimental, even loving."
—Glenda Jackson

"I found it fascinating that this grotesquerie [her layers of makeup], was probably ignored by everybody, including herself. Inside this terrible old hag of 69 lived a 17-year-old beautiful girl. Elizabeth believed she was beautiful and everybody had to tell her so." —Glenda Jackson

UPDATE

Glenda Jackson has given up her throne—and indeed her acting career—for a seat in Parliament, where she serves as the esteemed member from Hampstead and Highgate.

first episode to celebrate her ascendancy: "I will survive because I have the heart of a lion—and I am a lion's cub!"

Survive she did—and so did Glenda Jackson, who prepared for the role by soaking herself in the Tudors. She read everything she could find and came to have a deep understanding of Elizabeth. "She was like a chameleon, altering to suit the circumstances and the people she was with, keeping her central self very much to herself," Jackson says. "She couldn't afford to betray herself, because she was an absolute monarch with power and authority of a sort that not even dictators possess today. And yet at the same time she capitalized on being a weak and feeble woman, so that the sentiments surrounding her apparent vulnerability helped to increase her power still further."

As with *The Six Wives of Henry VIII* (which was really the first part of this two-series Tudor history), each episode was written by a different author and focused on different aspects and relationships of the sovereign.

First we see Elizabeth as a young princess flirting with the husband of one of her father's former wives. Next we see her as a 25-year-old monarch caught up in her great romance with the Earl of Leicester, then as Europe's most eligible queen, fending off suitors. We follow her as a shrewd schemer playing cat and mouse with her cousin, Mary Queen of Scots, then as the heroine who inspires England to defeat the Spanish Armada. Finally we see her sad end as an aging dowager, when most of her courtiers desert her deathbed to ride north toward Scotland to greet their new king, James I.

No Locks, No Nudity

In Tudor times bathing was not yet considered necessary or even safe. Elizabeth had bathed only twice in her life—when she was baptized and when her body was prepared for burial in Westminster Abbey 70 years later, thereby eliminating the possibility of a nude bathing scene, which has been a staple of historical movies ever since Cecil B. DeMille placed Claudette Colbert in a bathtub full of milk in Cleopatra. The scriptwriters attempted to sneak in a nude shot where King Philip of Spain peeks through the keyhole and sees her royal highness in the buff, but Jackson was saved from the task of removing all those brocades and petticoats on camera by the intervention of historical researchers who claimed that the palace doors had no locks, therefore no keys, and consequently no keyholes.

Every Inch a Queen

History records that Elizabeth I left 2,000 dresses when she died. For the series, 200 were made specially for Jackson, all with an eye to authenticity. Some costumes were so solidly padded that Jackson could hardly bend her arms; others were so heavy that she had to remain seated. The tightly cinched and padded corsets meant that she had to sit up straight, so bones wouldn't dig into her. "I had to breathe through my back," she said. Some costumes were so enormous that Jackson had great difficulty steering herself through doors. Weights were used to retain the shape of the gowns and, at the end, Jackson was wearing six pounds of kapok around her waist and so many yards of material that her shoulders were rubbed raw.

The scriptwriters cleared up many of the questions that viewers might have asked about Elizabeth's private life. Marriage was impossible because an English husband would have made her move over on the throne, and a foreign marriage with the Roman Catholic families of Spain or France was unthinkable. But the associations between sex and tragedy throughout her life may also have helped maintain her as the "virgin queen." As Jackson explains, "The fact that sex and sudden, violent, willful death were so caught up together in the lives of the people who came close to this girl must have marked her deeply, not just in her youth but all through her life, right up to her relationship with Essex, which also ended in violence." (She cut off his head.)

Jackson delivers some of the grandest lines ever heard on television, spitting them out with venomous relish. In one scene, when a foreign ambassador begins to threaten her by saying "Madam, I must warn you," she interrupts immediately: "No, sir, you must *not!* You must guard your rattling tongue lest I have my hangman pluck it out." Any way you look at her, Jackson (winner of the 1970 Academy Award for her role in *Women in Love* and in 1972 for *A Touch of Class*) was a perfect Queen Bess. She saw the possibilities, took the bit, and ran with it.

Elizabeth was quite a piece of work. She managed to forge a nation that was destined to become, for a time, the greatest power on the globe. When she came to the throne, as Alistair Cooke explains, "England was a rebel outcast from Rome, a second-rate

Jackson refused to wear a bald wig because she believed that they never look like real skin—a decision applauded by viewers who have often winced at faux baldness bestowed by saboteurs in the makeup department. That she chose to shave her head is yet another sign of her great dedication to her craft.

trading nation off there on an island in the North Atlantic. When Queen Elizabeth died, the Church of England was established once and for all, and England was a first-rate European power, with a great navy, prospering commerce and industry, and a rosy future as a colonial power." Glenda Jackson managed to leave viewers with an unforgettable image of Her Highness.

Makeup to Die For

Makeup was a prime consideration for *Elizabeth R.* It was reliably reported that when Elizabeth died, her face was caked with a half-inch mask of white-of-egg, powdered eggshells, alum, borax, and poppy seeds. Dentists didn't exist in those days, and toothbrushes hadn't been invented yet, so teeth turned black from decaying food particles. This accounts for the fact that no one in the history of royal portraiture was ever painted smiling. Tooth-conscious Hollywood would never tolerate a black—or even midnight blue—smile, and a less dedicated actress than Glenda Jackson might have bolted at the thought as well. Instead, she darkened her teeth as the series progressed, leaving an unforgettable image that, in less skillful hands, could have teetered on the edge of high camp.

Vanity Fair

5 EPISODES

October 1–October 29, 1972
Produced by *BBC*
Producer *David Conroy*
Based on the novel by *William Makepeace Thackeray*
Writer *Rex Tucker*
Director *David Giles*

CAST

Becky Sharp *Susan Hampshire*
Rawdon Crawley *Dyson Lovell*
Amelia Osborne *Marilyn Taylerson*
George Osborne *Roy Marsden*
Captain Dobbin *Bryan Marshall*
Jos Sedley *John Moffat*
Emmy Award *1972–1973*
**Outstanding Continued Performance in a
Leading Role, Drama/Comedy Within a
Limited Series** *Susan Hampshire*

IN PILGRIM'S PROGRESS *John Bunyan, an English lay preacher, created a mythical fair in the city of Vanity, which had been established by Beelzebub, the ancient prince of devils. It's a fair that never closes and where all manner of unusual things are sold—houses, lands, honors, titles, countries, kingdoms, lusts, pleasures, and delights of every description.*

William Makepeace Thackeray seized Bunyan's idea for the title of his novel VANITY FAIR, *satirizing the weaknesses and follies of human* nature in early-19th-century England. More than a century later, a dramatized version of Thackeray's novel opened the second season of Masterpiece Theatre, part of its continuing examination of the English social classes.

This time viewers are introduced to a lively cast of characters situated somewhere in the affluent vacuum between the hardworking middle classes and the idle aristocracy—playboys, bankers, socially acceptable gamblers, slightly soiled peers, flashy army officers, and the women they attract. Their counterparts are still with us today: those demi-celebrities the public finds vaguely detestable but endlessly fascinating.

In approaching either the novel or the BBC dramatization, it helps to understand that Thackeray's vast comic panorama has no hero; indeed, the novel's subtitle is *A Novel Without a Hero.* Instead we are given a heroine, Becky Sharp (convincingly played by Susan Hampshire), who is one of the most selfish, deceitful, unfaithful, manipulative, and generally untrustworthy women in all of literature.

"[Becky] is one of the most accomplished bitches known to fact or fiction between the fall of Rome and the rise of Las Vegas." —Alistair Cooke

In Living Color

In 1935 *Vanity Fair* was paid a high compliment when it was chosen to be the first all-talking feature to be filmed in color. In a cunning admission that Hollywood understood the marquee attraction of an overgrasping social climber, the title was changed to *Becky Sharp,* with Miriam Hopkins in the title role. Like Susan Hampshire, Hopkins was an attractive actress with a bright and original personality that enabled her to catch the essence of Becky's allure. As if to follow in the footsteps of *Becky Sharp,* the BBC selected *Vanity Fair* to be its first color television production.

Vanitas Vanitatum

The plot is gloriously complicated. The story opens when gentle and kind Amelia Sedley invites a schoolmate to come home with her for a visit. This is Amelia's first big mistake because her school chum is Becky Sharp, an orphan

who had been working her way through Miss Pinkerton's academy by teaching French to the other girls.

From the Sedley household, Becky moves on to a governess position. To engage Becky to teach children is a bit like asking Henry VIII to lecture on table etiquette. She charms everyone, as usual, and when her employer's wife dies he asks Becky to marry him, but she can't; she is secretly married to his son, the handsome Captain Rawdon Crawley of the Horse Guards, who is abruptly disinherited by the old man for beating him to the boudoir.

When word comes of Napoleon's escape from exile on Elba, Rawdon is called to duty in Brussels, and Becky goes with him. It's party time there and before long Becky becomes the toast of the town. Amelia has meanwhile married George Osborne (played by Roy Marsden, more currently Adam Dalgliesh in P. D. James' series on Mystery!), who has an eye for Becky.

The Big Moment in *Vanity Fair,* the great ball given by the Duchess of Richmond in Brussels, demonstrates that the BBC scenic and costume departments were not idle. Indeed, they must

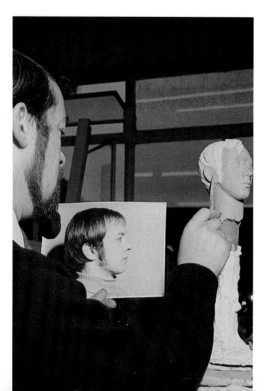

The puppets used in the BBC title shots for each episode are modeled on a device Thackeray used in the novel to introduce his characters. "The famous little Becky Puppet," Thackeray says, "has been pronounced to be uncommonly flexible in the joints, and lively on the wire."

"As we bring our characters forward, I will ask leave, as a man and a brother, not only to introduce them, but occasionally to step down from the platform, and talk about them; if they are good and kindly, to love and shake them by the hand; if they are silly, to laugh at them confidentially in the reader's sleeve; if they are wicked and heartless, to abuse them in the strongest terms politeness admits of. Otherwise you might fancy it was I who was sneering at the practice of devotion, which Miss Sharp finds so ridiculous; that it was I who laughed good-humouredly at the railing old Silenus of a baronet—whereas the laughter comes from one who has no reverence except for prosperity, and no eye for anything beyond success. Such people there are living and flourishing in the world— Faithless, Hopeless, Charityless: let us have at them, dear friends, with might and main. Some there are, and very successful too, mere quacks and fools; and it was to combat and expose such as those, no doubt, that Laughter was made." —William Makepeace Thackeray, *Vanity Fair*

have worked overtime to create such a glittering spectacle of chandeliers, champagne, dazzling gowns, and officers in uniform—a scene that is suddenly shattered by the sounds of cannon announcing that Napoleon's army is at the gates.

After the war Becky and Rawdon go to Paris, then London, and live beyond their means in both cities. When busy little Becky is discovered in a compromising position with the rich but sleazy Lord Steyne, her husband decides she's not worth fighting for and abandons her. The ever-resourceful Becky relocates to the continent, where she shacks up with Amelia's brother, Joseph, who dies mysteriously, leaving her half his life insurance. This enables her to live out her shallow life as a virtuous widow with a reputation for piety, benevolence, and generosity.

If anything is to be learned from this elegantly produced BBC drama, it's that the rats often win the race—a lesson that is taught frequently in literature but almost never in school.

$\mathcal{U}$PSTAIRS,

SERIES 1
13 episodes, January 6–March 31, 1974

SERIES 2
13 episodes, November 3, 1974–January 26, 1975

SERIES 3
13 episodes, January 4–March 28, 1976

SERIES 4
16 episodes, January 16–May 1, 1977

Series created by *Jean Marsh and Eileen Atkins*
Produced by *London Weekend Television*
Producer *John Hawkesworth*
Writers *Fay Weldon, Jeremy Paul, Rosemary Anne Sisson, Alfred Shaughnessy, Terence Brady, Charlotte Bingham, Anthony Skene, John Hawkesworth, Deborah Mortimer, Elizabeth Jane Howard*
Directors *Raymond Menmuir, Cyril Coke, Bill Bain, Christopher Hodson, Derek Bennett, Lionel Harris, Simon Langton, James Ormerod*

CAST
Richard Bellamy *David Langton*
Lady Marjorie Bellamy *Rachel Gurney*
James Bellamy *Simon Williams*
Elizabeth Bellamy Kirbridge *Nicola Pagett*

Hudson *Gordon Jackson*
Rose *Jean Marsh*
Mrs. Bridges *Angela Baddeley*
Edward *Christopher Beeny*
Sarah *Pauline Collins*
Alfred *George Innes*
Roberts *Patsy Smart*
Lawrence Kirbridge *Ian Ogilvy*
Lady Southwold *Cathleen Nesbitt*
King Edward VII *Lockwood West*
Hazel Forrest Bellamy *Meg Wynn Owen*
Georgina Worsley *Lesley-Anne Down*
Edward *Christopher Beeny*
Ruby *Jenny Tomasin*
Daisy *Jacqueline Tong*
Virginia Hamilton *Hannah Gordon*
Sir Geoffrey *Raymond Huntley*
Lady Prudence *Joan Benham*
Lily *Karen Dotrice*
Frederick *Gareth Hunt*
William Hamilton *Jonathan Seeley*
Alice Hamilton *Anne Yarker*
Sir Guy Paynter *Robert Hardy*
Lady Newbury *Celia Bannerman*
Marquis of Stockbridge *Anthony Andrews*

Emmy Award *1973–1974*
Outstanding Drama Series
Emmy Awards *1974–1975*
Outstanding Actress in a Drama Series *Jean Marsh*
Outstanding Director in a Drama Series *Bill Bain*
Outstanding Drama Series
Special Award *Host, Alistair Cooke*
Emmy Awards *1975–1976*
Outstanding Limited Series
Outstanding Supporting Actor *Gordon Jackson*
Emmy Awards *1976–1977*
Outstanding Drama Series
Outstanding Continuing Performance by a Supporting Actress in a Drama Series *Jacqueline Tong*
Peabody Award *1978*

DOWNSTAIRS

*S*INCE UPSTAIRS, DOWNSTAIRS *was first shown on Masterpiece Theatre on January 6, 1974, the lives of the people at 165 Eaton Place have become entwined with our own in a remarkable television love affair shared by an estimated one billion people in 40 countries speaking 16 languages, making the show the most popular dramatic series in history. Who*

"You can't keep on playing a character who is losing without feeling very low yourself. James was a failure and a pretty gloomy and miserable failure at that. I hope people realize I'm not at all like James. Although we served each other well, he was typical of the dreadful priggy types that were around then.... He is the worst sort of Englishman: arrogant, rude, snobbish, and not even very bright."

—Simon Williams

can forget the evening the king came to dinner? Or the terrible night that the *Titanic* sank and we learned that Lady Bellamy was aboard? Or the bittersweet romance of Ruby the kitchen maid, or the suicide of James Bellamy? They were our friends, and we had come to know them and love them. Even in the reruns we knew that we could always stop by and spend an hour at 165 Eaton Place as neighbors do, without calling ahead.

The series begins in the Edwardian era on November 23, 1903, and goes through the first World War, the Roaring Twenties, and ends just before the stock market crash. It covers births, deaths, divorces, the changing of rulers at Buckingham Palace, the women's suffrage movement (Elizabeth and Rose join the Women's Social and Political Union), the general strike, the beginning of the motion picture industry (Georgina works on a film), and much more.

To keep viewers abreast of what was happening beyond Eaton Place, host Alistair Cooke begins and ends each episode with a brilliant essay on the Edwardian era, complete with period photographs. It's a rich portrait of the period Cooke paints, dropping such names as Havelock Ellis, Somerset Maugham, Max Beerbohm, John Singer Sargent, George Bernard Shaw, H. G.

Rehearsals About Town

For each episode the cast had eight days' rehearsal outside the studio—in drafty halls, boys' club gyms, and even a rat-infested army barracks on King's Road, Chelsea. This was followed by two days in the studio—one for setting up and fussing with their costumes and wigs and one for taping. Some of the more scholarly members enjoyed reading vintage copies of the *London Times* chosen to coincide with the date of the script.

"I'd make a terrible butler. When I first played Hudson, I had to get used to keeping my arms straight to my sides. I felt like a penguin. Another difficulty is the fact that a butler must never show his feelings. His master can order him to do the silliest things and he must keep a poker face and get on with it." —Gordon Jackson

Wells, and John Galsworthy. By giving historical and cultural context to the episodes, Cooke's thumbnail essays help viewers better understand what drives the characters.

For the second series, Cooke is in a brand new setting—the Players' Theatre, the last surviving Edwardian music hall in London. Authentic turn-of-the-century music hall songs, performed by contemporary artists, replace his concluding pictorial essays. The song that Cooke felt best expressed the downstairs' view of Edwardian England was "It's the rich what gets the pleasure, it's the poor what gets the blame."

From Swimming
Pool to Eaton Place

Upstairs, Downstairs was conceived in a swimming pool on the French Riviera by two young English actresses who were splashing in the warm summer sunshine of 1971. Jean Marsh and Eileen Atkins figured the only way they could ever afford to have a pool like that was to invent a television series—and that's just what they did. They called their idea *Upstairs, Downstairs*. Marsh's mother had been in service as a maid, and Atkins' father as an underbutler, so the two were familiar with

"Ruby and I both have this Northern intuition about people—Ruby was the first to suspect that Welsh maid of stealing. And I suppose we both try hard to please. But Ruby has been trained not to think. She'll cut the parsley when asked, but not wash it first." —Jenny Tomasin

> "I like Daisy. She was allowed to make her mark as an individual in the last series when she dared to strike up a friendship with Lady Georgina."
> —Jacqueline Tong

Replicating a Rail Scene

When the plot called for a scene at Charing Cross Station, circa 1914, to show wounded troops returning from the front lines, the crew found ingenious solutions.

Marylebone Station substituted for Charing Cross, which was too modern. "All we had to do was take down the modern signs and cover up the current posters with replicas of 1914–1918 posters we bought at the Imperial War Museum," explained prop hand Rex Dutton. "Then we built an old newspaper and confectionery kiosk and put up dummy gaslamps." The crew next made a plywood engine and stuck it on the front of the first carriage, while a modern diesel locomotive did the pushing from behind, well out of camera range. One woman who happened upon the set fainted when she caught sight of all the bloody corpses.

the real estate from the ground up and could easily imagine the upstairs-downstairs life in Edwardian England and how nice it must have been—if you lived upstairs.

They took their proposal to London Weekend Television, and it was picked up immediately, with John Hawkesworth, a man of great taste and personal sensitivity, as producer and writer. Eileen Atkins had other acting commitments, but Jean Marsh was free and took the part of Rose, the upstairs maid, whose face became the emblem for the series.

Unlike countless dramas about landed English aristocrats in grand estates staffed by uniformed servants who vastly outnumber their masters, *Upstairs, Downstairs* gives the staff equal time. Indeed the scales are weighted in their direction, while the flaws appear more frequently on the upstairs characters—possibly because they have more time and money to get flawed. Only Hazel stands in the middle, as the shy, graceful wife of James Bellamy whose compassion for those below stairs is demonstrated in her affectionate treatment of Rose in the episode where her Australian romance is crushed.

Part of the success of *Upstairs, Downstairs* is due to the strict attention the producer and directors paid to the authenticity of every prop, piece of furnishing, and article of clothing. But the true test of theatrical reality is in the familiarity with which the props are used, and the actors in this series are remarkably successful in this. Mrs. Bridges handles her heavy copper pots and pans as if she has cooked with them all her life. When Rose sets a tray to be carried upstairs you can see her pause to make sure that everything on it is in the right place. These are not accidental movements, according to Simon Williams (James Bellamy), who said the cast often spent more time deciding which was the proper side for serving tea than they did discussing how to read their lines. The "bible" the production team consulted to ensure the authenticity of props, furnishings, and clothes was a rare 1907 catalogue from London's famous (and extant) Army & Navy store. Even scholars, apparently, used the series for reference. Cooke once ran into an American diplomat and scholar who was writing a history of British diplomacy from 1880 to 1939. "There's one thing I've come on that shows much more ruthlessly, much more accurately why it was the upper classes and not the lower that cracked," he told Cooke. "It's the television series *Upstairs, Downstairs*."

A House Divided

Hawkesworth and his writers knew their way around Edwardian London. Jean Marsh says she's probably read "everything that has ever been written about the period." Writer Alfred Shaughnessy based a lot of dialogue on phrases he found in letters written between his parents. Of the upstairs manner born, Shaughnessy had the perfect model in mind for the episode when Edward VII comes to dinner: a dinner at his grandmother's, which the king also attended.

"It was a fascinating era," Hawkesworth notes. "There was glitter and glamour, but also the most appalling squalor and poverty." It was a time when dinner parties often consisted of 17 courses, while one Londoner in three suffered from malnutrition; when children of the rich were raised by nannies and tutors, while one in four working-class children died in infancy. It was a time when lower-class men and women worked for

"I really think the further from Europe you go, the more likely you are to attract viewers who still think of England as a country of rich eccentrics and quaint cockneys, and that's partly the appeal of the series."

—Producer John Hawkesworth

A Royal Fan

When Angela Baddeley (Mrs. Bridges) went to Buckingham Palace to receive the C.B.E. (Commander of the British Empire) awarded to her in the Queen's 1975 New Year's Honours List, she discovered that *Upstairs, Downstairs* was Queen Elizabeth's favorite television program and Mrs. Bridges her favorite character.

"The Queen was very interested in the series," Baddeley reported. "She kept saying it was 'greatly enjoyed, greatly enjoyed.'"

"Mrs. B. and I are both disciplinarians and can't stand bad manners. My grandchildren call me Queen Victoria, and I think that's nice. But Mrs. Bridges is a terrible snob—which I hope I'm not—and a fairly static character who doesn't move with the times. We had a cook just like Mrs. Bridges when we were children, and I've modeled her on my memories. I can cook, but I don't like it. Mrs. B. has taught me plenty." —Angela Baddeley

starvation wages and died in the streets of London's East End. The Bellamys' domestics worked 90 hours a week, often for as little as $50 a year, wages that some two million men, women, and children in service toiled for during the Edwardian era. As Alistair Cooke explained, "It sounds like a dog's life, but it was better than the rat's life of the mines and the factories and what William Blake called 'the dark Satanic mills.'"

The only character to break through the up-down barrier is Sarah, the delectable parlor maid, during her affair with James Bellamy. When the family finds out about it, they send junior off to India with the Army to harass the natives, British style, and send Sarah to the country to have the baby, heartbreak style. Throughout its seasons *Upstairs, Downstairs* handled its domestic dilemmas with intelligence and discretion.

American viewers who accepted the series solely as entertainment are likely to have overlooked the underlying theme of

Upstairs, Downstairs, which is the collapse of a class system that had separated the downstairs from the upstairs in England for centuries. In episode after episode there are small indications of the arrogance of the Bellamys—and their apparent ignorance of it—such as James Bellamy's indifference toward Rose after he has lost her life savings in the stock market crash, or his insensitivity in brusquely asking her to serve tea when she has joyfully told of her engagement and given notice of her departure after 15 years of service to the family. Coupled with the upstairs callousness is the patient acceptance of it downstairs.

"The war, as it was for so many who live downstairs, was the great turning point in Edward's life. Before he decided to volunteer he'd been completely submissive."
—Christopher Beeny

Some Impressive Statistics

❧ *Upstairs, Downstairs* regularly captured 12 percent of the market, one of the highest ratings ever for a PBS offering.

❧ It won 25 major TV awards, including the rare Peabody Award and 8 Emmys.

"I miss Rose as though she were a member of my family. I adored her, but when the series ended it was like being let out of school." —Jean Marsh

"Richard Bellamy was no kept toady—even though Marjorie supported him in the early days, he still dared to vote against the Southwolds in Parliament on a point of honor. And he remained loyal to his wife when she had that scandalous affair. Bellamy hated hypocrisy and injustice—and I'd like to think there's some of me in him."—David Langton

"The plight of Elizabeth Bellamy brings up a typical Edwardian contradiction—between the way life was and the way it was supposed to be, between the doctrine of respectability and the awkward facts that mocked it. It was a conflict carefully disguised in the life of the Court: the loose morals of the king's social set, and the very tight morals of the rest of society." —Alistair Cooke

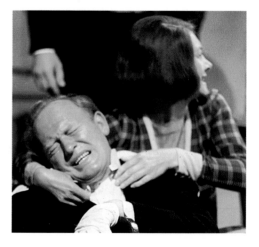

"Georgina is happier than I am—more able to cope with life, more resilient. But then she's a Sagittarius and I'm a Pisces—depressed one minute and cheerful the next."

—Lesley-Anne Down

Over There

Reactions from some BBC viewers indicate that the reported demise of "downstairs" may have been premature. A duke wrote to complain about the time of the telecast because the kitchen staff watched the show and it interfered with his dinner. A noblewoman congratulated the producer on the title and assured him that she watched it upstairs and her staff watched it downstairs.

"But can't you see, Mr. 'Udson, the war has chinged all that!" says Edward the Cockney footman, returning from the front in uniform. And indeed it had. Not only had men from downstairs served in uniform beside men from upstairs, but women took on new roles. "It was ironic that the insatiable demand for men and more men at last gave women the chance they had been waiting for," Hawkesworth comments. "House-maids, kitchen maids, and scullery maids came up from the basements to take on men's jobs, from bus drivers to coal heavers, while the young ladies from upstairs took more readily to nursing, driving ambulances, or running canteens."

Even James Bellamy notices the changes and eventually makes an admission to his father that might serve as a time capsule for the series: "I believe there is one spark of hope—just one—that came out of the hideous waste of that war. And that was the courage, the fellowship, the sheer bloody good sense chaps like me saw for the very first time in the working man. If we can just hold on to that common ground and keep trusting each other we can build something good in peace time."

Gordon Jackson's splendid portrayal of Mr. Hudson brought him the Queen's Order of the British Empire. The fact that she honored, at the same time, Olivia Newton-John and a manufacturer of spark plugs does not lessen in any manner the honor she bestowed upon the world's most distinguished butler.

After 68 episodes Hawkesworth and his team of writers agreed that they had said all there was to say about the characters and the times in which they lived. Although there is no specific date when families like the Bellamys stopped living in big town houses with large staffs of servants, the stock market crash of 1929, felt on both sides of the Atlantic, served as a convenient stopping point.

When the end finally comes, it is bittersweet. The Bellamys are alone. Elizabeth left long ago and lives in Canada. Both James Bellamy and his wife, Hazel, have died—she in a flu epidemic and he by his own hand. Georgina lives with her husband, the Marquis of Stockbridge. Hudson and Mrs. Bridges announce plans to marry and open a boardinghouse. In the final scene, the home on Eaton Place is being closed. Mrs. Bridges is supervising the packing of the kitchen things while Hudson is directing the moving man. Outside, Ruby sits forlornly at the curb alongside a stack of luggage. Rose crosses the street, then pauses for a moment, and turns to look at the For Sale sign on 165 Eaton Place. There are tears in her eyes, and in ours as well.

Eternal Youth

Although *Upstairs, Downstairs* spans nearly three decades, its characters never age. Producer John Hawkesworth believed that the addition of rubber wrinkles and gray wigs would only get in the way of the stories, and surely he was right. Instead the members of the Bellamy household show their age less obtrusively—as we all hope to do. It was a brilliant decision that bestows the gift of eternal youth upon the cast.

"Rose is conservative—an archetypal house-parlor maid who knows her place. But as the series develops she begins to question the old order. Certainly, the great turning point in the last series was her falling in love and very nearly heading for Australia. She chickened out, but the seeds of unrest had been planted." —Jean Marsh

Lord Peter Wimsey

Clouds of Witness

5 EPISODES
October 7–November 4, 1973
Produced by *BBC*
Producer *Richard Beynon*
Based on the novel by *Dorothy L. Sayers*
Writer *Anthony Steven*
Director *Hugh David*

CAST
Lord Peter Wimsey *Ian Carmichael*
Detective-Inspector Parker *Mark Eden*
Bunter *Glyn Houston*
Lady Mary *Rachel Herbert*
Duke of Denver *David Langton*

The Unpleasantness at the Bellona Club

4 EPISODES
December 2–December 23, 1973
Produced by *BBC*
Producer *Richard Beynon*
Based on the novel by *Dorothy L. Sayers*
Writer *John Bowen*
Director *Ronald Wilson*

CAST
Lord Peter Wimsey *Ian Carmichael*
Detective-Inspector Parker *Mark Eden*
Bunter *Derek Newark*
Robert Fentiman *Terence Alexander*
Ann Dorland *Anna Cropper*
George Fentiman *John Quentin*
Mr. Murbles *John Welsh*

Murder Must Advertise

4 EPISODES
October 6–October 27, 1974
Produced by *BBC*
Producer *Richard Beynon*
Based on the novel by *Dorothy L. Sayers*
Writer *Bill Craig*
Director *Rodney Bennett*

CAST
Lord Peter Wimsey *Ian Carmichael*
Chief Inspector Parker *Mark Eden*
Mr. Armstrong *Robin Bailey*
Major Milligan *Peter Bowles*
Mr. Tallboy *Paul Darrow*
Lady Mary *Rachel Herbert*
Pamela Dean *Gwen Taylor*
Miss Meteyard *Fiona Walker*

The Nine Tailors

4 EPISODES
April 13–May 4, 1975
Produced by *BBC*
Producer *Richard Beynon*
Based on the novel by *Dorothy L. Sayers*
Writer *Anthony Steven*
Director *Raymond Menmuir*

CAST
Lord Peter Wimsey *Ian Carmichael*
Chief Inspector Parker *Mark Eden*
Bunter *Glyn Houston*
Warder *Edwin Brown*
Deacon *Keith Drinkel*
Reverend M. Venables *Donald Eccles*
Inspector Frost *Robin Wentworth*

Five Red Herrings

4 EPISODES
December 19, 1976–January 9, 1977
Produced by *BBC*
Producer *Bill Sellars*
Based on the novel by *Dorothy L. Sayers*
Writer *Anthony Steven*
Director *Robert Tronson*

CAST
Lord Peter Wimsey *Ian Carmichael*
Bunter *Glyn Houston*
Matthew Gowan *Russell Hunter*
Sandy Campbell *Ian Ireland*
Mr. Alcock *John Junkin*
John Ferguson *David McKail*
Jock Graham *David Rintoul*

Mysteries

URDER HAS FASCINATED writers for centuries, but it wasn't until 1841 that the detective story was invented by an American—Edgar Allan Poe in "The Murders in the Rue Morgue"—just a few years after the job of crime detective was created by the police. Over the next century, thousands of detective stories and novels were written with increasingly difficult clues which finally became so complex that Robert Graves observed: "The crime could have been

Putting on the Monocle

What about that monocle? In *Whose Body?* Lord Peter does agree with Inspector Parker's observation that the Wimsey monocle is "a powerful lens." But he's quick to add "and jolly useful when you want to take a good squint at somethin' and look like a bally fool." All of this makes some close Wimsey observers suspect that Lord Peter may very well have had minimal—if any—eye trouble, and that he used his monocle as a ploy, or a put-on—and a "powerful" one at that. "The point is that Wimsey is putting on his facade," Ian Carmichael explains, adding that the monocle has long been a tradition of the English nobility. "Wimsey is cunningly adopting the misleading mantle of the classical English twit."

committed only by someone with a knowledge of Chinese, in desperate need of money, who could persuade a left-handed dwarf to train a monkey to climb up a ventilator pipe and squirt a rare type of South American poison into the victim's hot bath with a syringe through the keyhole at that one brief moment when the French maid's back is turned." (And Graves should know: He wrote *I, Claudius*.)

Dorothy Sayers had a different idea. In the 1920s she turned her detective stories into novels of manners rather than crossword puzzles, and to do so she created a new type of detective, giving him the name Lord Peter Wimsey. She made him a private detective, rather than a police detective, so that he could operate unrestrained by department rules. She also made him an aristocrat, bibliophile, music lover, epicure, and bon vivant. In addition, she gave him the richest peer in the realm for a brother, which ensured that Wimsey would never be short of money and she would never be limited in inventiveness. It is the Duke of Denver's money, for example, that enables Wimsey to hire an airplane and cross the

"The great beauty of Lord Peter, however, is that he is a super sleuth. He is of a Sherlock Holmesian turn of mind. His Lordship has been accused of being cosy and he is as cosy as mutton before an open fire, but he is also the only truly superbrain on the video 'tec scene and it is a welcomed change, old port and vintage motor cars and all." —Stanley Reynolds, *The Times* (London)

Wimsey's occasional use of "ain't" puzzled Americans until we learned that it was fashionable in those days for educated sophisticates and the "in" crowd to enjoy a kind of linguistic slumming.

Atlantic in *Clouds of Witness,* which predated Charles Lindbergh's solo flight. In this case it is the duke's neck that needed to be saved: He is the prime suspect in the murder of his house guest in the conservatory of his Yorkshire hunting lodge, a situation that causes Lord Peter to comment characteristically, "It *is* rather convenient to have the murder in the family."

Despite some initial confusion regarding Lord Peter's sexual bent, he became a favorite with the Masterpiece Theatre audience, brightening five miniseries between 1973 and 1977. As envisioned by Sayers in 1923 in the first Wimsey novel, *Whose Body?,* Lord Peter is more than what he appears to be. He is interested in many things and knowledgeable about almost everything. His detective work aside, you get the feeling that he would be good company, and Sayers soon discovered that she had invented a man of such alluring taste and languid sophistication that she was in danger of falling in love with him. "His affairs are more real to me than my own, and I find myself bringing all my actions and opinions to the bar of his silent criticism," she said.

A Seductively Clever Dottiness

Clouds of Witness is the first of Sayers' novels for which the BBC acquired television rights and the first to reach Masterpiece Theatre. Viewers are introduced not only to Ian Carmichael in the Wimsey role but to his two permanent sidekicks, manservant Bunter (Glyn Houston) and Detective-Inspector Parker of Scotland Yard (Mark Eden). They set about their duties with a zest that approaches camp of a very high quality, and the air is peppered with such lines as: "I say old chap, you cahnt be serious. Lady Mary is not the sort of woman to be in the conservatory at such an early hour."

It also established the series' reputation for being true to the period and to the original author. One critic wrote, "As usual with BBC presentations, the period details of the 1920s are realized superbly in a whirl of damp mansions and potted palms, monocles and tweeds, billiard rooms and long cigaret holders. And the Sayers style, rooted in a seductively clever dottiness, is retained to a remarkable degree."

By the time *The Unpleasantness at the Bellona Club* was shown on Masterpiece Theatre, it was apparent that Wimsey was just the man to solve the mystery of who died first—the old general in the club chair or his sister who died at home the same morning. Although the staunchly patriotic old general had apparently left

"To Dorothy Sayers, Wimsey was a very real person. I'm certain of that. After the last series, I was sent a copy of *The Papers Pertaining to the Family Wimsey* [written by Sayers], which traced his ancestry right back to the first Duke of Denver—all totally fictitious, of course. It was never publicly printed, so why did she do it? The only answer is that she was quite carried away with the character." —Ian Carmichael

---

UPDATE

The Sayers' stories were continued in Masterpiece Theatre's sister series Mystery! with Edward Petherbridge as Lord Peter and Harriet Walter as Harriet Vane, the outspoken, independent artist (and Lord Peter's love interest) who is perhaps Sayers' alter ego.

"Sayers carefully made Wimsey an apparently effete Englishman. He assumes the facade of being a complete silly ass, but beneath this there is a great depth of character, steely resolution, amazing erudition, and an astonishingly able brain. He has been to Eton and Balliol College, Oxford. He is quite deliberately able to hide behind his mask of buffoonery, with the result that he can decoy people away from the intensity and skill of his detection." —Ian Carmichael

this world on Armistice Day, only Lord Peter noticed that he was not wearing a poppy.

The third show was *Murder Must Advertise*. For two years Sayers worked as a copywriter at Bensons, one of the largest advertising agencies in London, an experience that soured her to the point that she began the novel by having a young ad man tossed down a spiral staircase. To discover who tossed the chap downstairs, the head of the ad agency hires detective Death Bredon (Wimsey in disguise) to pose as a copywriter. "Death" is pronounced "deeth," and it takes him exactly four weeks of television time to tie the crime to a drug-smuggling ring operating out of the agency. Written in the thirties, the tale remains a satisfactory, though uncomplimentary, guide to the advertising business.

The Nine Tailors followed, but they didn't sew; they are the nine church bells that signal death in country towns, followed by a bell for each year of the decedent's life. But this time the man in the coffin has been strangled with the rope of the bell ringer.

The last of the Wimsey series, *Five Red Herrings,* returns us to the artists of Scotland where the only one of six suspects with an alibi is the killer. The rest are red herrings, and the clue that traps the killer is a tube of flake white artists' paint. Lord Peter has done it again. And so has Sayers. When one of the local residents in her home town of Kirkcudbright angered her, a friend of hers suggested, "Why don't you write a book and murder him in it?"

Sayers was born in 1893 and educated at Oxford (she was among the first women ever to attend), where she specialized in medieval history. After graduation she translated Dante's *Inferno* and wrote a cycle of radio dramas on the life of Christ called *The Man Born to Be King,* never suspecting that one day she would return to the airways with the man born to be a detective. It was to indulge herself in the low-paid intellectual pleasures of religious writing that she turned to the higher-paying life of literary crime. At times she seems to flaunt her erudition, as in the *Clouds of Witness* scene in the Anglo-Soviet Club, when a revolutionary asks her companion, "Ever know a sincere emotion to express itself in a subordinate clause?" and he agrees: "Joyce has freed us from the superstition of syntax." Obviously this was heady stuff for viewers who were not accustomed to associating scholarship with homicide.

Sayers had enormous financial success with her detective stories, but at the outbreak of World War II, after writing 14 Peter Wimsey novels that sold 10 million copies, she returned to books on religious themes, which she attempted to popularize but never vulgarized. She died in 1957, with her place in the history of detective literature secure and enhanced by television.

Shoulder to Shoulder

HERE IS PERHAPS *no scene in all 25 years of Masterpiece Theatre programs that remains as powerfully imprinted* in people's memories as that in which the frail suffragette Lady Constance Lytton is force-fed in prison in the moving series SHOULDER TO SHOULDER. *We see her held down by sadistic wardresses while two doctors shove 20-inch-long tubes into her nostrils and down her throat and pump food into her. We see her face contorted in pain and shock, and we are revolted by the barbarity, incensed that such a gruesome tactic*

6 EPISODES

October 5–November 9, 1975

Produced by *BBC and Warner Bros. Television*

Producer *Verity Lambert*

Created by *Georgia Brown, Midge Mackenzie, Verity Lambert*

Writers *Ken Taylor, Alan Plater, Douglas Livingstone, Hugh Whitemore*

Directors *Waris Hussein, Moira Armstrong*

CAST

Emmeline Pankhurst *Sian Phillips*

Christabel Pankhurst *Patricia Quinn*

Annie Kenney *Georgia Brown*

Sylvia Pankhurst *Angela Down*

Dr. Pankhurst *Michael Gough*

Lady Constance Lytton *Judy Parfitt*

Emmeline Pethick-Lawrence *Sheila Allen*

Frederick Pethick-Lawrence *Ronald Hines*

Keir Hardie *Fulton MacKay*

"Mrs. Pankhurst displayed all the zest for life, all the sudden storms and deep affections which her contemporaries found in her. One could readily imagine her taking a delight in what she once called 'the sportingness' of it all."
—Brian Harrison,
The Times (London)

Art Imitating Life

It could have been 1914. Ten women were marching in the rain toward Holloway Prison carrying banners that said "Stop Force-Feeding." But it was 1974. The demonstrators were actresses who had marched straight off the set of *Shoulder to Shoulder* to protest the force-feeding of IRA prisoners Marion and Dolours Price. Shortly thereafter force-feeding was banned in Britain. "We helped do the job," said Georgia Brown. "It was an incredible thing to feel—what we felt was coming through our work, and what was coming through our work we felt."

should have been used. The strength, conviction, and dedication of the suffragettes confronted by the brutality and the senseless cruelty of the prison officials represents so clearly the extremes to which individuals will go for their beliefs and, on the opposite end, the horrific extremes to which those in power will go to maintain their power. We've seen this theme in several Masterpiece Theatre productions, but never as graphically or as emotionally as here.

Shoulder to Shoulder chronicles the struggle for the enfranchisement of women. It begins in 1895 when Manchester barrister Dr. Richard Pankhurst stands for Parliament with women's suffrage as part of his platform, and ends 23 years later when women over 30 years of age have gotten the vote, due in large part to the indispensable role women played in war work. "The war has brought us victory," Emmeline Pankhurst claimed at the time. The series focuses on the activities of the Women's Social and Political Union which, after years of politely petitioning, writing letters, and holding meetings—to no avail—takes the battle to the streets. From this vantage they finally gain attention for their struggle, though often not the kind they were seeking: they are beaten by the police, arrested en masse, and derided in the press.

"They were very gutsy ladies who were treated with enormous brutality and who have been blatantly ignored by historians. I find it hard to understand why I wasn't taught about this in school... after all these women were my grandmother's generation.... The issue of the vote united women in a way that no issue had ever done before and is likely to again."
—Co-creator Midge Mackenzie, *TV Week*

Shoulder to Shoulder is far more than a historical drama about significant events. It shows the lives, the motivations, and the relationships of a group of women who played such an important role in history. It is an honest rendering, showing brilliant speeches, tender exchanges, major revelations as well as jealous outbursts, petty meanness, and arch superiority.

The Women Behind the Banners

The central figure is Emmeline Pankhurst who, after her husband dies, together with her daughters helps found the Women's Social and Political Union. She is warm, charismatic, driven, and classist (and superbly portrayed by Sian Phillips, who played a different sort of *mater familias* in *I, Claudius*). Her middle daughter Sylvia, an artist, gradually moves away from the others, who feel, at first, that working women have no part in their movement, and so she organizes East End women around the suffrage movement as a way out of their poverty. One working woman recruited to the cause is Annie Kenney, a mill worker who gradually becomes a fiery, dynamic speaker for the movement. The class issue also angers Lytton, who abhors receiving special treatment in prison because of her title and social position. So she disguises herself as a working woman. The ruse works—she is force-fed like the others and leaves prison as a semi-invalid. Christabel Pankhurst, the eldest daughter, was trained as a lawyer

The Long-Lived Suffragettes

Despite the torture the suffragettes endured in prison, many lived to ripe old ages, supporting, perhaps the belief that an active, productive life can lead to a long one. Emmeline Pankhurst, who died in 1928 at the age of 70, visited Russia in 1917 to observe the effects of the revolution, lectured in Canada on child welfare, and shocked her socialist friends by joining the Conservative Party and running for office. Sylvia Pankhurst wrote a book on Russia (she was a supporter of the revolution) and one on her mother, and settled in Ethiopia, where she campaigned for African independence. She died in Addis Ababa at the age of 78. Her sister Christabel also lived to the age of 78, after having run for a house seat in Parliament during the first election open to women candidates (she lost). She later moved to the States, where she proclaimed her belief in the second coming of Christ. Ethel Smyth, composer of "The March of the Women," lived to be 86, Emmeline Pethick-Lawrence to 87. Leonora Cohen was 102 when *Shoulder to Shoulder* first aired in Britain. (She was the woman who hurled an iron bar through a glass case housing the crown jewels in the Tower of London.) She was distressed that women weren't doing more with the vote, from gaining more seats in the House of Commons to overcoming prejudice in the workplace. "The vote is the one essential thing. It includes every other liberty," she said.

UPDATE

Although a statue of Emmeline Pankhurst stands in the Victoria Tower Gardens, in full view of Parliament, 77 years after women gained the vote in Britain, only 63 women held seats in the House of Commons, as opposed to 588 men. Appropriately, the statue marks the very spot where the suffragettes were often kicked, beaten, and clubbed by the police.

and becomes the political genius of the group, directing the logistics from exile in Paris.

As the suffragettes adopt more militant tactics—smashing windows in the West End, setting fire to many buildings and mailboxes, bombing the Coronation Chair, slashing Velázquez's nude *Venus* in the National Gallery—the young suffragette Emily Wilding Davison flings herself under the king's horse at the Derby and is killed. While some believe that she meant to kill herself in the act, others point out that she had a return train ticket in her pocket. Though weakened by their prison ordeals and beatings and demoralized by the government's intransigence, these brave women nevertheless carry on in the struggle until they finally get the vote.

The television series was created by three equally dedicated women: producer Verity Lambert, script editor Midge Mackenzie, and the late actress Georgia Brown (Annie Kenney). Brown had complained to the BBC

"What was strange—and decisive—however, about the English pioneers was that they, of all people, were militant. Like many later advocates of populist causes, they discovered something that has terrified our own time: the success of violence."
—Alistair Cooke

about the paucity of meaningful roles for women, and they told her to find a series she would like to be in. She and Mackenzie, who had been researching the suffrage movement, talked about that as a possibility. Then when Brown was waiting to get an award at a banquet, and the lights suddenly went out, she began talking with Lambert about their idea. Shortly thereafter she went back to the BBC, which approved the project. Although, Brown said, "we desperately tried to get women writers who could deal with this subject on a historical level, it broke our hearts that we couldn't. There's no space in the media for women today." Four men were hired. "We had to sit on their heads, literally," Brown recalled. The male point of view kept creeping in—innuendoes, such as the assumption that Christabel Pankhurst had to be a lesbian because she was unmarried, or the portrayal of the working-class Annie Kenney as a music-hall-type character. "We had to make them understand she wasn't a joke," Brown explained.

The writers clearly got the message, as did the British government when it granted women the vote. And so did viewers as they watched the six gripping episodes in 1975.

The More Things Change

A letter to the *Radio Times* noted that many English wives were forced to forego the last 20 minutes of the final episode of *Shoulder to Shoulder* so their husbands could watch the European Cup Finals. Maybe Emmeline Pankhurst was right nearly a hundred years ago when she said, "Next to property, the thing most sacred to Englishmen is sports," and dispatched a group of suffragettes to pour acid on their putting greens.

Prolific Producer/Writer

John Hawkesworth

JOHN HAWKESWORTH is one of the most imposing figures in the history of British television—and the most successful writer-producer in the first 25 years of Masterpiece Theatre with an amazing 127 hours of programming to his credit.

Originally a painter—he still exhibits his latest work in London galleries—Hawkesworth started his show business career after completing his military service in 1946. He was picked by British movie giant Vincent Korda as his personal assistant at London Films and later served as a designer/art director on some of the greatest films of the postwar era, including Carol Reed's *The Third Man* (1949) and *Outcast of the Islands* (1951), David Lean's *Breaking the Sound Barrier* (1952), the classic Alec Guinness films *The Detective* (1954) and *The Prisoner* (1955), and Ronald Neame's *The Man Who Never Was* (1956). In 1957 he produced his first film, *Windom's Way,* then wrote and produced *Tiger Bay* (1959), giving a very young Hayley Mills her first acting role.

Turning to television in the 1960s, Hawkesworth wrote scripts for *The Rivals of Sherlock Holmes, The Elusive Pimpernel,* and dozens of other programs. In 1967 he teamed with John Witney to form Sagitta Productions, which immediately made its name through a series of programs for Masterpiece Theatre. These include the phenomenally popular *Upstairs, Downstairs, The Duchess of Duke Street, Danger UXB, The Flame Trees of Thika, The Tale of Beatrix Potter,* and *By the Sword Divided.*

In the 1990s Hawkesworth has concentrated on painting, completing his book *The Making of Upstairs, Downstairs,* and writing TV movies for his friend Angela Lansbury (*Mrs. 'Arris Goes to Paris,* for example).

When you first saw the rough concept for Upstairs, Downstairs, *what made you think it might make a good television series?*

Hawkesworth I thought the pearl in the oyster was the idea that the people below stairs were of equal weight and value dramatically as the people who were upstairs. That was original and something new.

Legend says Upstairs, Downstairs *almost was killed by the studio before it ever went on the air. What's the true story?*

Hawkesworth The controller of television changed at London Weekend Television and the new man, Cyril Bennett, came in like a new broom. We had finished the first series of episodes, but he still hadn't looked at them. I asked him to look at the first episode with me, but halfway through he said, "Honestly, John, I'm very fond of you, but they'll switch this off by the thousands. I shouldn't show it, but I'll put six of them on Sunday nights at 10:30 next winter."

When the series became a huge hit anyway, what did Bennett say?

Hawkesworth He became a very great supporter. In fact, after we had done five series and 68 plays and I told him we had all decided to stop before it started to decline, he exploded. I had an incredible hour with him screaming and shouting and dancing around and crawling on his knees, saying, "Here's a contract for the next 10 years! We've got a gold mine that hasn't begun to be excavated yet!"

How did you choose the marvelous acting ensemble that became the core of Upstairs, Downstairs?

Hawkesworth I had an extremely experienced casting director, Martin Case, and I knew quite a lot about casting myself. Quite honestly, there's such richness of talent in this country for that sort of series that you'd have to be pretty stupid not to cast it well. We had quite a few people who were right for each part.

I think the hardest part to cast was Georgina. After Elizabeth (Nicola Pagett) left, we needed a young female lead to take her place by bringing in a bit of glamour. I must have seen about 40 actresses. I thought it would be better to cast an unknown and bring out a latent talent. It finally came down to just two: Jane Seymour and Lesley-Anne Down. Lesley-Anne had virtually no acting experience, but she was a very pretty girl and was very enthusiastic. I thought it would be a challenge, so I picked her to play Georgina. I was very disappointed at first and thought I'd made a silly mistake, but suddenly she blossomed and was marvelous from then on.

How did you decide who would write each episode?

Hawkesworth Freddy Shaughnessy and I actually wrote each series in outline. We sat together for hours and worked out all 13 episodes like a novel. We then decided, sometimes wrongly, which writers would work on which plays.

Some of your writers also were novelists, like Fay Weldon, who wrote the first episode. How did they work out as television writers?

Hawkesworth The problem with a novelist working on a long-running series is that the writers have to compromise. They have to accept other people's characters and styles. Fay Weldon certainly wrote a very good first episode, which gave us a big push forward and inspired all of us. The problem was that Fay's style was so different from the others that it didn't work well in the end.

The closeness of the Upstairs, Downstairs *cast and crew is another television legend. How did that come about?*

Hawkesworth A long-running series like that is a bit like the war. You're in the heat of battle, and friendships forged in that kind of atmosphere are more powerful than any other sort and last forever. Almost all the people involved were friends. I was particularly fond of Angela Baddeley and Gordon Jackson.

What was the worst crisis during the making of Upstairs, Downstairs?

Hawkesworth Christopher Beeny, who played Edward, the footman, was very nearly killed one morning. It was a bright November day and there was a railway strike on. Christopher lived about 25 miles outside London, so he rode a motorcycle to work that morning, because of the strike. Some woman ran straight into him, and he was very seriously injured. On the desk in the control room, there was a red telephone that I guess was like the one in the White House. It had never rung before, but it did that morning, and I jumped about a foot. The person on the phone said a man named Christopher Beeny had recovered consciousness just long enough to give this telephone number. They said, "We hope he'll live until lunchtime."

By lunchtime that day, we had rewritten his part for a girl, found an actress we liked, and put her through wardrobe and makeup. She had learned her lines by 2 and we'd recorded the episode by 7 o'clock. That was quite a day. Beeny only recovered because he was young and tough. He came back to do the next series.

Fans of Upstairs, Downstairs *know you and your colleagues still refuse to authorize any further stories, but there's a persistent rumor that you wanted to do an* Upstairs, Downstairs *feature film. Is there any truth to this rumor?*

Hawkesworth During the second year, I decided we could make a wonderful film in between the series. In fact, I wrote an outline, and Rosemary Sisson wrote the film script. It could have been great fun. We got the money to do it and everything. By the time we were off on the third and fourth series, though, the film became curiously out of date because it was all about 1909. In a way, I regret we didn't make it. But we were just too busy to fit it in.

How did London innkeeper Rosa Lewis inspire you to create The Duchess of Duke Street?

Hawkesworth I met Rosa Lewis during the war when I was very young and in uniform. I went into her hotel, the Cavendish, once or twice. She was a marvelous, funny woman—a great sort of lady of my generation. Years later, after the success of *Upstairs, Downstairs,* the BBC's head of drama asked me to join the BBC to do another *Upstairs, Downstairs.* I said I'd just done it and didn't want to do it again. So, he said, "Well, something like it then."

I'd been doing a lot of research, and Rosa Lewis and her hotel kept coming up. She struck me as being a most unusual character, especially with her history with Edward VII, so I decided her story might make a great television series, and the BBC agreed. However, I thought it might be safer to change her name and the name of the hotel and make the whole thing fictional. Then we could do what we liked.

Is it true that Hayley Mills was your first choice to play Louisa?

Hawkesworth Yes. I was very, very fond of her. I thought she was a neglected talent. She'd had a very tough life for the last few years and was just getting divorced. She's a great natural comedian, so I offered her the lead. She read the first episode for me—and did it brilliantly. But her agent called me the following morning to say that right after her reading for me, Hayley went to the doctor and found out she was pregnant, so she couldn't do the part. Also, she didn't want anyone to know about the baby. She hadn't even told her parents, John and Mary Mills. But I'd already told the bosses at the BBC that she was going to do the part, so I had egg on my face. In desperation, I put together a short list of other actresses and, just by luck, Gemma Jones was available and enthusiastic. She was absolutely marvelous in the part, and later I was able to cast Hayley as the lead in *The Flame Trees of Thika.*

Your next project, Danger UXB, *was based on Major Bill Hartley's account of the brave soldiers who disarmed unexploded German bombs that fell on England during World War II. What inspired you to turn it into a TV series?*

Hawkesworth My partner, John Witney, got interested in it originally. I read the book, then met Hartley, who was a marvelous man and a great raconteur. He told me many more stories than were in his book. Sadly, he died before we made the series. Some of the characters in my scripts were based on men from the Royal Engineers unit attached to my armored unit during the war. I was full of admiration for them. I found it a fascinating drama on two levels: the battle between German and British scientists, each trying to outwit the other with more cunning and lethal fuses, and the men on the ground, having to cope with increasing danger every week.

How were you able to duplicate the bomb mechanisms so realistically and simulate the look of bomb-scarred London more than 30 years after the war?

Hawkesworth I had the cooperation of the Army and a very good technical man, so we were absolutely accurate scientifically. At that time, the East End of London was still enormously derelict. The London docks were not in use, and they said we could do anything we liked there, even explode a real bomb. They were going to bulldoze the whole thing anyway.

For the scenes where Anthony Andrews is blown into the sea by a bomb on a pier, we went to a town in Norfolk which had that kind of pier. The real incident happened at Brighton, and the officer was blown into three bits. They removed him to this marvelous hospital in Sussex, where he was sewn back together, more or less. He came on location with us the day we filmed that scene. He was blind, but he sat with me while Tony did the stunt and after the explosion told me, "That sounds about right."

You met Elspeth Huxley during the war. Is that what inspired you to film her memoir, The Flame Trees of Thika?

Hawkesworth No. That came about because John Witney and I and our wives decided to go on safari in Africa for a holiday, and my wife told me I should read the book before we went. It's a nine-hour flight from London and I never can sleep on airplanes, so I read it during the flight. By the time we got to Nairobi, I knew it could be a wonderful television series and had already divided it into six or seven episodes.

How did Elspeth Huxley assist you in the filming of her story?

Hawkesworth She was a great help. Elspeth has become a dear friend. She came over when I was doing the script and told me all about her life when she was young. During the filming, I arranged for her to come out on location for two to three weeks. This was a marvelous boost to the whole crew. With great difficulty, I found a very good young actress, Holly Aird, to play her, and they got on together very well indeed.

What was the biggest problem you faced filming Flame Trees *on location in Kenya?*

Hawkesworth The only real tough thing was the pressure of time. We had to film one 50-minute episode every two weeks. Then, at the very last moment, the board of directors of the studio, Euston Films, told me we had to cut £500,000 out of the budget and cut back from two directors to just one. These were very severe blows and seriously affected the quality of the production. We had to cut out all the scenes about this young family arriving in Africa.

Your next project, The Tale of Beatrix Potter, *seems a surprising choice for you. What interested you in the woman who created Peter Rabbit?*

Hawkesworth My grandfather was the vicar of Ambleside, a town very near where Beatrix Potter lived. When my father was young, he used to bicycle over and see her, and they became great friends. All my life, I was brought up to think she was a friend of the family. I also started out as a painter and I loved her paintings. It was incredible to me that she was more or less confined to her nursery until she was 30 by her terrible parents. That's really what forced her into writing and painting. I didn't think most people realized what an extraordinary life she led. That's why I did it, and it's my favorite production.

Your last projects for Masterpiece Theatre were the two By the Sword Divided *series, chronicling the English civil war. What led you to that subject?*

Hawkesworth Again, it's something personal. My family came from Yorkshire and were divided by the civil war. Sir Charles was a squire and lived at Hawkesworth. He was for the king, so his estate was confiscated and he wound up a loser. On the other branch, Joseph became an officer in Cromwell's army. Cromwell was determined to destroy all trappings of the monarchy. My ancestor was ordered to go to Kenilworth Castle and blow it up, which he did with 500 barrels of gunpowder. He kept the gatehouse, which is still in perfect order today, to live in with his mistress. That's why Britain is the land of ruined castles. Cromwell did more blowing up than the Germans did.

I'd always wanted to tell this story. The British people are incredibly ignorant about their own moment of truth, which was the civil war. It's the moment we became a democracy, but it's a story that sort of got lost in history.

Do you miss working in television regularly?

Hawkesworth Television is pretty rough in Britain at the moment, but I am planning another series, and I've been writing some movie scripts for Angela Lansbury. I've written *Mrs. 'Arris Goes to New York* for her, but they keep offering her so much money to go on with her *Murder, She Wrote* series that she never has time to do it. ❧

Madame Bovary (BBC)
October 10–October 31, 1976, 4 episodes
Based on the novel by Gustave Flaubert

How Green Was My Valley (BBC in association with
20th Century Fox Television)
November 7–December 12, 1976, 6 episodes
Based on the novel by Richard Llewellyn

Five Red Herrings (BBC)
December 19, 1976–January 9, 1977, 4 episodes
Based on the novel by Dorothy L. Sayers

Upstairs, Downstairs, Series 4 (London Weekend
Television)
January 16–May 1, 1977, 16 episodes

Poldark, Series 1 (BBC)*
May 8–August 21, 1977, 16 episodes
Based on the novels by Winston Graham

Dickens of London (Yorkshire Television)
August 28–October 30, 1977, 10 episodes

I, Claudius (BBC in association with London Film
Productions Ltd.)*
November 6, 1977–January 29, 1978, 13 episodes
Based on the novels by Robert Graves

Anna Karenina (BBC)
February 5–April 9, 1978, 10 episodes
Based on the novel by Leo Tolstoy

Our Mutual Friend (BBC)
April 16–May 28, 1978, 7 episodes
Based on the novel by Charles Dickens

Poldark, Series 2 (BBC)*
June 4–August 27, 1978, 13 episodes
Based on the novels by Winston Graham

The Mayor of Casterbridge (BBC)
September 3–October 15, 1978, 7 episodes
Based on the novel by Thomas Hardy

The Duchess of Duke Street, Series 1 (BBC)
October 22, 1978–January 28, 1979, 15 episodes

Country Matters, Series 2 (Granada Television)
February 4–March 4, 1979, 5 episodes
Based on two stories by A. E. Coppard and three
stories by H. E. Bates

Lillie (London Weekend Television)*
March 11–June 3, 1979, 13 episodes

Kean (BBC)
September 9–16, 1979, 2 episodes
Based on the play by Jean-Paul Sartre

Love for Lydia (London Weekend Television)*
September 23–December 9, 1979, 12 episodes
Based on the novel by H. E. Bates

The Duchess of Duke Street, Series 2
(BBC/Time–Life Television)
December 16, 1979–April 6, 1980, 16 episodes

My Son, My Son (BBC/Time–Life Television)
April 13–May 25, 1980, 7 episodes
Based on the novel by Howard Spring

Disraeli: Portrait of a Romantic
(Independent Television/ATV Network)
June 1–June 22, 1980, 4 episodes

Crime and Punishment (BBC)
September 28–October 19, 1980, 4 episodes
Based on the novel by Fyodor Dostoyevsky

Pride and Prejudice (BBC)*
October 26–November 23, 1980, 5 episodes
Based on the novel by Jane Austen

Testament of Youth (BBC in association with
London Film Productions Ltd.)
November 30–December 28, 1980, 5 episodes
Based on the autobiography by Vera Brittain

Danger UXB (Thames Television)*
January 4–April 5, 1981, 13 episodes
Based on the book *Unexploded Bomb* by Major Bill
Hartley

Thérèse Raquin (BBC in association with London
Film Productions Ltd.)
April 12–26, 1981, 3 episodes
Based on the novel by Emile Zola

---

*Available on video   §Video out of print
*Video cassettes of many Masterpiece Theatre programs are
available at public libraries and video rental stores. For
information about the availability of any program or about
purchasing videos, call VideoFinders, a service of public television station KCET, at 1-800-343-4727.*

Seasons 6–10

SERIES 1, 16 EPISODES
May 8–August 21, 1977

SERIES 2, 13 EPISODES
June 4–August 27, 1978

Produced by *BBC*

Producers *Morris Barry (Series 1); Richard Beynon,*
Tony Coburn (Series 2)

Based on the novels by *Winston Graham*

Writers *Peter Draper, Jack Pulman, Jack Russell,*
Paul Wheeler, Alexander Baron, John Wiles, Martin Worth

Directors *Paul Annett, Christopher Barry, Kenneth Ives,*
Philip Dudley, Roger Jenkins

CAST

Ross Poldark *Robin Ellis*
Elizabeth Warleggan *Jill Townsend*
Demelza *Angharad Rees*
George Warleggan *Ralph Bates*
Francis Poldark *Clive Francis*
Caroline Penvenen *Judy Geeson*
Mr. Pearce *John Baskcomb*
Jud Paynter *Paul Curran*
Dr. Dwight Enys *Richard Morant*
Ellen *Tilly Tremayne*
Prudie *Mary Wimbush*
Drake Carne *Kevin McNally*
Sam Carne *David Delve*
Agatha Poldark *Eileen Way*
Dr. Enys *Michael Cadman*
Reverend Osborne Whitworth *Christopher Biggins*

POLDARK

*I*N THE SPRING *of 1977 Masterpiece Theatre replaced the Bellamys of Eaton Place with Captain Ross Poldark. The battle-scarred male chauvinist came as a breath of fresh air to viewers longing to see a romantic hero fighting for survival against a pack of dastardly villains and making out with all the women in the neighborhood (plus a few from out of town). To give us such a man, Masterpiece Theatre ventured back two centuries in time to the rugged tip of England aptly called Land's End.*

"There's a sense of danger about Ross. And of course he's good-looking. He's a strong man who makes the right decisions for the right reasons — even if they bounce back on him. He's the man with everything, and it's difficult to separate Ross Poldark from Robin Ellis who plays him." —Angharad Rees

Like the Scotland of *Sunset Song* and the Wales of *How Green Was My Valley,* the Cornish coast of England where the winds are wild and the rocky bluffs drop into a foamy sea was the rightful setting for *Poldark* (though the bulk of the filming was done in the BBC's London studios).

The year is 1783, and the audience is introduced to Captain Poldark as he rides in a stagecoach across the rough Cornwall countryside. From his conversation with the other passengers, we learn that he is returning home after fighting in the American Revolutionary War, trying to keep the colonies safe for taxation without representation. He is now ready to claim his deceased father's estate.

Poldark's friends and family have presumed him dead, and his rat-tailed Uncle Charles has claimed the estate. The farmlands and copper mines have been allowed to deteriorate and are being sold to the Warleggans, a scheming local family of down-and-dirty villains in the classic sense. The news of his old girl friend is even more gloomy. As often happens in wartime, she has not waited for the armistice or even checked the official death list and is now engaged to marry another man who is—to make things worse still —his cousin Francis. It's enough to discourage British enlistment in overseas wars for all time.

"Tonight we begin a new series called Poldark … and I can only say that now is the time for the party to settle in to a spate of loving, dueling, poaching, smuggling, wenching, marrying—not to mention banking and copper mining." —Alistair Cooke

After such an introduction anyone who enjoys a good story would find it very difficult to switch channels, and apparently very few did because *Poldark* was one of the most popular dramas in the Masterpiece series up to that time. It also had a tremendous following in Britain. As Shaun Usher of the *Daily Mail* said, "Committee meetings were delayed, bridge games deserted in mid-rubber, family visits paid only on condition that it could be watched. *Poldark* … may have been the best-loved serial since *The Forsyte Saga.*"

In the first series of 16 episodes we see Poldark work to pay off his father's debts, replant his land, rebuild his copper mines, and care for his tenants. The series was such a success that it was followed by a second batch of 13 episodes that gave scriptwriters plenty of opportunities for more disasters: ship wrecks, mine explosions, fiery furnaces, gout, politics, bankruptcy, house burnings, the death of a child, and the French Revolution.

In many historical romances the hero is torn between two loves, and Poldark is no exception. One is Elizabeth, his old girl friend (played with icy coldness by Jill Townsend), who goes through with her marriage to Ross' cousin. The other is Demelza (Welsh actress Angharad Rees), a perky teenage urchin whom he befriends and marries shortly afterward because Elizabeth is no longer available and Demelza is with child—his. Demelza is illiter-

"Ross Poldark was a man outside his time. He was exceptional because he dealt in human beings rather than establishment creeds. He was willing to break barriers down. He cared about his miners and knew conditions were bad because he went down into the mines. That in itself was unusual. He was often ashamed of his fellow gentry, of their atrocious behavior. His marriage to Demelza proves that he was prepared to go against convention and marry out of his class." —Robin Ellis

ate but has sufficient other attractions to push literacy toward the bottom of his list of requirements for happiness in her company. By the end of the series, however, she has grown into an intelligent and sophisticated woman. Their marriage is a tempestuous affair, played in the shadow of Poldark's continuing attraction to his first love, providing the series with sufficient romantic interludes with both women to relieve the strain of the melodramatic action.

The characters are played by a grand collection of actors who deliver their lines with great relish in the robust Cornwall accent. For American viewers there is many a slip twixt the ear and the lip, but the accent barrier is never serious enough to get in the way of the plot, and the occasional language confusion tends to enrich the sensation of being transported to the stony southwest tip of England that points toward America.

ℛoldark and Handsome

The series stars Robin Ellis in the title role, fresh from losing his head as Essex in *Elizabeth R.* Although he is not handsome in the traditional leading-man sense, his command of the language, his rugged masculinity, his soulful eyes, and cleft chin led to his being dubbed by the British Press as "the sexiest man on the telly" in his homeland.

During the location shooting in St. Ives for the first season, the cast was able to walk around without being recognized because no one in Cornwall had seen the show. But when they returned the following year to film the second series, the cast couldn't move outside the hotel without attracting a crowd.

The immense popularity of the series with the locals was not exactly accidental, particularly in Port Quin, where the fishermen and their families were used as extras in one grand Cecil B. DeMille–style recreation of the starving 18th-century townspeople rushing into the bay to scavenge the wreckage of a ship with a cargo of corn and brandy. The costume department had dressed the crowd in the rough and ragged clothes of their ancestors, and the property department scattered the surface of the water with barrels and bottles bobbing in the surf. On the director's signal the crowd of perfectly normal men and women from all walks of life went out of their minds and rushed, screaming, into the surf, nearly overturning the camera platform. It took three shouts of "cut" to stop them. When the episode reached the air, it looked authentic indeed.

Twenty-nine episodes may be a little too long for some viewers to spend in Cornwall, but when it is over the Warleggans have been thwarted, Elizabeth has died in childbirth, Ross and his devoted Demelza have each other, and the world is safe once again for sex and copper. And the gallant Captain Poldark is overwhelmingly voted favorite Masterpiece Theatre hero by viewers.

"Even when their aim is merely to tell an entertaining yarn, the British are painstaking about it. We're assured the Cornwall locations are authentic for the period. Certainly the costumes, settings and furnishings create a spell-casting sense of place and time. A scene in a country marketplace was so pungent in detail you could all but smell it. I once asked an English friend how his countrymen managed such an array of excellent television. 'I don't know, old boy,' he said. 'Something to do with the playing fields of Eton, I reckon.'"

—Robert MacKenzie, *TV Guide*

I, CLAUDIUS

✦✦✦✦✦✦✦✦✦✦✦✦✦

13 EPISODES
November 6, 1977– January 29, 1978
Produced by *BBC in association with London Film
Productions Ltd.*
Producer *Martin Lisemore*
Based on the novels I, Claudius and Claudius, the God
by Robert Graves
Writer *Jack Pulman*
Director *Herbert Wise*

CAST

Claudius *Derek Jacobi*
Livia *Sian Phillips*
Augustus *Brian Blessed*
Tiberius *George Baker*
Caligula *John Hurt*
Antonia *Margaret Tyzack*
Herod *James Faulkner*
Drusilla *Beth Morris*
Drusus *Ian Ogilvy*
Livilla *Patricia Quinn*
Germanicus *David Robb*
Sejanus *Patrick Stewart*
Agrippina *Fiona Walker*
Julia *Frances White*
Messalina *Sheila White*
Silius *Stuart Wilson*
Nero *Christopher Biggins*

*A*FTER WATCHING THAT *snake slither across the mosaic tile floor at the beginning of each episode of* I, CLAUDIUS, *viewers realize that all those Hollywood tales of ancient Rome with Victor Mature and Kirk Douglas are merely sentimental garbage. The British brought us the real garbage instead. But they did so with such style that it was impossible* for even the most fastidious viewers to protest or tune out. The PBS was, nevertheless, a bit apprehensive as to what the reaction of viewers might be to the graphic smorgasbord of sexual couplings, rape, incest, adultery, and nudity of every extreme. After all, a number of problems had been raised by the baring of a single breast in *Jude the Obscure* (which caused the series to be referred to as Jude the Not-So Obscure).

Undoubtably Alistair Cooke's introduction to the first episode helped to allay any negative response. He said: "Some people are going to be more shocked by this series than most of the dramas that we've shown on Masterpiece Theatre. But Robert Graves did not make it more cruel or more gamey than the manuscript

of Suetonius from which he worked.... Graves left in only what is essential to the historical plot. Violence is not shown for titillation. And there's no pretense that a sexual orgy is some sort of

"We none of us knew for the first fortnight how to play the parts. As soon as [writer] Jack Pulman said 'Mafia,' we all got into our parts immediately. I suddenly started to touch people, smile at people. And then when their backs were turned, say 'I can't stand him.' Suddenly, the Mafia note was the key."

—Brian Blessed

launch pad into a liberating Playboy philosophy. Vice is shown for what it is, and even the monster Caligula described his court as a sink of degradation—he did not think of incest or group sex as a new form of freedom. He knew it as a certain sign of the decadence of his times."

The Roman emperor of the title who plays dumb and fools all his relatives had already stuttered his way through two successful novels *(I, Claudius and Claudius the God)* by Robert Graves, a writer with a scholarly sense of humor and a humorous sense of scholarship. Graves had invented an ancient manuscript secretly written by Emperor Claudius and buried for centuries, which told the true story of the life and crimes of four emperors: Augustus, Tiberius, Caligula, and Claudius, covering the years 24 B.C. to A.D. 54. As fantastic as the tale is, it is based on historical documents—the writings of Suetonius, whose modern translator is Graves. Suetonius, who was born twenty years after Claudius' death, had access to all the records of the time. He was also able to verify the accuracy of those documents by questioning people who had actually been in the courts of Tiberius, Caligula, and Claudius.

"I, Claudius is about the marketplace. The desires and the way people behaved then are exactly the way they behave today.... You see the workings of a city today—business, politics, the dirty tricks they play upon each other. It's all there. It's just a bit more overt, because it was more fashionable and the power was absolute. But it is totally relevant today and completely recognizable." —Director Herbert Wise

"Having decided that we wouldn't be spending any money on battles and great, huge crowd scenes, the whole idea was going to be, as in the book, that Claudius is a man on the inside looking out, the fly on the wall, the man looking through the keyhole. In the same way would we, as the camera, be on the inside, always looking out."
—Director Herbert Wise

"You can hardly class Livia as a woman. She was freakish.... Livia had no boundaries.... I thought to myself, at first, I'll find a nice side to Livia somewhere. But she was totally evil.... Fortunately, there was a lot of humor in the part, even if it was black humor, and that finally made Livia almost bearable." —Sian Phillips

The Family That Slays Together

At the beginning of each episode we see Claudius scribbling away with a quill pen on his bloody story of the pleasures and sins that humankind is heir to. Claudius is a family man—and what a rotten family it is. His grandmother Livia poisons her way to a position of power, leaving a list of Latin obituaries that includes her own daughter, Claudius' brother Germanicus, and eventually her husband Emperor Augustus. All this, just so that her son Tiberius can become emperor. There is no reason for Claudius to love or even like his grandmother. She kills his 13-year-old son, drives his mother to suicide, and poisons his first girl friend. On top of all that, she forces him to marry Urgulanilla, whom he hates and who hates him. She is soon removed so he can be married off to another unhappy woman.

It is unfortunate enough for Claudius to have a grandma like Livia, but he also has a crazy nephew named Caligula who kills his own father at the age of seven and becomes emperor after he smothers Tiberius, his lecherous predecessor. Caligula proclaims himself a god, appoints a horse to the Senate, marries his sister, and even has the head of a child cut off to stop him coughing. He forces Claudius to marry his cousin, Messalina, a notoriously immoral teenager who makes a specialty of murdering her lovers when she tires of them. Claudius ignores her playfulness until she playfully marries another man, and then unwittingly has her executed.

The Praetorian Guard, a 12,000-man army, watch with amused disgust as the loonies in the palace destroy one another in

> *"Nineteen hundred years or near, Clau-Clau-Claudius shall speak clear."*
> —The Sybil, prophesying Claudius' historical manuscript

"It was a bit like juggling. With a twitch and a stammer, and a limp going all at the same time." —Derek Jacobi

their lust for power during the reigns of Augustus and Tiberius, when the empire stretches from Scotland to the Euphrates and owns everything in it, from the pyramids to the Parthenon. But Caligula is too much for them, so they storm the palace one afternoon and murder Caligula. When they find old Claudius cowering behind a curtain, in a burst of affectionate hilarity, they salute him as a half-wit to succeed the monstrous Caligula and carry him off to the Senate to be approved. This leads to one of the most satisfying scenes in the series.

*Q*uality of Wits

At first we see only a frightened, stammering old man, but slowly it becomes apparent that we are watching someone who is going to make a wise leader. To a senator who says he's not fit to be emperor, Claudius replies: "It is true I'm huh-huh-hard of hearing, but you'll find it's not from want of listening. As to speaking, it's t-t-t-true that I have an impediment, but isn't what a man says more important than how long he t-t-t-takes to say it? As for being half-witted, what can I say except that I have survived to middle age with half my wits while thousands have died with all of theirs intact. Evidently quality of wits is more important that quantity."

Claudius rules the empire for 13 years, striving for a return to the Republic. But his just and sensible rule is ruined by the rampant ambitions of the power-mad around him. Nevertheless, he revolutionizes the provincial governments, broadens the Senate, builds bridges. He also adds three letters to the Latin alphabet and

The Curse of Claudius

Many involved in the production feel there was a curse on *I, Claudius,* evidenced by seven unsuccessful earlier attempts to film the story, including the 1937 film produced by Alexander Korda, directed by Josef von Sternberg, and starring Charles Laughton and Merle Oberon. After only a few scenes had been shot, Oberon was in a serious automobile accident and the film was canceled.

The first evidence of a "jinx" on this version was the locked neck Derek Jacobi got (presumably from too much twitching). Although Jacobi went to an osteopath, it was only after Robert Graves, responding to an urgent appeal from producer Martin Lisemore, said that he needed the money, that Claudius had always taken care of him, and that it would be all right, that Jacobi's problems miraculously ended. But it didn't prevent new ones. An extra died of a heart attack.

Then there was the time the electricity on the film set suddenly and inexplicably went out for three or four minutes during the scene in which Livia, who has poisoned Augustus, watches as he draws his last breath. Then, just as inexplicably, the electricity came back on.

At an end-of-filming luncheon, producer Lisemore rejoiced that the jinx was broken. "We've done it, we've broken the curse," he said. A few months later he died in an auto crash.

"I tried to play Caligula as sane as possible. A madman is not necessarily a raver, and although Caligula has fits of screaming, I tried to make him sound as though he's being completely rational because to me that's more frightening. It's the content of what he says that is out of this world."
—John Hurt

"Historical plays in English are usually written in a style that is stilted, painfully archaic, and meant to convey dignity through distance. What Graves did was to make his characters talk a vernacular and a confident, upper-crust slang that was totally familiar to his audience of 60 years ago: it was the vernacular of the British empire builders, public school Conservatives, the Tory establishment, and to me it perfectly fits the character and the easy exercise of power of the emperors and their cronies. It also gave us my favorite line in the whole 13 hours: When Tiberius expressed shock at finding his trusted friend Sejanus a traitor, Caligula (of all people) said, 'Aren't people awful?'" —Alistair Cooke

writes 20 books on Etruscan history. (Roman historians of later years have noted that Claudius was intelligent and sensitive, a scholar in an age that honored only soldiery. While Graves' ruse of having Claudius engaged in writing a family memoir was only a stroke of the novelist's imagination, Claudius was, nevertheless, quite up to the task.)

Like many rulers—including modern presidents—Claudius decides to boost his popularity by over-running a neighboring country. In A.D. 43 he invades Britain, appearing in person at the crossing of the Thames, thereby bringing his story to the British people 1,934 years before they would see it on television.

Derek Jacobi called the part of Claudius the role of a life-time and quickly made it his own. In less skillful hands the stammering spastic might have been almost too much for viewers to accept, but Jacobi never allows the physical tricks to get in the way of the storytelling. Any actress in her right mind would kill for a role like Livia, but Sian Phillips got it through sheer talent instead, and plays it with a brilliant iciness. Brian Blessed as Augustus gives a solid sense of the emperor's wisdom coupled with foolishness. John Hurt almost steals the show with a portrayal of Caligula as a cunning madman always on the razor's edge of hysteria.

Of all the shows presented on Masterpiece Theatre, *I, Claudius* is the one viewers most ask to have repeated. And indeed it was, in 1991, with the snake slithering 13 more times across the tile floor.

Anna Karenina

10 EPISODES
February 5–April 9, 1978
Produced by *BBC*
Producer *Donald Wilson*
Based on the novel by *Leo Tolstoy*
Writer *Donald Wilson*
Director *Basil Coleman*

CAST
Anna Karenina *Nicola Pagett*
Alexei Karenin *Eric Porter*
Count Vronsky *Stuart Wilson*
Levin *Robert Swann*
Kitty *Caroline Langrishe*
Countess Vronsky *Mary Morris*
Dolly *Carol Nimmons*
Stiva *David Harries*

*O*NE OF THE MOST *dramatic episodes in world literature takes place on an almost deserted platform at a Russian railway station on a winter's night. A beautiful well-dressed woman of the upper classes gazes at the railroad tracks, hypnotized, listening to the sound of an approaching train. Suddenly she remembers something that happened at the station years before, on the day*

> "Nicola Pagett has created the classic Anna. She doesn't appear to be acting. She *is* Anna Karenina."
> —*Evening News*

she first met her lover: She had seen a workman run over by a train. The sound of the approaching engine is now like thunder in her ears. She carefully measures the distance and then throws herself onto the cold steel tracks in front of the oncoming train.

Leo Tolstoy had once witnessed such a scene and it left an indelible impression on him. He wondered what would cause a beautiful woman to end her life in such a sordid manner, and from that puzzlement he created one of the greatest novels of modern realism: *Anna Karenina,* the story of a married matron who is in love with Count Vronsky—a man who is not her husband— and faces the tragic consequences of such a love. The size and enthusiasm of the television audience demonstrated, once again, the enduring appeal of this tragic story, particularly when played against the backdrop of a beautiful production with settings that drew viewers into the mansions and private landscapes of 19th-century Russia and the luxurious society that was the equal of any in Europe.

Because of restrictions imposed by the cold war, the exteriors were filmed in Budapest—in corn-fields, outside of stately homes, on snow-covered ponds—and in England.

ℋot Love in a Cold Climate

Anna's story is quite simple. A young society woman of impeccable character, she had been happily married to a cold-blooded older man for ten years when she falls in love with the handsome young count and gives up her husband and son to live openly with him. In the first episode Anna comes from St. Petersburg to Moscow to comfort her sister-in-law, who has learned that her husband is having an affair with their governess and is devastated at the discovery. The conversation between the two women provides a good assessment of the moral climate in which the ensuing drama takes place. Anna explains to her sister-in-law that men of the world have a special way of looking at affairs of this sort:

"They may be unfaithful but their homes and their wives are sacred. If they take other women, they look upon them with contempt. They draw a line—one that cannot be crossed—between their mistresses and their families. The longer a man lives with his wife, the higher she rises in his esteem. Compared to love of that kind, what is an infidelity?"

Those guidelines for extramarital love affairs have perhaps not changed much since Tolstoy's novel was

"It goes almost without saying that the show is marvellous to look at. The scenes at the railway station—presumably shot in Hungary—were worthy of Monet."
—*Financial Times*

"Vronsky's heroic growth from an incredibly superficial person interested only in the pleasures of life is fascinating. When he falls in love with Anna, his whole character undergoes a traumatic change. He becomes an interesting person. He grows in stature. He gives up his whole career, his way of life. He reforms." —Stuart Wilson

published in the 1870s, and they would seem to apply equally well across international borders. If so, Anna's story may have some relevance as a cautionary tale even in the permissive moral terrain of contemporary America.

Her story also serves as the anchor for Tolstoy's gloomy reflections on Russia's troubled upper-class society in the later half of the 19th century. Tolstoy himself had been born to wealth (like his Vronsky, he was a count), but he rejected the trappings of the aristocracy in the later years of his life. *Anna Karenina* is the story of a woman shackled by her social class and the incongruities of its rules.

In contrast to Anna and her count, there is a second pair of lovers, Konstantin and Kitty, the young daughter of the family into which Anna's brother has married. Konstantin Levin is an aristocrat who understands more clearly than the others his responsibility for the peasants on his estates and represents Tolstoy's newly found sympathy for what he perceives as the new Russia. The two stories run on one tether throughout the book as a suggestion of the author's splintered life. Most dramatic adaptations have tended to soft-pedal the second plot because Anna's story is quite enough to handle in the tight time frame of a two-hour movie, but once again Masterpiece Theatre demonstrates the great advantage of a television series that provides more time to tell the story. Viewers were invited to dig in for a long Russian winter—which they did—to watch the classic drama of hot love in a cold climate.

"You could call this novel 'The Three Faces of Tolstoy.' Tolstoy had been very much like Vronsky, a hellion, until he grew tired of the strict military life and the debauchery on the side…. Through Levin, Tolstoy begins to examine and doubt his own life as a prosperous landowner tied to the peasants and the land. Through Karenin, Tolstoy marks his own move away from a life of strict respectability and duty to what he calls a life of Christian forgiveness." —Alistair Cooke

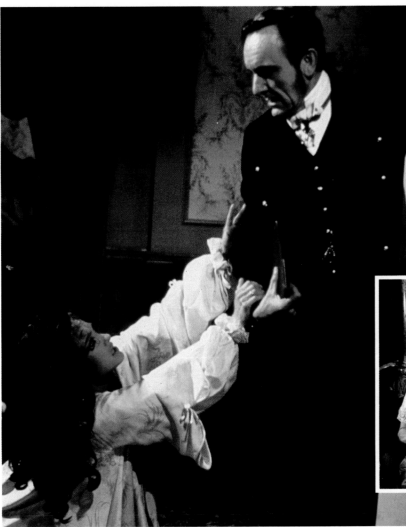

"Anna is one of the greatest parts ever written by anyone, and I include Shakespeare. It's just so enormous in emotion. Anna's so many things— mother, wife, mistress. She's kind, she's neurotic, she's got a bit of all women in her." —Nicola Pagett

Anna Karenina has been filmed many times—twice with Garbo and later with Vivien Leigh, plus a previous BBC production starring Claire Bloom as the unfaithful wife of old Russia. In the Masterpiece Theatre production, the repertory players are in full array. Nicola Pagett (Anna) is instantly recognized as Elizabeth Bellamy, the suffragette of *Upstairs, Downstairs.* Pagett has a luminosity and a sensuality her predecessors did not. Vronsky is played by Stuart Wilson (Helen Mirren's love interest in parts five and six of *Prime Suspect*). No one has ever explained why foreign counts are always dashing and handsome, but Vronsky is one of these, and Wilson fills the description quite nicely. The late Eric Porter, who plays Anna's husband, is remembered as Soames Forsyte, a character very much like Alexei Karenin: Both men are conservative, status-conscious, and affluent, and they live with spirited young wives who leave them for younger, more attractive lovers.

The appeal of Tolstoy's story—in print as well as on television—is universal. Each generation of new audiences finds its own truth in the tale, beginning with the first sentence of the novel: "Happy families are all alike; every unhappy family is unhappy in its own way."

"Adultery had not been used as a serious theme in Western literature for almost 200 years, until it was re-introduced to a shocked world by Flaubert with Madame Bovary *in 1857—and that was 20 years before* Anna Karenina." —Alistair Cooke

The Duchess of Duke Street

SERIES 1

15 Episodes, October 22, 1978–January 28, 1979

SERIES 2

16 Episodes, December 16, 1979–April 6, 1980

Produced by *BBC (Series 1);*
BBC/Time–Life Television (Series 2)
Producer *John Hawkesworth*
Writers *John Hawkesworth, Jeremy Paul, David Butler,*
Jack Rosenthal, Rosemary Anne Sisson,
Julia Jones, Bill Craig,
Julian Bond, Ken Taylor, Maggie Wadey
Directors *Bill Bain, Cyril Coke, Raymond Menmuir,*
Simon Langton, Gerry Mill

CAST

Louisa Trotter *Gemma Jones*
Charlie Tyrrell *Christopher Cazenove*
Mary *Victoria Plucknett*
Mr. Merriman *John Welsh*
Mr. Starr *John Cater*
Major Smith-Barton *Richard Vernon*
Augustus Trotter *Donald Burton*
Mrs. Leyton *June Brown*
Mr. Leyton *John Rapley*
Prince of Wales *Roger Hammond*
Lady Adam *Angharad Rees*
Diana Strickland *Elizabeth Bennett*
Marcus Carrington *Anthony Andrews*
Margaret *Joanna David*
Lottie *Lalla Ward*
Violet *Holly de Jong*
Professor Stubbs *Freddie Jones*
Thomas Prince *Kevin McNally*
Mr. Appleby *Jeremy Clyde*
Sophie Applegate *Anna Calder-Marshall*

*M*OVIE AUDIENCES OF *this century have been treated to an endless parade of Hollywood films about chorus girls who become stage stars.* THE DUCHESS OF DUKE STREET *is a refreshing change of occupational*

"Louisa was plain, very plain, and saucy, vulgar, and free. I think the Prince of Wales just found her a marvelous person to be with, to relax with, someone he didn't have to behave with. He didn't have to pretend to be royal in her presence."

—Gemma Jones

venue, but there's a big difference: Scullery maids don't become culinary stars overnight—even by staying overnight, although that may expedite the process, as shown in this delightful series.

In the opening program of *The Duchess of Duke Street*, viewers are introduced to the "duchess" of its title, Louisa Leyton, a Cockney-born woman at the turn of the century who goes into service as a skivvy at the age of 12. Through pluck, beauty, and culinary prowess, she becomes the hostess, entertainer, and intimate friend of peers, princes, kaisers, and eccentrics.

Gemma Jones, one of England's finest young actresses, plays the role of Louisa with a tight-lipped relish as she comes to work in the house of Lord Henry Norton and soon rises to cooking assistant. "All I want to be is the finest cook in London," she says, and her on-job training makes joyful viewing as the delights of cooking are eventually linked to the upstairs pleasures which often follow a good meal—even in England, where overcooked Brussels sprouts are considered gourmet fare.

Louisa is a quick learner and therefore is prepared for her big break, which comes one night when Chef Alex is away and his lordship returns unexpectedly saying that an important person is

"Rosa Lewis never lost a Cockney vowel or picked up an aitch. And she handled her whole crew, whether staff or guests, baronets or busboys, like a Pirate King." —Alistair Cooke

"Actually, it would be fair to call the Cavendish a 'house of assignation'—a meeting place for lovers—where ladies and gentlemen married to other ladies and gentlemen could get together discreetly.

"However, it was in no way limited to such trysts. It was a favorite London residence for many Englishmen and foreigners in town for business or pleasure, with no romantic overtones."

—Producer John Hawkesworth, *Pittsburgh Post-Gazette*

"To show you the sort of standard Rosa Lewis set herself, I've come on this menu which is: Cavendish Hotel Dinner, June 20, 1908. It's nothing special. This is the ordinary day-to-day hotel dinner: consommé with chicken wings, followed by cold trout Cavendish, whitebait, soufflé of quails, beef in aspic, Polish ham with fava beans, cold chicken parisienne, salad, asparagus en branches, poached peaches with chestnuts, ice cream mold, friandaises (little glazed fruits), macaroons and so on, and finally a savory—an oyster on a bed of minced mushrooms wrapped in bacon." —Alistair Cooke

"In those days, the early 1900s, there were very few hotels that upper-class people could stay in, and respectable people did not dine out. So Louisa decided there should be no public dining room. The place was divided up into suites, each having its own drawing room, dining room, bedroom, bathroom. This was a tactful and a comfortable arrangement. It offered the maximum temptation with the minimum of publicity." —Alistair Cooke

coming for dinner. After the superb meal, the guest of honor asks to have the chef brought to the table to accept his congratulations. Giving Louisa a gold coin, he says: "Here is a new sovereign from a future sovereign." When Louisa realizes that the generous guest is the future king of England, she faints dead away, as any proper Victorian girl would have done in 1900.

The prince is impressed by more than Louisa's cooking and eventually and discreetly he becomes her lover—after she is persuaded to marry Augustus Trotter the butler because, after all, His Royal Highness does not compromise single women. When the prince becomes Edward VII, this dalliance ends, though not before news of Louisa's culinary competence has gotten around and she is catering dinners for fashionable people, including the new king, the Churchills, and the Kaiser, whose other needs she catered to also. Louisa sells her house and purchases the Hotel Bentinck on Duke Street. She battles bankruptcy, ill health, and a drunken husband, whom she eventually throws out. Her hotel nevertheless becomes an international meeting place for statesmen, artists, aristocrats—even a few crooks—with Louisa reigning as its duchess, staunchly holding on to her Cockney accent.

This apparent fairy tale is based on the life of Rosa Lewis, whose rumored affair with the Prince of Wales supposedly gave her the money to set herself up as mistress of London's Cavendish Hotel, which was known for its fine fare and good company from the early part of the century through two world wars. Lewis' clientele ranged from the affluent aristocracy to eccentrics she favored for personal reasons and whose bills she was apt to transfer to the accounts of patrons she disliked. Producer and co-writer John Hawkesworth actually knew Lewis. "She used to be kind to me because she knew my father," he says. "It was a private hotel and she was a real old dictator. She was a terrible snob—she would only have people she liked in the hotel, and she used to throw people out. It was a unique, zany kind of place, and when I knew her she was well into her 70s and still spoke with a strong Cockney accent, and used the strongest language you can imagine." So Rosa of the Cavendish was given a rebirth as Louisa of the Bentinck nearly a quarter of a century after her death in 1952.

"Louisa is a shrewd businesswoman with guts, determination, and arrogance, and very much her own boss. She really pre-empts women's lib." —Gemma Jones

Lewis never cashed any of the hundreds of servicemen's checks she'd accumulated during World War I—even when she needed the money desperately. "That's my war work," she was fond of saying.

Lillie

---

13 EPISODES
March 11–June 3, 1979
Produced by *London Weekend Television*
Producer *Jack Williams*
Writers *David Butler and John Gorrie*
Directors
John Gorrie, Christopher Hodson, Tony Wharmby

CAST

Lillie Langtry *Francesca Annis*
Edward Langtry *Anton Rodgers*
Prince of Wales *Denis Lill*
Prince Louis of Battenberg *John Castle*
Oscar Wilde *Peter Egan*
Princess/Queen Alexandra *Ann Firbank*
Dean LeBreton *Patrick Holt*
Patsy Cornwallis-West *Jennie Linden*
King Leopold *Derek Smith*
Mrs. LeBreton *Peggy Ann Wood*
Charles Longley *David Rintoul*
Mrs. Henrietta Labouchere *Annette Crosbie*

*M*ANY WOMEN—*in fact or in fiction—could be called serial lovers. What made Edwardian-age courtesan Lillie Langtry unique was the respect she commanded and the high caliber of the men she attracted, from those she turned down, like King Leopold of Belgium,*

Denis Lill, the New Zealander who played Francesca Annis' lover once before on Masterpiece Theatre, in *Madame Bovary,* is in her arms once more as Edward VII.

to those she turned up, including Prince Rudolph of Austria and King Oscar of Sweden. But the biggest trophy on the Langtry bedside mantelpiece was Bertie the Prince of Wales, who would even-

tually succeed his mother, Queen Victoria, on the British throne as Edward VII. "Kings, princes, and millionaires have made love to me," Lillie said, "but I have never really found the right man." Heaven knows she tried. Most of her attempts to find Mr. Right are pictured in *Lillie,* a lush and lavish 13-episode series. Also portrayed are her wit, boldness, intelligence, and playfulness.

The pattern of Lillie's conquests is straightforward: love him, take his money, leave him, and replace him. She even ducks out on the Prince of Wales—after four expensive years as his first officially acknowledged mistress—and takes on his cousin Prince Louis of Battenberg, who is young, titled, rich, and handsome. Luckily, Louis (the present Prince Philip's grandfather) is Bertie's favorite cousin, and Bertie figures if anyone is to follow him into Lillie's bed it might as well be a relative. In later years, both Bertie and his wife continued to demonstrate their affection for the woman

Some Famous Reflections on Lillie Langtry

❦ "I resent Mrs. Langtry. She has no right to be intelligent, daring, and independent as well as lovely. It is a frightening combination of attributes." —George Bernard Shaw

❦ "I would rather have discovered Mrs. Langtry than have discovered America." —Oscar Wilde

❦ "There shines in Lillie Langtry a purity of spirit. Therein lies the essence of human poetry." —Walt Whitman

❦ "Sure we named a town after her. I dare any man alive to tell me a better name for a town than Langtry." —"Hanging" Judge Roy Bean

❦ "To look at Lillie is to imagine one is dreaming. She is so extraordinary that not even I can do her justice in a painting." —James Whistler

❦ "What I find so astonishing about Mrs. Langtry is that she has a genuine talent on the stage." —Mark Twain

❦ "That woman is a real marvel, and she's so pretty she takes away a man's breath." —Theodore Roosevelt

who had declined to take unfair advantage of her position. When Edward VII died in 1910, Lillie Langtry was summoned by the Queen to pay her last respects.

Eventually, motherhood puts an end to Lillie's stint of carefree indiscretion. To avoid scandal, the handsome Louis ships out on a two-year cruise—like Lieutenant Pinkerton in *Madame Butterfly*—and Lillie raises her daughter in the Bournemouth house the king had built for her. When the child is old enough to ask who her daddy is, Lillie has more possible answers than any woman in the British Isles, but she tells her his name was Maurice and he had been killed in India while hunting tigers.

The Look of Lillie

- More than 1,000 performers (150 of them playing principal characters) were involved in the project.

- Nearly 100 studio sets were used, each one painstakingly and meticulously designed to match the original stately ballrooms, elegant salons, cluttered artists' studios, and each one decorated with period props worth thousands of pounds.

- Exterior scenes were filmed on period racing yachts, at Euston and Waterloo stations, in Hyde Park, along Rotten Row.

- Francesca Annis wore 200 costumes, each one specially designed and fitted. All told, 3,000 costumes were used in *Lillie,* each an original, trimmed where appropriate with lace and ribbon of the period and complemented by handbags, shoes, and gloves. Under each dress the actresses wore underwear of the period—the corsets, the bustles, and the petticoats.

"Once you were married you could roam as much as you liked. They were a very promiscuous lot.… In an age when women were dreadfully exploited by men, Lillie Langtry reversed the situation. She exploited sex."
—Francesca Annis

An Icy Retort

At a fancy dress ball, Lillie commits a faux pas by wearing a costume that exactly matches Bertie's. The Prince fears this "coincidence" will distress his wife, and when he reproaches Lillie, she drops some ice down the royal collar.

At age 29, Lillie finds another rich admirer who builds her a theater and she launches a career as an actress, attracting audiences curious to see what sort of woman had caused all the gossip. Oscar Wilde was at his height as England's most famous playwright, and like all the rest he falls for Lillie—in the theater if not in bed. He advises her on everything from gestures to jewelry.

"She exploited everything and everyone, but she still managed to retain their respect. I don't know if I would have gone to bed with a man to get what I wanted, even if I had been born in her era, when women had so little freedom. But I can think of far worse things people have done to succeed." —Francesca Annis

A Modern Woman

The first society woman to go on stage, and also the first to endorse commercial products (Pear's Soap, Watt's Glycerine Jelly of Violets), Lillie makes her American stage debut in 1882 and is rewarded with 12 curtain calls. In her late forties, Lillie marries a handsome but ineffectual baronet and lives with him for the rest of her long life.

In the eyes of British critic Clive James, Lillie "was one of those rare women who help to forge the shaky but enduring alliance between high society and the upper reaches of Bohemia." Calling

"The marvelous thing about her was she never felt intimidated by society. She set precedents which have become acceptable today. That took courage."
—Francesca Annis

her "a kind of walking poem," James looks beyond her notoriety: "She fascinated not only the nobs, who are always easily fascinated, but the artists, who in many cases can be fascinated only against their will.... That the Prince of Wales went to bed with her means nothing at all: Who cares about him? But that she appealed to the imaginations of men like Wilde and Whistler is a fact not without significance, and the proper mainspring of any story about her life."

Francesca Annis was given the almost impossible task of bringing to life this extraordinary woman who was beautiful, self-assured, witty, intelligent, headstrong, and magnetic—and who ages from 16 to 76. According to writer-director John Gorrie, "Lillie Langtry… retained her beauty throughout her life. This was the real problem faced by Francesca Annis…. She portrays advancing age in a subtle way. It is an attitude of mind rather than what the eye sees, slight differences in movement and reaction. It stems from her own skill…. [Francesca] simply became Lillie Langtry." The British agreed: They awarded Annis the equivalent of an Oscar.

Lillie proved that when it comes to historical preservation, television, not diamonds, could be a girl's best friend, because 50 years after her death on the French Riviera, Lillie Langtry was the talk of the town all over again.

"Lillie had enormous stamina and didn't feel too many creaks when she was old, because she was so incredibly fit. She was Britain's first jogger. She used to run through the park every morning at 7 a.m. and she would go riding and have cold baths." —Francesca Annis

Lillie was the first society woman to go on stage and the first to endorse commercial products.

LOVE *for* LYDIA

*L*YDIA WAS A *jazz-age flapper who made love as easily as she danced the Charleston,*" pronounced the promotional material for LOVE FOR LYDIA. *That single sentence served as a splendid enticement for viewers to watch this compelling story of an English heiress and the four men who loved her.*

12 EPISODES
September 23–December 9, 1979
Produced by *London Weekend Television*
Producer *Tony Wharmby*
Based on the novel by *H. E. Bates*
Writer *Julian Bond*
Directors *John Glenister, Piers Haggard, Christopher Hodson, Simon Langton, Michael Simpson, Tony Wharmby*

CAST
Lydia Aspen *Mel Martin*
Edward Richardson *Christopher Blake*
Alex Sanderson *Jeremy Irons*
Tom Holland *Peter Davison*
Blackie Johnson *Ralph Arliss*
Aunt Juliana *Rachel Kempson*
Aunt Bertie *Beatrix Lehmann*

Smoke and Mirrors
(or Salt and Plastic)

Many of the early scenes were filmed in an abandoned airfield in Northamptonshire. But the lake on which Lydia and her friends skate is no more real than the field of daffodils. The lake was fashioned from tons of granulated white plastic and salt sprinkled liberally over a square mile of special sheeting, transforming the former Battle of Britain airbase into a winter wonderland. And the skates on which Lydia glides her way out of shy repression and into flirtatious flapperhood have hidden wheels inside the blades—an early version of rollerblades. Because spring needed to be filmed well before it actually arrived, a truckload of daffodils was set rootless in a still-cold field.

"The sensitive cameras dwell exactly where they ought—on faded drawing rooms and exquisite winter landscapes, on the palatial interiors of Daimlers and on the vividness of the human gaze. The social landscape is deftly sketched in—the decaying local dynasties, the seediness of small town civic life, the sanatorium's long shadow across everything that happens. The story opened, and continues to unfold, at a leisurely pace, and indeed, why hurry? The interest throughout lies in the revelation of how people change, interrelate, love and destroy each other."

—Michael Church, *The Times* (London)

"It was important to get the taste of the countryside. Bates' characters grew out of that countryside and are dominated by it. At the start, it is cold and icy, people are hunched up against the weather and Lydia is little more than a child. But as the characters mature and their relationships strengthen, the landscape changes.... Lydia blossoms into a woman."

—Producer Tony Wharmby

In the opening sequence Lydia Aspen's wealthy father breaks his neck in a fall from his horse, leaving his shy, quiet daughter to be brought up by two eccentric aunts and an oddball uncle. Looking at bashful Lydia and recalling the PBS promise of love and Charlestons to come, seasoned viewers could recognize the reliable dramatic convention where the leading lady's timidity is a setup for a stunning turnaround. For Lydia the breakthrough occurs when she hears the first crank of the Victrola. By the end of the episode her shyness has melted. When she plants a kiss on a young reporter, it is apparent that he is to be but the first to fall victim to love for Lydia. The others are a farmer, a chauffeur named

Blackie, and a man-about-town, played by Jeremy Irons three years before *Brideshead Revisited* and 12 years before his Oscar award.

The late 1920s and early '30s were a time of giddy prosperity in England when rich folks danced to the latest American jazz, young men called each other "old chap," and young women were sweet and flirtatious. Lydia was an exception. She was fascinating but

"*Love for Lydia is a slow, bitter, relentless tale, Hardy with gall and wormwood.*"
—Alistair Cooke, in response to a publisher who had dismissed Bates' early writings as "Thomas Hardy with water."

arrogant, and she could win and ruin any man she chose. Mel Martin was excellent in the title role, convincingly moving from bashful teen to spoiled princess to alluring temptress to liberated woman while retaining the audience's intense interest in her. Like many English actresses, she seemed to American audiences to have

Alistair Cooke found his memory pleasantly refreshed by much of the music in *Love for Lydia*. Though only a child during the period portrayed in the series, he's a jazz buff and an accomplished pianist who has cut several records.

"I understand Lydia, why she behaved as she did. Suddenly, the whole world was before her, and she wanted to see and do everything. She was an innocent, untutored in the ways of the world. She behaved instinctively." —Mel Martin

"My father had a prodigious memory and once in the twenties he saw a very elegantly dressed lady waiting to catch a train to London on a very dingy railway platform in a Midlands leather town. He stored the image away for 25 years, wondering who she was and what she was doing in such a place. The whole book is built on finding the answer." —Richard Bates

come suddenly from nowhere. In fact, Martin came to the role after several years at the Bristol Old Vic and the Royal Shakespeare Company—neither place usually considered a training ground for nabbing the role of a spoiled provincial heiress with a thirst for fun and an eye for men.

A Family Affair

The series was adapted from a novel by H. E. Bates, who approved the concept shortly before his death and left the task to his son, Richard, an experienced TV producer. After seven years of working to keep his father's poetic images intact, producer Bates sold the project to London Weekend Television, the company responsible for *Upstairs, Downstairs.* A disagreement over the first two episodes led to the dismissal of Bates and the resignation of the original director. The price tag for scrapping the two episodes and sacking young Bates was more than a million pounds. Even as the producer, the director, and the controller argued about whose artistic vision should prevail, the show aired in Britain and was a smash hit.

The ultimate responsibility for turning the very short novel into a 12-part series fell to scriptwriter Julian Bond. "There were about 17 pages of the book—much of that description—to draw on for each one-hour episode," he explained. "*Love for Lydia* is shaped as a recollection, illuminated by shafts of hindsights from a mature narrator (the 'I' of the book) reflecting on the vulnerability, the shortsightedness, the passion, the carelessness and illogic of

youth, and the unbearable happiness and sorrow of young love. It uses time very fluidly, with an interlude of two years dismissed in a line. Much of it is internal: about how people felt in retrospect, rather than what they actually did or said. There is relatively little dialogue, most of it fragmentary. There is a great deal of descriptive writing." Regardless of these difficulties, Bond succeeded in writing a fascinating script about a very perplexing person.

From the music to the clothing, the series was handsomely produced with great attention to the details of English jazz-age life. Such hotsy-totsy songs as "You're the Cream in My Coffee" and "Button Up Your Overcoat" rolled off Victrolas, while the costumes were so authentic that viewers could almost feel the soft sensation of short silk dresses swishing across the thighs of pretty young women on the dance floor. To get the right look, the costumers raided the secondhand shops, then cleaned and restored their finds. But under the hot arc lights of the film studio, the old dresses quickly disintegrated, especially those that were shredding to begin with. When the series was over, most American viewers felt they had been on a slow but pleasurable trip—like taking a cruise ship instead of an airplane.

"Lydia didn't want to hurt people. She would have been staggered if she knew she was hurting. She was flirting outrageously, just having a good time. Lydia never realized the devastating harm she was causing because of her lack of experience." —Mel Martin

PRIDE *and* PREJUDICE

5 EPISODES
October 26–November 23, 1980
Produced by *BBC*
Producer *Jonathan Powell*
Based on the novel by *Jane Austen*
Writer *Fay Weldon*
Director *Cyril Coke*

CAST

Elizabeth Bennet *Elizabeth Garvie*
Mr. Darcy *David Rintoul*
Jane Bennet *Sabina Franklyn*
Mr. Bingley *Osmund Bullock*
Mr. Bennet *Moray Watson*
Mrs. Bennet *Priscilla Morgan*
Lydia Bennet *Natalie Ogle*
Mary Bennet *Tessa Peake-Jones*
Mr. Wickham *Pete Settelen*
Lady Catherine de Bourgh *Judy Parfitt*
Mr. Collins *Malcolm Rennie*
Charlotte Lucas Collins *Irene Richard*
Caroline Bingley *Marsha Fitzalan*

JANE AUSTEN'S *working title for her comedy of manners was "First Impressions," a phrase that emphasizes a key theme of her novel: that first impressions may be lasting, but they are often false or misleading—a lesson that is usually learned too late in life to make much difference. Austen wrote* PRIDE AND PREJUDICE *when she was 21 years old and revised it 16 years later for publication. It was intended solely for the pleasure of her parents and sisters at a time when families would entertain themselves by reading aloud.*

Pride and Prejudice is the story of the Bennet family, who live in a modest but comfortable country house in rural England at the beginning of the 19th century. The principal business of Mrs. Bennet's life is to find suitable husbands for her five daughters, and being good daughters, they are equally devoted to the project. Jane is the Bennet family beauty, but the brightest of the girls is Elizabeth, "as delightful a creature as ever appeared in print," according to her creator, and the novel pivots on her spirited intelligence. The other three are crazy for uniforms and take long walks into nearby Meryton, headquarters of the local regiment, and we all know what *that* can lead to.

When the story opens, Mother Bennet has her eye on Netherfield Park, the grandest country house in the neighborhood, which has been rented for the season to a Mr. Bingley of London. She is pleased to learn that he is rich, and overjoyed to hear that he is a bachelor. Her daughters are quick to realize the possibilities, and the resulting hubbub throws the excitable cast into one of those giggly scenes where no one sits very long in one place and the din is deafening.

At this point Father Bennet, a clergyman, suggests that perhaps Bingley is not moving into the country for the single purpose of

"I think we're very alike. Elizabeth Bennet is such a determined person. She's absolutely honest, says exactly what she thinks. I can't cover up if something isn't the truth or isn't honest, either. She's Jane Austen's liberated woman. She knew what she wanted, but she lived in a time when you couldn't be so radical and outspoken as you are today."
—Elizabeth Garvie

"I have often said that certain great novels are difficult to adapt for stage or screen or even for radio.... They are difficult because their whole is greater than their parts—more than dialogue, incident, scene-setting; more, indeed, than what I can loosely call their philosophy. The novel at its best can do things that cannot be done, or done only approximately, on stage or screen....

"I would say of Fay Weldon's adaptation that it preserves much of what one thinks of as characteristically Jane Austen.... Jane Austen's main interest as a novelist was in human relationships—relationships which she rightly regarded as complex, irrational, and fluid. The primary virtue of this production, which stems, I think, from Fay Weldon's adaptation, is that." —Bernard Davies, *Broadcast*

marrying one of the Bennet girls. He does this with the dry humor and the obedient demeanor of a man accustomed to living in the same house with six women. Just when things are starting to quiet down it is revealed that Bingley will make his first local appearance at a ball— news that sends the sisters into another decibel-raising frenzy. At the party we meet the handsome Mr. Bingley and his close friend Mr. Darcy, who is even more handsome.

Although Elizabeth Bennet is a charming role, she represents the "prejudice" part of the title, though she manages to shake it off as her admiration for Darcy grows, particularly after sipping tea in his drawing room, which is the size of your local supermarket. The rich, snobbish Darcy represents the "pride" of the title, but eventually he learns that there is more to people than money and social standing, a discovery that appears more often in Regency novels than in real life.

In the end, after a series of ups and downs and turnabouts, Jane gets Bingley—probably because neither of them has ever said an unkind word about anyone and they are therefore vulnerable to romance. Elizabeth changes her mind about Darcy and they become engaged. Pride has been humbled and prejudice dissolved. And a feminist voice is heard 100 years before the suffrage movement: Elizabeth gets her man by what scriptwriter Fay Weldon calls "unconventional means—audacity rather than compliance."

The settings for the production of *Pride and Prejudice* have been selected from what must be, by now, the BBC Architectural Digest of Stately Homes of England whose real owners—if they exist at all—probably cowered in some remote turret while the filmmakers swarmed over the antique premises like Norman invaders. Longbourne, the Bennet house, is actually Thorpe Tilney Hall, and Mr. Bingley's Netherfield Hall is Well Vale, both in Lincolnshire. Mr. Darcy's imposing Regency pile called Pemberley is Renishaw Hall in Derbyshire, the family home of Osbert, Edith, and Sacheverell Sitwell, the eccentric sibling

The role of Elizabeth was won by 23-year-old newcomer Elizabeth Garvie, who was just out of drama school when the producer saw her photograph on a talent agent's wall and auditioned her the following day. The English critics flipped over her dimples and her expressive brown eyes, and she returned to Masterpiece Theatre three years later in *The Good Soldier.*

poets who filled its halls with costumed artists and other post-Edwardian oddballs in a manner Darcy might enjoy and Austen would satirize.

No Room of Her Own

Although Austen lived through the turbulent years of the Napoleonic wars, her focus was the social and moral wars at home, and her understanding of herself and those around her is complete and assured. She realized that the lives of most people didn't turn on high ideals and historic events but mainly on money, property, and marriage, which might involve, if possible, a little love. As Alistair Cooke explains, "Austen was content mainly just to sit back and observe the fusses and follies of the people around her. And in the process to invent a quite new form, a short, exquisite satirical novel."

Austen never married, and she never had a room of her own, but she managed to write six novels in the midst of the daily confusion of the household. She died at the early age of 41. Literary critics who marvel at her knowledge of life, given how little of it she had seen, are forgetting that the things that interested her most are "those little matters on which the daily happiness of private life depends." This BBC adaptation transfers them easily to the television screen.

Although it was inevitable that Weldon would be criticized for what she left out of a well-loved classic and what she added to it, she stated her aim in Austenian simplicity: "I hope it makes *Pride and Prejudice* accessible to those who might never read the book and pleasurable for those who know it well."

DANGER UXB

✦━━━✦━━✦━━✦━━✦━━✦━━━✦

13 EPISODES
January 4–April 5, 1981
Produced by *Thames Television*
Producer *John Hawkesworth*
Based on the book Unexploded Bomb by
Major Bill Hartley
Writers *John Hawkesworth, Jeremy Paul,*
Don Shaw, Paul Wheeler, Kenneth Clark
Directors *Ferdinand Fairfax, Roy Ward Baker,*
Jeremy Summers, Henry Herbert,
Simon Langton, Douglas Camfield

CAST
Brian Ash *Anthony Andrews*
Susan Mount *Judy Geeson*
Dr. Gillespie *Iain Cuthbertson*
Lieutenant Rodgers *Jeremy Sinden*
Sergeant James *Maurice Roeves*
Sapper Salt *Kenneth Cranham*
Sapper Powell *Robert Pugh*
Sapper Wilkins *George Innes*
Corporal Horrocks *Ken Kitson*
Norma Baker *Deborah Watling*

OF ALL THE SIGNS *in wartime England, none was dreaded more than "DANGER UXB," which* marked the site of an unexploded bomb. The series of the same name set off an explosion of its own when Masterpiece Theatre dropped this lively wartime suspense series into the comparative tranquility of its tenth season.

Brian Ash is portrayed by Anthony Andrews, who was introduced to American viewers in the brief role of the Marquis of Stockbridge, the man who married Georgina in *Upstairs, Downstairs*. Ash was his first big role in a career that would take off brilliantly in *Brideshead Revisited*.

Bombs Away

Between 1939 and 1945 nearly 250,000 bombs were dropped on the United Kingdom by Nazi bombers; more than 20,000 unexploded bombs were moved by disposers during the war.

The 13-part series opens in September 1940. War has raged on the continent for more than a year, and the Germans have overrun Poland, Luxembourg, Belgium, the Netherlands, and France. New weaponry enables Hitler's troops to deliver brutal bombs at British targets from launching sites across the English Channel. The blitz of London—the longest and most vicious attack against a civilian population in human history—has begun.

The bombs that explode on impact created pockets of destruction in London and nearby cities. But the unexploded bombs presented a new problem that the English were not prepared to handle at first. Within three months 2,500 unexploded bombs lay scattered across southeast England. Some were buried as deep as 30 feet, at the bottom of holes they

had burrowed. Others had lodged in walls or bounced into gardens. The British were confused: Why had so many of the German bombs failed to explode? It was a question that was soon answered. The mere presence of DANGER UXB signs on highways and around railroad stations could paralyze transportation at vital points. Then, as the attacks increased, the Germans delivered more delayed-action bombs intended to kill the bomb defusers. Whenever the English figured out how to defuse a new type of bomb, the news got back to the Germans with such astonishing rapidity that a total security and news ban was eventually placed on all bomb-disposal activity.

A Perfect Landing

One World War II veteran recalls a 500-pound bomb that scooped four feet off the surface of a road in Seaford, went through the wall of a garage, through the front window of a car, out through the back wall, over a graveyard, through a school wall, over the desks of a classroom, and through another wall before it came to rest on the lavatory seat of an outside privy next to a bar. "It was a perfect position to be defused," he said.

𝒟ead Man's Shoes

The series follows six men of section 347, a Bomb Disposal Unit of the Royal Engineers, particularly Brian Ash, a young officer initially assigned to the 27th Tunnelling Company who learns in the first episode that his unit is in the new business of defusing bombs, not building tunnels. The episode is ominously subtitled "Dead Man's Shoes," referring to

"In its own chin-up-while-socializing-for-merrie-olde-England way, Danger UXB *could conceivably be criticized as 'blitz-chic.' But that is not meant as a criticism.... It is brittle, exciting entertainment at the same time that it explores its own fascinating world of wartime England."*
—Arthur Unger, *Christian Science Monitor*

"I remember, only a dozen years ago, the case of a golfer walking along a fairway, a famous golf course in the South of England, [and] his ball landed a few yards away from an oak tree, and when he came to it, he took out an iron club and the moment he touched the ground with it, the tree blew up. Miraculously he was unharmed. Incidentally, he was allowed a free drop with no penalty." —Alistair Cooke

A Deadly Job

During World War II some British soldiers volunteered for bomb-disposal duty, while many were selected for it on a "you, you, and you" basis. The earliest defusing techniques were extremely crude, relying on hammers and chisels. Between August and December 1940 the bomb-disposal men died at the rate of one a day, mostly officers because only officers did the defusing. The on-the-job life expectancy was ten weeks, making an assignment to a bomb squad the equivalent of a death sentence. After six months the survivors were given the option of a transfer, but few chose to desert their comrades.

To ensure accuracy and authenticity of this film, specialists from the Royal Engineers were consulted and present at filming whenever the program showed one of the characters working against time to defuse a bomb.

Ash's predecessor, who was killed the day before when he made one wrong move in disarming a bomb—a grim scenario played over and over as the series progresses.

Along with other officers of the unit, Ash is billeted with the Baker family, whose house has been commandeered by the Royal Engineers for living quarters. On his first night Ash discovers that one of the amenities of Mrs. Baker's household is her baby-faced blond daughter Norma (played by Deborah Watling), who finds air raids sexually arousing. This proclivity coupled with her natural patriotism enables her to help the war effort in ways that are immediately apparent to all the servicemen, but not to her mother.

During the six months of filming *Danger UXB* in 1980, German bombs were still being defused on an average of two or three a week, which caused problems for onlookers who didn't

"I didn't want to portray Brian in any sense as a James Bond who defies the impossible ... he's the kind of hero who gets his hands dirty and who doesn't come out whiter than white all the time." —Anthony Andrews

know whether they were watching a film in production or the real thing. The filming locations included London (the Thames docks, Wimbledon Theatre, Whitechapel Road, and the Fulham Power Station), Stow-on-the-Wold, and Cromer, an east-coast resort where the pier was partially dismantled, to the consternation of residents and fishermen. An old school building on the south side of Clapham Common was used as a base

of operations for the series. With its windows taped, the building doubled as barracks and dozens of other interiors.

The inspiration for *Danger UXB* was an account, *Unexploded Bomb,* by a veteran of the bomb-disposal units, Major Bill Hartley. Producer-writer John Hawkesworth saw in the book the possibilities for a television series of continuing suspense and character development. He chose to leave the 13th episode open-ended, to allow for a possible sequel, but that project never materialized, despite the series' success in keeping viewers at the very edge of their seats.

UPDATE

When *Danger UXB* aired in England, one viewer realized that the "souvenir" in his daughter's toy cupboard was actually a butterfly bomb which, as he had learned from an episode of the program, cannot be defused. He buried it in his garden in Sussex—and 400 homes had to be evacuated when a Royal Engineer Major finally came to detonate it.

Writer of Relevance

Andrew Davies

ANDREW DAVIES is one of the most sought-after English television writers of the 1990s, following the enormous success of *House of Cards* (1991), its first sequel, *To Play the King* (1994), and the elaborate production of *Middlemarch* (1994).

Davies began writing freelance radio plays in 1960 and didn't even own a television set until he married, had children, and began staying home nights. After watching innovative programs by writers such as the late Dennis Potter (*Pennies From Heaven, The Singing Detective*), Davies decided to try writing for television. His third attempt at a script sold in 1965, but it took him seven years to sell his next two scripts. In the meantime, he taught high school and at Warwick University.

His popular British medical series, *A Very Peculiar Practice* (1986), finally brought Davies to the attention of the general public. Among his many other credits are Masterpiece Theatre's *To Serve Them All My Days* (1982) and *The Final Cut* (1996), (third in the Urquhart trilogy), *Mother Love* (1989) for PBS' Mystery! series, a new BBC version of Jane Austen's *Pride and Prejudice* (1996), the British sitcom *Game On!* (written with Bernadette Davis), the London stage hit *Fearless Frank,* which also had a brief Broadway run, and the international hit feature film *Circle of Friends* (1995). His latest screenplay is for a feature film version of the Gothic novel *The Monk.*

Your television adaptations of period novels are often praised for their relevance to contemporary issues. For example, many American critics saw a parallel between the problems of the shell-shocked World War I veteran trying to resume his civilian life in To Serve Them All My Days *and the plight of Vietnam War veterans in the United States. Do you purposely look for that kind of contemporary relevance?*

Davies I'd be very reluctant to take a project like that on if I didn't feel it had some kind of relevance. And if it has, I like to point it up. I think the audience should include more than just people who think this is great literature, but also much younger people who might never read a novel by someone like George Eliot. I wouldn't want to adapt anything unless I felt it really involved me personally in some way, so that I could identify with the author's feelings and put some of my own feelings into it.

Many reviews of Middlemarch *said you had discovered a sense of humor few had ever noticed in George Eliot. But your own sense of humor is keen. Whose sense of humor were we getting—yours or Eliot's?*

Davies I think it really is there in the book. It's one of the more overlooked things about George Eliot. Because she's this formidable thinker and takes life very seriously, people tend to overlook the sly wit. Some of her lowlife types are quite rich comic characters, and the dialogue is very funny. It's a question of just pointing up the humor where it is. I don't think I put in humor that wasn't there, although I suppose what I might have done is omitted great chunks of her more sententious comments on life and people, so the proportion of humor was different from the proportion in the book.

Do you have a standard approach to breaking down a long novel into episodes?

Davies No. They're great writers, after all, so I usually hope the way they've constructed it will work on television, but often it doesn't quite work out that way. With *Middlemarch*, finding episodes wasn't a problem because George Eliot published in serial form, so her long chunks did almost correspond to dividing the book into episodes.

You had to trim a lot of Eliot's scenes even for a multipart version of Middlemarch, *and you invented some scenes that weren't in Austen's* Pride and Prejudice. *How do you decide where to depart from the original?*

Davies There's usually a different problem with every book. Eliot takes up a couple of characters for quite a long period, then goes back and picks up the characters she has left behind. She's a bit like somebody trying to carry five suitcases along a railway platform when she can only manage two at a time. If you do that on television, people are going to forget the characters you left behind and they're going to be irritated when you stop to go pick them up. So it was a question of interweaving the stories much more than Eliot does.

Austen's *Pride and Prejudice* is a beautifully constructed book. It's only when I started adapting it that I realized the first half is full of vivid scenes that almost just need copying out, but in the second half everybody goes off to different parts of the country to write each other letters. That was extremely difficult to adapt. One had to actually cheat a little and invent a few scenes that weren't there or dramatize other scenes they were just writing letters about.

Does that get you in trouble with literary purists?

Davies It really hasn't. With *Middlemarch,* I was invited to meet with the George Eliot Fellowship, a society dedicated to Eliot and her works. They were very suspicious of the project before it went out, but they were very generous about it after they'd seen it. They were very understanding that a certain amount of cuts had to be made and some of their favorite bits have disappeared. Although I didn't want to offend them, I certainly wasn't writing every scene with them in mind.

What about adapting the works of living authors?

Davies I find it a little bit more nerve-wracking with living authors. I suppose one of the more interesting cases is Michael Dobbs, who wrote the novels on which *House of Cards* and *To Play the King* were based.

Dobbs is very right-wing in his politics and has worked for the Conservative [Tory] Party. I tend to take a sharply satirical view of the Tory party, and I'm always pushing my adaptations of his books much further in that direction than he wants them to go.

In *To Play the King,* Dobbs was very reverential about the monarchy, while I wanted to show the king as a sympathetic character we could like, but also as a man who's in a ridiculous position, quite unaware of his immense privileges and out of touch with the way ordinary people really live. Dobbs worried about that because he thought the palace might not like it.

One day I told him I couldn't understand why the people in his books seem to get into such a desperate state about getting a knighthood. I told him I personally wouldn't want a knighthood, and he said, "God, I'd die for one! Of course I want a knighthood! Imagine not wanting one!"

We have quite a good time together, but we don't really understand each other at all. He always has been very complimentary about my work. But he does tend to say, "I wish his political education had been as good as his literary education," which is quite witty, I think.

Are you kept busy rewriting your scripts all through the long period of filming?

Davies No. Usually we hope to get the script pretty solid before they start filming. I go to the rehearsal period, where any difficulties are thrashed out. Once filming starts, it's rare that they'll ask me for a rewrite—and that usually would be something to do with the actual conditions during filming, like maybe there's six inches of snow on the ground and they think perhaps we should make some reference to it.

How important is it for you to know who's going to play one of the roles you're writing?

Davies Oddly enough, I hadn't imagined Ian Richardson or anyone like him playing Francis Urquhart in *House of Cards*. I'd always imagined Urquhart as a big, burly man, someone who dominated people both physically and mentally. So I had to readjust quite quickly when Ian was cast. Of course, as soon as I heard him do it, I couldn't imagine it done any other way.

It was enormously helpful when I was writing the second and third series. You know who you're writing for and what he does best—things like those little looks he gives in those asides to the camera. Ian can do so much with a little look that I found I was writing fewer lines and just writing down something like: "Urquhart gives us one of his looks."

How often do you have to rewrite a scene because the actor doesn't like it?

Davies I can hardly remember any instance of that. Occasionally, they'll tell you it would be more comfortable if the order of words were changed, and that's something one always agrees to. But there was one striking example in *House of Cards*. The actress we originally cast to play Mattie Storin, the journalist who has an affair with Urquhart, objected to saying, "I want to call you Daddy." She found that offensive and expected it to be changed. But we told her that was the core of the perverse relationship they both enjoy. In fact, the decision became hers: Either play the part as written or resign. So she resigned, and we cast Susannah Harker, who was actually jolly good.

How do you think that dispute would have been resolved if you had been working in American television?

Davies I've heard of awful things happening to writers in America. What seems to happen is they pay you a lot, then treat you like dirt. Is that right? We don't get paid riches beyond the dreams of avarice, but certainly we do get our work treated with respect, which is worth a lot more.

On the other hand, you created quite a sensation when you blasted the British television industry during a public lecture for "narcotizing the viewing population with tired old drama formulas."

Davies I got a tremendous number of letters and phone calls in support, mostly from creative people and program makers. But the top management at the BBC were terribly hurt, upset, and angry with me. I was directing my attack much more at independent television than at the BBC, but the press chose to focus on the bits that were critical of the BBC and ignored all the rest.

In fact, I wasn't saying British television is rubbish. I was just trying to sound a warning note of a tendency that seems to be developing. There's so much emphasis on ratings at the expense of almost everything else that program makers are tremendously tempted to just imitate the last thing that was successful.

One of the things I've complained about is that the freedom for talented, creative producers to back their own taste at the BBC and the independent companies seems to be eroding. There are too many committees creeping in and referrals upwards. Nobody seems to be able to take a decision on his own. They're now subject to a decision by somebody higher up the line.

Do you think this is something the British networks are learning from their dealings with American television or from co-financing arrangements like the ones with Masterpiece Theatre?

Davies I don't think it's spreading like a disease from your culture to ours. I've certainly seen no signs of it. The co-producers we've dealt with are extremely supportive and, if anything, tend slightly toward the reverential and traditional.

Which of the programs that you've written have been your most popular in England?

Davies Probably *House of Cards* and *To Play the King,* although the one with the biggest cult following is *A Very Peculiar Practice.* They tried to do an American version. Terrence McNally wrote a pilot, but I didn't think it worked. Neither did the American networks.

Anyone in America with your success as a television writer would have started producing his own shows by now, just to retain control of them. Why are so many top British television writers still freelancers?

Davies There's still much opportunity for writing serious, thoughtful, intelligent drama on television here. We complain about it becoming more formulaic and commercial, but one can still do things like *House of Cards* and *Middlemarch.* There isn't so much the feeling, as there must be in the States, that you've got to go into the movies in order to do quality work. ❧

A Town Like Alice (Alice Productions Pty Ltd. in association with The Seven Network Australia, The Australian Film Commission, and The Victoria Film Corporation)*
October 4–November 8, 1981, 6 episodes
Based on the novel by Nevil Shute

Edward and Mrs. Simpson (Thames Television)
November 15–December 27, 1981, 7 episodes
Based on *Edward VIII* by Frances Donaldson

The Flame Trees of Thika (Euston Films in association with Consolidated Productions for Thames Television)*
January 3–February 14, 1982, 7 episodes
Based on the memoir by Elspeth Huxley

I Remember Nelson (ATV Network)
February 21–March 14, 1982, 4 episodes

Love in a Cold Climate (Thames Television)
March 28–May 16, 1982, 8 episodes
Based on the novels by Nancy Mitford

Flickers (ATV Network)*
May 23–June 27, 1982, 6 episodes

To Serve Them All My Days (BBC in association with the Australian Film Commission)
October 10, 1982–January 2, 1983, 13 episodes
Based on the novel by R. F. Delderfield

The Good Soldier (Granada Television)
January 9, 1983, single 2-hour episode
Based on the novel by Ford Madox Ford

Winston Churchill—The Wilderness Years (Southern Pictures)
January 16–March 6, 1983, 8 episodes

On Approval (BBC)
March 13, 1983, single 2-hour episode

Drake's Venture (Thames Television)
March 27, 1983, single 2-hour episode

Private Schulz (BBC)
April 3–May 8, 1983, 5 episodes

Sons and Lovers (BBC in association with 20th Century Fox Television)
May 15–June 26, 1983, 7 episodes
Based on the novel by D. H. Lawrence

Pictures (Central Independent Television)
October 2–November 13, 1983, 7 episodes

The Citadel (BBC)
November 20, 1983–January 22, 1984, 10 episodes
Based on the novel by A. J. Cronin

The Irish R.M., Series 1 (Little Bird in association with Ulster Television and RTE)
January 29–March 4, 1984, 6 episodes
Based on the novels by Edith Sommerville and Martin Ross

The Tale of Beatrix Potter (BBC in association with Consolidated Films)
March 25–April 1, 1984, 2 episodes
Based on the biographies by Margaret Lane

Nancy Astor (BBC/Time-Life Films)
April 8–May 27, 1984, 8 episodes

Barchester Chronicles (BBC)
October 28–December 9, 1984, 7 episodes
Based on *The Warden* and *Barchester Towers* by Anthony Trollope

The Jewel in the Crown (Granada Television)*
December 16, 1984–March 17, 1985, 14 episodes
Based on *The Raj Quartet* by Paul Scott

All for Love (Granada Television)
March 31–April 28, 1985, 5 episodes
Based on the stories by Elizabeth Taylor, Francis King, Rumer Godden, Susan Hill, and Philip Oakes

Strangers and Brothers (BBC)
May 5–June 16, 1985, 7 episodes
Based on the novels by C. P. Snow

The Last Place on Earth (Central Independent Television)*
October 20–November 24, 1985, 6 episodes
Based on the book *Scott and Amundsen* by Roland Huntford

Bleak House (BBC)*
December 1, 1985–January 19, 1986, 8 episodes
Based on the novel by Charles Dickens

Lord Mountbatten: The Last Viceroy (George Walker Television)
January 26–March 2, 1986, 6 episodes
Based on the book by Alan Campbell-Johnson

By the Sword Divided, Series 1 (BBC in association with Consolidated Productions)
March 23–May 18, 1986, 9 episodes
Series created by John Hawkesworth

The Irish R.M., Series 2 (Little Bird in association with Ulster Television and RTE)
May 25–June 29, 1986, 6 episodes
Based on the novels by Edith Somerville and Martin Ross

---

*Available on video §Video out of print
Video cassettes of many Masterpiece Theatre programs are available at public libraries and video rental stores. For information about the availability of any program or about purchasing videos, call VideoFinders, a service of public television station KCET, at 1-800-343-4727.*

Seasons 11–15

⊷⊷⊷⊷⊷ ⊷⊷⊷⊷⊷

6 EPISODES

October 4–November 8, 1981

Produced by *Alice Productions Pty Ltd. in association
with The Seven Network Australia, The Australian Film
Commission, and The Victoria Film Corporation*
Producer *Henry Crawford*
Based on the novel by *Nevil Shute*
Writers *Tom Hegarty, Rosemary Anne Sisson*
Director *David Stevens*

CAST

Joe Harman *Bryan Brown*
Jean Paget *Helen Morse*
Noel Strachan *Gordon Jackson*
Sergeant Mifune *Yuki Shimoda*
Mrs. Frith *Dorothy Alison*

A Town Like Alice

*I*N THE FIRST EPISODE *of* A TOWN
LIKE ALICE *a group of English
women and children are being force-
marched on a dusty Malaysian road as prisoners
of the Japanese in World War II. They come
upon a truck being repaired by two soldiers in
khaki uniforms. The women are startled at the
sound of male voices speaking their own language. One of the women approaches the vehicle
and asks cautiously, "Are you English?" A
healthy young man appears from under the
truck, smiles, and answers in jaunty soldier jargon, "Na bloody fear, we're Aussies!"*

"*A Town Like Alice* is a story of courage in a terrifically traumatic situation—war. And it's also about the breaking down of class and cultural barriers. There's also a great sense of joy in it too." —Helen Morse

The bravado of that response provides viewers with an immensely exhilarating image of people caught in a desperate wartime situation but managing to hold on to their humor, their pride, and their optimism.

A Town Like Alice is adapted from Nevil Shute's novel of the same title (though called *The Legacy* in Britain), a bold and believable interweaving of fact and romance played against the turmoil of Japanese-occupied Malaya. The Australian television production tells the story partly in the present, several years after the war, and partly in the past. One flashback takes viewers to early 1940, to show the colony of British rubber planters and their families gathered for a pleasant day of tennis, cocktails, and ordering the natives around. They are living in Malaya, as they have for years, under the protection of the British navy and land forces, which include Australian troops. This happy picture is shattered when the Japanese overrun the Malay peninsula and the British naval base at Singapore in a surprise attack. It is the first great Allied disaster in

"Shute was an aeronautical engineer before he was a novelist. His narrative was scientifically stressed, tested in the wind-tunnel and commercially practical. He was also an Englishman who fell deeply, but not uncritically in love with Australia and the Australian people: hence, the real and sympathetically observed tussle for the heroine's affections between uncouth salt of the earth in the outback and po-faced professional men in London."

—Philip Purser, *The Sunday Telegraph*

"I felt it was an opportunity to play the definitive Australian.... The characters accept responsibility for having found themselves in a situation, and just set about fixing it in the most positive way. They're game and I like that." —Bryan Brown

"In this production no shortcuts were taken. The Asian locations were the real thing. The Japanese were real Japanese. Above all the Australia on show was the real Australia, with all its colours uncorrected. You could hear Jean's skin drying as she stood outlined against the red earth." —Clive James, The Observer

"I couldn't resist it. I was in England to look at something else and there was this Australian series literally stunning the entire country, and I knew from just looking at the first episode that we had to start off in the fall with this one."

—Joan Wilson, Executive Producer, Masterpiece Theatre

the Pacific war zone. The Japanese army sends the male captives—both civilians and soldiers—to work camps. Because no Japanese commander wants to assume responsibility for the women and children, they are sent on a forced march across Malaysia in search of a nonexistent family prison camp. During the six-month trek disease, hunger, and exhaustion claim all but the hardiest of the group.

Their ordeal is lessened for a brief time by the kindness of Joe Harman, a lanky Australian from Queensland who trades gasoline from his stalled truck for medicine and soap for the women. He is attracted to Jean, and she to him, and they have a few precious hours together one night exchanging stories of home.

It is a poignant moment in the tropical night stolen from their captors. The two fall in love without touching and without a word of endearment. Everything is in their eyes, and it breaks your heart.

Joe's truck is repaired, but before he leaves he steals some chickens from a Japanese Army captain and sends them to the women. For this he is captured, tortured, and crucified. The women and children are made to watch and Jean is devastated.

As the exhausting march continues, the women trade their few possessions for food and eventually adopt the sarongs and the lifestyle of the Malaysians. When the sergeant who guards them dies of sunstroke, they find a village that gives them sanctuary in return for work in the rice paddies. After the war, Jean returns to build a well for the villagers in gratitude for their wartime friendship. Upon hearing the wonderful news that Joe survived his ordeal and is alive in Australia, she sets out to find him. He, meanwhile, is on his way to London looking for her.

The death march in the novel is based on a true story, though Shute changed the locale and the nationality of the prisoners, and added the romance. In truth, 80 Dutch women and children were rounded up by the Japanese and forced to cross Sumatra on a death march that lasted two and a half years. The character of Joe is based on a manager of an Australian sheep station who survived crucifixion by the Japanese in Malaysia, and Jean is based on a Dutch woman who endured the death march in Sumatra. But the two never met.

Going Down-Under

A Town Like Alice was the first Masterpiece Theatre series made outside of England. It was produced by Henry Crawford with backing from three Australian companies and the BBC, and it was filmed entirely on location in Australia, New Zealand (standing in for Scotland), England, and on Langkawi, a small island off the northwestern coast of Malaysia. Before filming began on Langkawi the native gods had to be appeased with singing, dancing, and a $100 nondeductible contribution to the local witch doctors (this may account for the perfect weather the crew encountered).

Co-stars Helen Morse and Bryan Brown were already famous in Australia, where the film and television industry was burgeoning. Their pleasant, straightforward style quickly endeared them to Americans as well. Morse might be considered rather ordinary looking, but when she speaks and laughs she projects an unmeasurable beauty and radiance that reaches right through the television screen. Likable Brown was a big hit with Americans (he had also been in *Breaker Morant*) and became Nancy Reagan's second favorite actor—next to you-know-who—and he moved directly from the role of Joe to film another Australian story, *The Thorn Birds*.

As in so many love stories, there is a third person tugging at the heartstrings of one member of the principal couple. Noel Strachan is a middle-aged barrister hired to sort out Jean's inheritance when she returns to England. He is very much in love with her. Gordon Jackson played this role six years after his great success as Hudson, the unflappable butler in *Upstairs, Downstairs*.

Despite the suffering the characters endure, the story ends happily for Joe and Jean. They are reunited along the Great Barrier Reef. They settle in Willstown, a tiny fictional spot in the Australian outback on the road to Alice Springs. But it is difficult for them to bridge the gap of years until Jean puts on her old Malay sarong and their relationship becomes simple and easy again. After an initial period of adjustment to Joe's rough and dusty life, they marry and set out to build Willstown into a better place. Maybe, someday, it might even become … a town like Alice.

"Getting 50 people and 12 tons of equipment into the country alone took us 12 months of negotiations with the government, and I think we ended up dealing with about seven different departments, and all wanted to read the script, and all had editorial comments to make on the scripts, and we had to try and appease all of these people.… One of the reasons we went to Malaysia was for the rice paddies, and when we arrived there had been a four-month drought, so there was no water in evidence. If we were in Australia we would just put a pump in some water and fill up the rice paddy to do the scene. But the problem there was that you just can't do that; you've got to go to the Department of Agriculture and several other government departments and get written permission, which is difficult, and then the god has to be consulted again to make sure that you're not upsetting the balance of nature." —Producer Henry Crawford

A Town Like Alice *Was:*

❦ The first non-British miniseries to air on Masterpiece Theatre

❦ The first Australian-made drama series ever seen on PBS

❦ The first Australian-made drama ever seen on the BBC in Britain, where it drew an audience of more than 16 million, outranked only by *Holocaust* and *Roots*

"Jean Paget is a humanist, a pioneer, with a sense of humor. She's trying to survive by her wits. She's not a hard person, but she becomes strong and resourceful. The thing I admire about her is her strength of character, and her spirit." —Helen Morse

"Noel Strachan's a silly old boy who should have known better. He's solid and tremendously reliable, but there's a glimmering of romance in the old boy yet.… I also missed out getting the girl in *The Prime of Miss Jean Brodie*. A director once told me I held a girl like someone with a time bomb in his hands. I'm just not a sex symbol."
—Gordon Jackson

EDWARD AND MRS. SIMPSON

7 EPISODES
November 15–December 27, 1981
Produced by *Thames Television*
Producer *Andrew Brown*
Based on Edward VIII by *Frances Donaldson*
Writer *Simon Raven*
Director *Waris Hussein*

CAST

Edward *Edward Fox*
Mrs. Simpson *Cynthia Harris*
Queen Mary *Peggy Ashcroft*
George V *Marius Goring*
Walter Monckton *Nigel Hawthorne*
Duff Cooper *Trevor Bowen*
Lady Diana Cooper *Patricia Hodge*
Lady Thelma Furness *Cherie Lunghi*
Winston Churchill *Wensley Pithey*
Clement Attlee *Patrick Troughton*
Prime Minister Stanley Baldwin *David Waller*

*A*T WINDSOR CASTLE *on the cold winter night of December 11, 1936, the handsomest and most sophisticated king in British history committed royal suicide while his subjects listened in stunned silence all over the world. It was the last chapter in the romance of the century in which the Prince of Wales destroyed himself as King Edward VIII and moved into private life with the woman he loved. It had been the most complicated royal love affair since Archduke Rudolph of Austria* fell for Maria Vetsera a century before, and it provided Thames Television with the plot for *Edward and Mrs. Simpson,* a startling and elegant drama about the first voluntary abdication of an English king in the history of the monarchy.

It was a story the people of England had waited 45 years to see, and they went for it in a big way. Needless to say, the Royal Family was not as enthusiastic. It was reported that the queen refused to watch it, but it's difficult to believe that anyone could have that much willpower. After all, it was about her own Uncle Ed. It was also reported that when Prince Charles read the biography by Frances Donaldson upon which the series is based, he was "shaken rigid" by the similarity between himself and his granduncle. Both were princes-in-waiting, with cold fathers and domineering mothers, still unmarried at 30. Although he could not realize it at the time, Charles would choose as his wife a woman as unprepared for her public role as Wallis was for hers.

Edward could have had his choice of almost any woman on earth and particularly in England, but David—as his family and friends called him—wanted a woman who could mother him, and he preferred married ones with cooperative husbands. We're talking here "mistress," and the Royals had always tolerated mistresses, married or single, as long as they were discreet and didn't aspire to sit alongside the king on the throne. Masterpiece Theatre audiences had already seen such women in bed-and-breakfast series including *Lillie* and *The Duchess of Duke Street.*

ℐelevision Ties the Windsor Knot

Edward and Mrs. Simpson is filled with some deliciously amusing scenes, such as the one where Lady Thelma Furness, the Prince of Wales' current girl friend, is prepar-

"The best story since the Resurrection."
—H. L. Mencken

Two designers spent three months researching more than 70 sets and finding more than 30 locations, from a safari park in Kenya to a coal mine in South Wales.

"As Simpson, Cynthia Harris is magnificent. She grabs the character of Simpson, a callous, domineering woman who emerges as ruthlessly unattractive—in person and in character. Harris unveils Simpson as a schemer who thought she could browbeat the more timid Edward into making her queen. 'Remember who is king,' Wallis tells Edward."
—Frank Swertlow, *Chicago Sun-Times*

"As Edward VIII, Edward Fox, the jackal in *The Day of the Jackal,* strikingly captures the dashing qualities of the king. More importantly, Fox subtly keeps the king's inadequacies apparent. Edward was impetuous, even foolish. He admired Mussolini, seemed sympathetic to Hitler and, above all, blindly disregarded his responsibilities to family, crown and country."
—Frank Swertlow,
Chicago Sun-Times

ing to take a six-week vacation and is telling Wallis (Mrs. Simpson) about her first encounter with the Prince:

"I met him at a fair, of all places. He was pinning a blue ribbon on a cow and he came right over and asked me to dine with him when I was next in London and he named the day and time—eight o'clock, St. James Palace—just like that.... Will you be a perfect darling and look after him while I'm away?"

"I'll try," replies Mrs. Simpson with all the innocence of a child who has just been given keys to the candy store. It is Thelma's big mistake. When she returns six weeks later she discovers that Wallis has looked after him more thoroughly than she had envisioned, and it is obvious that the Prince has pinned the blue ribbon on a new mistress. Before she can say "God save the king," Thelma and all the rest are curtsying to the American girl from Baltimore.

The Prince is either a little stupid or he has in him what George Eliot referred to in *Middlemarch* as "spots of commonness." Perhaps it is both. He could surround himself with the most creative and brilliant people in the realm but he chooses, instead, the stylish but shallow playboys and -girls of London's nightclub circuit whose knowledge doesn't extend much beyond the Savoy Hotel and Van Cleef-Arpels. And Wallis Simpson is one of them.

The drama gives viewers a fascinating glimpse of the Prince's inner social circle in a series of beautifully staged scenes in hotel ballrooms, in town houses, at poolside, and in clubs. There, far from

public scrutiny, the couple and their coterie play out their private drama behind the government's protective screen.

But the ban on press coverage of his personal affairs does not last long. Edward ascends to the throne after his father's death and makes a bold move to elicit public support: He speaks to the miners in Wales and sympathizes with their miserable conditions—despite a centuries-old agreement that a British monarch cannot take sides in political matters. (This situation is explored in contemporary terms in the 1994 Masterpiece Theatre series *To Play the King*.) With the miners behind him, Edward has a splendid opportunity to be more than a figurehead—and to keep Wallis as well. His chances are dashed when the press begins to publish stories about his romance with that divorced American woman. The bishops blubber, government spokesmen howl, and the nation turns against him. All that is left in the drama is for Wallis to tie the Windsor knot and encourage the newly renamed Duke of Windsor to duck out and spend the rest of their days playing tennis in Biarritz or sailing off Cannes. And apparently David liked the idea.

Edward Fox approached the princely role with a boyish assurance quite like that of the real Edward, and he was totally believable. Cynthia Harris had a more difficult assignment convincing viewers that she was the sort of woman for whom a king would surrender his crown and, ultimately, his family.

Wardrobe and Jewels Fit for a Queen

Mrs. Simpson was often referred to as "the best-dressed woman in town," her dresses designed by Schiaparelli and later by Mainbocher. Re-creating that style for the television series was neither cheap nor easy. Diana Thurley, Thames Television's leading costume designer, spent six months researching, designing, and shopping for fabrics to make more than 40 outfits for Cynthia Harris, but only two (including a Mainbocher wedding dress) are facsimile copies, because actress and duchess are, quite simply, built differently.

The real secret to the dazzling authenticity of the series' wardrobe is in the detail—television's duchess, for instance, has to wriggle into her wedding dress because it, like the original, has no zipper. It is also made from the last existing bolt of the same type of 1930s material; researchers spent months searching before finding it on a dusty shelf. Mrs. Simpson's jewels were also a popular subject of gossip, and Collingwood of Conduit Street—jewelers to the Prince of Wales, don't you know—loaned gems worth several million dollars to the production.

The Duke of Windsor was also a fashion plate in his day, and Edward Fox is dressed in clothes painstakingly stitched by the same Savile Row tailors who dressed the other Edward 40 years ago.

Keeping the Public in the Dark

The Windsor Affair had happened right under the noses of the British on their tight little island without public knowledge of it. All stories about the royal romance in American magazines such as *Time* and *Life* were clipped before they were sold on English newsstands, and all the British newspapers and magazines were silenced by Lord Beaverbrook, Britain's press czar and a good personal friend of Edward's. Reporters were accustomed to these conditions and accepted them. Although the people's civil rights are very well looked after, England has no freedom of the press, no equivalent of the First Amendment. Ironically, the conspiracy of silence surrounding the royal romance was finally broken by a sleepy reporter on a rural newspaper who mistook a line in a bishop's sermon as a criticism of Edward's romance when the bishop was referring only to his lack of churchgoing. If the bishop could lecture the king about Mrs. Simpson, the reporter figured, the self-censorship lid was off. In a few months, so was the crown.

Dame Peggy Ashcroft breached the traditional English devotion to authenticity in her portrayal of Edward's mother, Queen Mary. In real life, Mary had a German accent so thick you could cut it with a sausage cleaver. In *Edward and Mrs. Simpson* Ashcroft's English is as polished as Eliza Doolittle's at the ball.

The dedication to historical detail was extraordinary. The House of Commons debates depicted in the series are taken verbatim from Hansard, the official parliamentary record; other dialogue is taken from the memoirs, diaries, and letters of the principals. Though the researchers received no cooperation from the Royal Family, they were able to take 200 photographs of royal interiors, from Buckingham Palace to the Royal Lodge in Windsor. Armed with these and the notes from hours of conversation with people who were there—and who remembered—production designer Alan Cameron and crew went to work, searching out a steam yacht for one scene, constructing the "Embassy Club," where the Prince liked to dance until dawn, choosing just the right little lampshade, finding $6,000 vases. Wallpapers of the period were reprinted, and suites of furniture recovered in period fabric. The swimming pool at Fort Belvedere, unused for ten years, was cleaned and filled.

In faithfully recreating the private scenes with Edward, Wallis, and their friends, the production was fortunate to have as an advisor Lady Diana Cooper. Then in her eighties, Lady Diana was one of the Windsors' closest friends during the happy days of their courtship and remained a loyal friend after their marriage. Her inside knowledge assured that the music, the food, and even the banter were true to life.

The fairy-tale story of the prince and the commoner was finally put to rest by the deaths of the duke in 1972 and his duchess a few years later. The passing of time is likely to show that Wallis was one of the fortunate ones on history's roster of Girl Friends of Kings-to-Be. Maria Vetsera died with Rudolph in a tragic suicide pact at Mayerling. Lillie Langtry, the mistress of David's grandfather, Edward VII, lost her sweetie to other women. Wallis Warfield Simpson was different. She kept *her* king.

"I was there in the humble, but absorbed, capacity as a reporter who was covering the ten days before the abdication—sometimes five, six times a day for an American network, a radio network in those days. And though I came to this docudrama bristling with doubts, I have to say it solves many a mystery. And the fidelity of the actors to the character and the bearing of a score of the main characters is astonishing." —Alistair Cooke

The FLAME TREES of THIKA

7 EPISODES

January 3–February 14, 1982

Produced by *Euston Films in association with Consolidated Productions for Thames Television*

Producers *John Hawkesworth, Christopher Neame*

Based on the memoir by *Elspeth Huxley*

Writer *John Hawkesworth*

Director *Roy Ward Baker*

CAST

Elspeth Grant *Holly Aird*
Tilly Grant *Hayley Mills*
Robin Grant *David Robb*
Ian Crawfurd *Ben Cross*
Hereward Palmer *Nicholas Jones*
Lettice Palmer *Sharon Mughan*

ELSPETH HUXLEY *was only six years old in 1913 when she left London with her parents, Tilly and Robin Grant, who were setting out to establish a coffee plantation in a remote part of Africa that Queen Victoria had claimed for England only 18 years earlier. The Grants were an educated city-bred English couple, not farmers, and they had answered their government's call for pioneers to settle a big chunk of East Africa that the British had grabbed from the natives. Elspeth was too young to remember everything clearly, but*

children are great observers and a child's mind is a storehouse of impressions. Forty-six years later, she combined her memories with the stories her parents had told her and wrote *The Flame Trees of Thika.*

Nearly 20 years after her memoir was published, an English television producer read it to pass the time on an airplane and fell in love with her story. Now, here she was, a grown woman, returning to Africa to watch her young life being re-created for a television series right before her eyes. It must have been an astonishing experience for the 71-year-old writer to come upon such a faithful replica of the house of her childhood memories: a small thatched bungalow of mud and wattle with three rooms and a veranda, floors of beaten earth, windows without glass, and a chimney made of flattened paraffin tins. She stepped inside and the furnishings were exactly as she remembered—tables made of packing crates, the familiar ironstone dishes, wash basins, jugs, and a gramophone with a big horn that the property department had borrowed from the descendants of early settlers in the area. They looked the same but now they were "period antiques."

"[I don't think the] enchanting Holly, the re-created Elspeth, [is] in the least, alas, like I was all those years ago. She is much, much nicer—more natural, more polite and self-composed, less awkward and a great deal more obedient, at any rate in the film. Her performance I thought a marvel— and a greatly idealised me."—Elspeth Huxley, *The Observer*

The Best-Laid Plans

At the outset the Grants envision a neat, fertile farm somewhere in the green hills of Africa where the coffee plants would grow like wildflowers and the natives would work for pennies. It is a familiar English colonial dream, but reality was quite different. The Grants begin from scratch on uncultivated land where they chop down trees, dam streams, and try to retain their English teatime graces in the face of native superstition and magic, man-eating leopards, and the hilarious challenge of carrying a grand piano from Nairobi into the bush. For city folks, they are reasonably successful at all these tasks but in the end they are, like the Danish Baroness Blixen in *Out of Africa,* only strangers in an alien land.

The Flame Trees of Thika was presented as a seven-part drama on Masterpiece Theatre in January and February 1982, three years before the movie *Out of Africa* was made and several decades after Hollywood introduced moviegoers to the African continent. But *Flame Trees* is different because it was produced by a staff that had become experts at perfectly

"Today, no wild animal may be legally killed, except under licence for crop protection. So ingenious tricks had to be employed. Stuffed leopards, snakes, and other creatures were used instead of real ones, ingeniously slotted in to shots of genuine wild creatures. In this land of 10 million goats, a stuffed goat was flown from Britain to do duty as a sacrificial animal in a witch doctor's ceremony."

—Elspeth Huxley, *The Observer*

"As soon as I read it I loved the story. It is a period in British history which has not been developed very much and I particularly liked it because it was about real happenings and real people. The women, like Tilly, who were pioneers in Africa were truly remarkable—and luckily not given to too much introspection. They coped because there was nothing to do but cope, there was no point in complaining about their lot."

—Hayley Mills, *Western Evening Herald*

"European clothing was unknown outside the towns in the period in question. Africans wore goatskin cloaks, or blankets knotted over one shoulder like togas, charms, and lots of beads. Today, Kenyan authorities forbid public exhibition of the semi-naked human body. There is an episode, for instance, in the book, where a posse of unmarried girls thatch a house, traditional women's work. They were naked to the waist, and below wore triangular mini-aprons. This was not permitted. In the film the girls wear cloaks which conceal their bosoms."

—Elspeth Huxley, *The Observer*

depicting people and places of another era.

The writer-producer who read the book on the airplane was John Hawkesworth, who set out to repeat the success he had found with *Upstairs, Downstairs, The Duchess of Duke Street,* and *Danger UXB.* He cast Hayley Mills (star of many Disney films from the time she was a child) as Tilly Grant, the young mother. It was a long-sought reunion: Mills had appeared 22 years earlier in Hawkesworth's feature film *Tiger Bay.* He chose David Robb, familiar to American viewers

from *I, Claudius,* to play her bush farmer husband Robin Grant, a man who had never plowed anything in his life before but was determined to succeed as a coffee farmer, having failed at everything else. After auditioning 500 child actors, Hawkesworth selected Holly Aird to play the daughter, and she did so without stepping over the line into obnoxious adolescence. She even rises to the occasion with such lines as "Mummy, I think something rather awful is happening" when she sees a hyena destroying a squirming but otherwise unidentified object just outside her bedroom window.

In contrast to the hard-up Grants, their upscale neighbors, the Palmers, another pair of English settlers, arrive in Thika with a piano, two Pekinese dogs, and other playthings. These still fail to provide Mrs. Palmer with enough home entertainment to prevent her from having a steamy love affair with Ian the local Great White Hunter (played by Ben Cross, fresh from *Chariots of Fire*). Her adultery—as well as problems such as crop failure, witch doctors' curses, and the red bumps caused by the bites of tsetse flies—is put to an end by the outbreak of World War I. The men go off to the battlefield, and the women and children await passage home to England. The film ends there, though the real Elspeth returned with her parents to the farm in Kenya and lived there for a number

"I am sure that Hayley Mills, with her elegant figure, her full skirts and clean blouse, a hairdresser just out of camera-range ready to adjust each errant curl, a makeup expert darkening her eyelids, doesn't look in the least like my mother looked when urging reluctant mules to draw a dilapidated buggy, bandaging an African baby seared by fire, pricking out seedlings under a broiling sun with dirty hands and sweating face."—Elspeth Huxley, *The Observer*

"Hayley gave me lots of advice…. She showed me how to say my lines and how to open my eyes really wide when the cameras were on me. I've learned so much from her. I've been a fan of hers ever since I saw her in *Tiger Bay*. I've always wanted to be like Hayley." —Holly Aird

"Like Hawkesworth's previous productions, The Flame Trees of Thika *is not in a hurry. It invites you into the world of a small band of settlers, lets you share their hopes, disappointments and fears and, like* Born Free, *gives you a taste of what life in Africa might have been like at that time."* —Kay Gardella, *New York Daily News*

Some Things Changed, Some Hadn't

In 1981 the mud-walled house of the Grant family was specially built by local labor for the filming. It took three weeks to construct and cost £5,000. In 1913 the identical house cost Robin Grant under £10 and was built in less than a week. But even in 1981, as in 1913, the Kikuyu men put up the wooden frame and left the thatching of the roof for the women to do.

of years. She wrote 20 books, married a cousin of British literary giant Aldous Huxley, and settled on a farm of her own in Wiltshire, England. She traveled to Kenya for the filming of her story and served as consultant.

The series was made entirely on location in a town in Kenya overlooking the great plain of Athi. Like the Grants in 1913, the 1980 production team wholly transformed the landscape, cutting roads, building new houses, and then aging them to account for the passing years. When the script called for rain but the weather failed to cooperate, the Nairobi fire brigade used their hoses. The production crew found the steam engine for the World War I departure scene in the Nairobi Railway Museum and filmed it right there. Getting the footage of the flame trees of the title was tricky because the showy flowers are temperamental and bloom only when they feel like it. Whenever the crew heard that one was blooming they sent someone off to film it, resulting in 5,000 miles of travel time that was chalked up to "blossom chasing." Given the extraordinary difficulties the Grants overcame to live among the Flame Trees, the effort to film the trees in bloom seems modest in comparison.

Barchester Chronicles

ᴇNGLAND HOLDS THE REPUTATION as the international center of droll humor, a dubious distinction because it is an honor that is not sought by any other nation on the planet. It is the small laugh, the tiny smile, the polite titter, and the wry observation made softly behind the hand of a nice old gentleman in a church pew. Moviegoers in the thirties heard it from actors like Eric Blore, the

7 EPISODES
October 28–December 9, 1984
Produced by *BBC*
Producer *Jonathan Powell*
**Based on the novels The Warden and
Barchester Towers by**
Anthony Trollope
Writer *Alan Plater*
Director *David Giles*

CAST
Signora Madeline Neroni *Susan Hampshire*
Septimus Harding *Donald Pleasence*
Archdeacon Grantly *Nigel Hawthorne*
Mrs. Grantly *Angela Pleasence*
Obadiah Slope *Alan Rickman*
Eleanor Harding *Janet Maw*
Mrs. Proudie *Geraldine McEwan*

somewhat naughty but ever-so-polite butler. It is a tradition carried on today by Frank Thornton as Captain Peacock on *Are You Being Served?* and by Stephen Fry as the humble but learned butler Jeeves. They are the people who can get away with saying the most insulting things to the worst sort of ruffian without being challenged to a duel because of the civilized manner in which the insult has been phrased.

In *Barchester Chronicles* the object of Anthony Trollope's humor, which sometimes extends beyond droll to blistering sarcasm and biting satire, is the small-town clergy of the Church of England, which has been a richly deserved target for generations and still is today because so little has changed in its devout playpen. Barchester is the name that the author has given to his fictitious cathedral town. The date is 1855 and under its peacefully pious exterior Barchester is seething with intrigue because the old duffers—both in and out of the churchyard—are trying to stand up for their muddled traditions against the assaults of three great and omnipresent dangers: progress, politicians, and the dreaded press. Screenwriter Alan Plater puts it this way: "The Barchester clergy are like the Borgias without murdering anybody."

"[*Barchester Chronicles*] is a deliciously satiric look at the ecclesiastic community in all its English glory—a rigid hierarchy of relics sacred and human, of scheming chaplains and bilious bishops and not-so-venerable bedesmen. At the centre of this incestuous circle, predictably surrounded by all manner of cant and hypocrisy, stands that rarest of creations. In fiction (no less than fact) a genuinely decent but still compelling figure is mighty hard to find. The Reverend Septimus Harding is just such a character, and his beguiling mix of meekness and audacity, apparent naivete and real virtue, is beautifully captured by Donald Pleasence." —Rick Groen

$\mathscr{B}$rouhaha in Barchester

The Reverend Septimus Harding (played with great sympathy by Donald Pleasence) is a sweet old clergyman in a very comfortable job. His church duties are largely confined to conducting the choir and fussing with sheet music, but he is also the warden of Hiram's Hospital, a home for old and impoverished wool-carders. The warden's duties there consist of leisurely afternoon visits with the 12 ancient occupants, whom he entertains by playing the cello. This pays him the princely salary of £800 a year and the use of a beautiful country manor house complete with servants and a carriage. He was appointed to this post by the bishop, who is the father of his daughter's husband.

Perks, nepotism, sinecures—does this sound like something in your town today? Of course it does. But suddenly in 1855 everything began to fall apart for the men of God who were toiling in great comfort for a self-satisfied Church of England, and Trollope

"Most of Trollope's characters can be recognized in modern life, scheming for jobs and money, while expressing noble sentiments. His comedy, says Alan Plater, is about the gap between aspiration and achievement. You can see Trollope types beavering away in the caring professions, in schools and trade unions, political parties, the Civil Service and the BBC—but they do seem especially awful (and awfully funny) in the church."

—D. A. N. Jones, *Radio Times*

"There's no malice in Madeline. Of course she schemes and plots, but she's the one who sorts everything out in the end, isn't she? She's the one who unmasks the villains and engineers the happily ever afters."
—Susan Hampshire

"Mrs. Proudie is a ridiculously horrible woman who has no redeeming features at all. They say this kind of role is a therapeutic thing—you get rid of all those horrible feelings you've really got inside you. I was very well behaved in my normal life when I was playing Mrs. Proudie."
—Geraldine McEwan

"Victorian audiences loved either elaborate saccharine romances or savage satires on the ways of the world. Trollope gave them both, but without the undiluted sugar and without the savagery. He could be as mischievously satirical about the romancing as about the skullduggery that can go on in the running of a cathedral."
—Alistair Cooke

makes this real-life crusade a pivotal event in the novels. An act of Parliament has sanctioned an inquiry into public corruption, such as the huge sums of money being given to churchmen for little or no work. The Reverend Harding is one of them, and *Barchester Chronicles* (adapted from two novels, *The Warden* and *Barchester Towers*) opens with a local investigation of the will that established Hiram's Hospital in 1434. A local doctor, John Bold, takes it upon himself to look into the matter.

The resulting brouhaha in Barchester consumes many characters and situations. Among them is the bishop's administrative officer, Archdeacon Grantly, who is also his son as well as the husband of Reverend Harding's eldest daughter (played by Pleasence's daughter Angela). The situation is perplexing as well to Harding's younger daughter Eleanor, who had been in love with Dr. Bold before he began attacking her father. She is now beset by alternating bouts of anger and worry. It is revealed that the old residents of Hiram's Hospital receive only a few pennies a day, the original allotment, which has never been adjusted to reflect the 416-year rise in the cost of living or the gigantic increase in the value of the trust. The public cry is "Out with the Warden!" Helping to create and ultimately to sort out the confusion is the meddlesome Madeline Neroni, played by Susan Hampshire. In the end, no one is exactly like what he or she seemed to be at first.

It is in the third and fourth episodes that the satire heats up. Trollope does not disguise his anger at the bullying tactics of investigative journalists, particularly those of the venerable *Times*—which he renames *The Jupiter*. As one of his characters declares: "What the Czar is in Russia or the mob is in America, that is what *The Jupiter* is in England.... It is the Vatican, a self-appointed Pope that can make you odious to your dearest friends and can turn you into a monster to be pointed at by the finger!"

The temperature continues to rise when the old bishop dies and the new one, a nitwit, arrives with two dogmatic and self-righteous "modernizers" who are among the most famous comic villains in the history of English literature: Mrs. Proudie, the masculine wife of the new bishop (handsomely played by Geraldine McEwan in costumes from the Victoria and Albert Museum), and the bishop's womanizing chaplain, Obadiah Slope, who is loathed by the men and loved by the women of Barchester. But he too is eventually replaced—along with the warden, and the nasty doctor who started it all in the first place.

When Trollope died at the age of 65 he thought he might be remembered as the inventor of the street postbox, but the world has forgotten that. The chronicles of the television title are only two of the more than 30 novels Trollope wrote during his 33 years as a post office employee. Every morning he rose at 5, wrote 2,500 words in two and a half hours, then went to work. The next time you wonder why your mail delivery is late, don't scream or write City Hall. Your postman may be another Anthony Trollope.

"Trollope is now confidently acknowledged to be one of the three or four great English novelists of the 19th century. Wherever he is, he would be astonished to hear this, because he was totally unknown until he was 40, and for the 40 years or so after he died in 1882, his reputation just about expired. The story that rescued him from obscurity in the first place was [The Warden]. *"*
—Alistair Cooke

"Eleanor is actually very independent but doesn't broadcast it. She is able to move into all different people's lives, which is why she becomes a sort of link figure, in the middle, not actually sitting on the fence watching it all. She's accepted by all these people and actually respected because people know she's no fool, she's very intelligent but it's very contained."
—Janet Maw

The JEWEL *in the* CROWN

14 EPISODES
December 16, 1984–March 17, 1985
Produced by *Granada Television*
Producer *Christopher Morahan*
Based on The Raj Quartet *by Paul Scott*
Writer *Ken Taylor*
Directors *Christopher Morahan, Jim O'Brien*

CAST
Ronald Merrick *Tim Pigott-Smith*
Hari Kumar *Art Malik*
Sarah Layton *Geraldine James*
Mildred Layton *Judy Parfitt*
Barbie Batchelor *Peggy Ashcroft*
Sergeant Guy Perron *Charles Dance*
Daphne Manners *Susan Wooldridge*
Lady Manners *Rachel Kempson*
Susan Layton *Wendy Morgan*
Count Bronowski *Eric Porter*
Major Jimmy Clark *Stuart Wilson*
Emmy Award *1984–1985*
Outstanding Limited Series
Peabody Award *1984*

No one enjoys *watching the decline and fall of the British Empire as much as the British, and no one pictures it better. They are particularly skilled at taking the dark chapters of their history and turning them into great entertainment. That is precisely what Granada Television did with* THE JEWEL IN THE CROWN, *a tour de force that never stops sparkling on the air and in our hearts and memories. As it had in Britain earlier in the year, it held viewers hostage for four months when it was shown on*

"This is the story of a rape, of the events that led up to it, and of the place in which it happened. There was no trial in the judicial sense, but as time went on, this rape became the core of a plot and a system that ended with the spectacle of two nations in violent opposition, not for the first time nor as yet for the last, because they were then still locked in an imperial embrace of such long standing and subtlety it was no longer possible for them to know whether they hated or loved one another, or what it was that held them together and seemed to have confused the image of their separate destinies."

—The Raj Quartet

Masterpiece Theatre in 14 stunning episodes in 1984. It dwarfs all other television series in its visual scope as well as in the richness of its characters, plucked from *The Raj Quartet,* four novels by Paul Scott that tell the story of England being shaken loose from India after centuries of unchallenged rule.

The story begins in 1942. India (the jewel in Queen Victoria's crown) is divided, as it has been for centuries, between two faiths, Hindu and Muslim, plus a sizable number of Sikhs and feuding splinter sects. Gandhi and his followers have been struggling for independence from Britain and are gaining ground. So are the Japanese, who have overrun neighboring countries, often finding volunteers for their army among anti-British Indians. This is the volatile background against which *The Jewel in the Crown* is set. Clips of old newsreel footage show the British view, further helping viewers to understand the mentality of the colonialists.

"There is no love; there is only contempt and fear."
—Ronald Merrick

The Thorn in the Crown

Unlike Scott's quartet, which is full of flashbacks and flashforwards, the series moves chronologically. The main thread of the story begins with the rape of Daphne Manners, a shy English woman who was meeting secretly with Hari Kumar, a handsome, upper-class Indian journalist, in the Bibighar Gardens. The sadistic British police superintendent Ronald Merrick believes Hari is responsible for the rape and tortures him viciously to get him to confess. Merrick's motives are quite mixed: He suspects Hari is a subversive but also resents Hari because Daphne has rejected Merrick and taken up with the better-bred, better-educated Indian. At the end of the series it's 1947, India has gained its independence, and the British are leaving. Daphne is dead (she died in childbirth), Hari is a broken man, and Merrick's ugly secrets have been revealed.

"What developed was a notion of racial superiority. That's what [Scott] uses Merrick to explore. Merrick has based his whole life on a misconception: that because he's white, he's superior to Indians. It's a pessimistic view [by Scott] but it's a valid one. In the end, Merrick becomes a tragic victim of his attitudes.... He fails to get a commission [in the army] because of his middle-class background and has to accept second best, which is the police force. He has had a lifetime of that class barbarity. What happens is that he hands on that contempt to the Indians." —Tim Pigott-Smith, *Los Angeles Times*

Interwoven, and some-
times running parallel to this
tale, are stories of other major
characters, all caught up in the
last throes of British imperialism. Daphne's aunt, Lady
Manners, who decides to rear
Daphne's half-caste daughter,
is one. The Laytons are her
neighbors at Lake Srinigar.
Mildred is the arrogant alco-
holic mother, whose husband

is in a German prisoner-of-war camp. Her daughter Sarah is one of
the most sympathetic characters in the series—kind, sensible,
strong, dependable, and one of the few non-Indians who questions
and breaks through the barrier separating the English from the
Indians. Her sister Susan is one of the least sympathetic characters—selfish, flighty, and weak. Susan marries Teddie Bingham, a
young officer whose new roommate is Merrick, transferred from
the police to the military. Shortly after the wedding, Teddie is
killed, despite Merrick's efforts to save him. Merrick is seriously
wounded, but survives. Susan, ever-grateful, eventually marries

"Apart from providing hypnotic entertainment about the British Raj, [*The Jewel in
the Crown*] has made people ponder afresh
over the unfashionable subject of our
imperial past."
—Gordon Brook-Shepherd,
The Sunday Telegraph

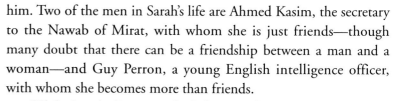

How Ashcroft Got the Part

One day, when Dame Peggy Ashcroft was waiting for a friend at the National Theatre in London, she overheard Christopher Morahan, then deputy to the director of the theater, talking on the phone about adapting *The Raj Quartet.* When he hung up, she asked if he was going to make the film, and when he replied yes, she said, "Well, I'll never speak to you again if you don't have me in it." When he asked what role she would be interested in, she replied, "Barbie, of course."

him. Two of the men in Sarah's life are Ahmed Kasim, the secretary to the Nawab of Mirat, with whom she is just friends—though many doubt that there can be a friendship between a man and a woman—and Guy Perron, a young English intelligence officer, with whom she becomes more than friends.

While Scott's dismay at the behavior of many of the British in India—Merrick and Mildred being extreme examples—is readily apparent, he also creates some very lovable and laudable characters, including Mabel Layton, Mildred's step-mother-in-law. Living with her is Barbie Batchelor, a warm, lonely, caring Christian missionary who becomes victim to Mildred's treachery and is eventually displaced by her. One of many memorable scenes is of Barbie riding through the rain in her rickshaw, uprooted, singing not "Onward Christian Soldiers" or some such hymn, as one might expect, but the song "Champagne Charlie," as the rickshaw careens around a slippery corner and overturns. In the end we see her in a hospital

"Somewhere in my childhood, in my past, I know various women—teachers, nurses, librarians—who to me are like Barbie. She's humble, but she doesn't lie down. She was a rebel in a way, an eccentric. And I like eccentrics."
—Dame Peggy Ashcroft

cell sitting in crazed silence, shredding her written notes while buzzards fly overhead outside. Barbie is played touchingly by Dame Peggy Ashcroft, who won a best actress award in Britain for her performance. She was a longtime friend of Rachel Kempson, who plays Lady Manners, and the two were inseparable during the arduous months of filming in India.

A Bloody, Senseless Mess

The series builds to its bold conclusion with the departure of the British and the murder of Merrick by an Indian youth, one of many he had abused, who leaves a word scrawled across a mirror: Bibighar—the scene of the rape Merrick had tried to pin on Hari Kumar five years and 12 episodes earlier. At the end of the series, in the tragic wake of British imperialism, it is left to Sarah, whom we hold on to for her compassion and her reasonableness, to offer some final words, but they are neither hopeful nor consoling—just truthful. She and Susan are in a train compartment en route to Ranpur. They have just seen her friend (and brother of the young Muslim leader) Kasim hauled off the train to be killed, and others massacred at the station. Susan is holding Merrick's ashes in a lunch basket on her lap. "There's nothing we could do," Sarah says. "Like Daphne Manners. Like Hari Kumar. After 300 years of India, we've left this whole damned bloody senseless mess ..."

The series gave the writer Ken Taylor (who won an award in Britain for his adaptation) ample time to define the characters, and the actors played their roles magnificently. Tim Pigott-Smith was so menacing as Merrick that his agent had to place newspaper stories and photos showing him as a loving family man who is kind to animals and has a number of Indian friends and acquaintances.

"What Americans seemed to have appreciated much more than British viewers was the sympathetic side of Merrick. They have gone for the reasons why he did what he did—and understood him in a much deeper way than in England. That is surprising to me, and it pleases me." —Tim Pigott-Smith

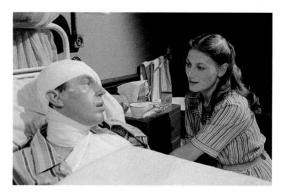

"I believe in Guy Perron. Most of the time he said things that I would say: behaved in a way that I would behave. There's a vulnerability, a questioning of his beliefs, his background, and his upbringing." —Charles Dance, *The Sun*

Pigott-Smith brought such depth to Merrick that, in spite of his brutality and treachery, one feels a bit of pity that this man should be so misguided, so full of self-loathing (Pigott-Smith says Merrick's "a man you hate to love"). He, too, won a best-acting award in Britain for his portrayal. Art Malik as Hari Kumar played his role with great understanding, perhaps because, as several reviewers noted, "Art Malik *is* Hari Kumar." Born in Pakistan, he, too, comes from an upper-class background and was educated in England in an uppercrust school. Like Hari, he feels the pull of the dichotomous cultures. Sarah, with her quiet sensibility, serves as the anchor in reality for viewers. So convincing is Geraldine James as Sarah that one cannot see her in another role, and, indeed, she has said, "Reading about Sarah Layton in *The Raj Quartet* was like getting a smack in the face. It was the first time I had ever come across a fictional character and thought, 'I know this person, this is me.'" Susan Wooldridge, on the other hand, is very unlike Daphne, yet convincingly conveyed her gawkiness and her quiet strength. The late Eric Porter as the Nawab's minister was suitably perplexing, his patched eye representing the shadow he keeps over himself.

Recognizing that the setting could easily detract from the characters, producer/co-director Christopher Morahan says that he very deliberately had the cinematographer focus tightly on the charac-

"Every novel is part soap opera. Scott's Quartet *has its fair share of doomed romance, random mayhem, suicide, and karma gone wrong. Every great novel has much more: social texture, moral choice, metaphysics, poetry, a sense of humor, revelation. Until now, no great novel has gotten a movie or a television program worthy of it."*

—John Leonard, *New York*

"It was an enormous privilege to know someone like Daphne, to be invited to meet her through the pages of the script. She falls in love and goes after her man, and it doesn't matter what color he is—she loves him deeply. It's amazing that a girl of that time—the 1940s—brought up in this incredibly strict upper-middle-class British life, which was like a corset, should have been so brave." —Susan Wooldridge

ters. Indeed, the cameras seem to often turn away from the pic-turesque scenery. In its understatement, India colors every scene, frames every line of dialogue. And when the background is shown—a pan across the misty lake, a view to the surrounding hills—it is captivating and poetic.

A Blessed Production

The problems of mounting such an ambi-tious production were enormous. First there was the £5.5 million budget, which Sir Denis Forman, chairman of Granada Television, was able to secure on the basis of his track record with the splendid *Brideshead Revisited*. Then there was the nearly insurmountable task of turning Scott's 2,000-page quartet into a 15-hour television series. Forman had the ingenious idea of chopping up wallpaper into yard-square segments, writing one episode on each sheet, and pinning the sheets around the walls of a large room, arranging the many events of the novels into chronological order. From these, the outline for each episode was drawn.

Rat Soup

Eventually even the actors became accustomed to the profusion of wildlife on location in India. When two rats were discovered running around the soup tureens one evening at dinner, no one panicked. Judy Parfitt, who played the flinty Mildred Layton, commented quietly, "You'd think the management would provide them with a separate dining room."

"Britain is full of desperate people watching the repeats on Sunday evening, half-pretending that they are seeing it for the first time so that the gap between episodes is reduced to two days." —Sean French, *The Sunday Times*

A Serendipitous Coincidence

By coincidence the three men chiefly responsible for *The Jewel in the Crown* were in the British armed forces in India at the same time: Paul Scott, who spent ten years writing *The Raj Quartet;* Sir Denis Forman, who conceived the idea of bringing Scott's novels to television; and Ken Taylor, who had the awesome task of adapting Scott's 800,000–word epic into a 15-hour series.

Transporting tons of equipment, props, costumes, food (yes, they brought lots of British food with them), and vintage vehicles, had its own set of problems, the stickiest of which was securing the customs clearances from India's thriving bureaucracy. Then there was the need for accommodations for a company of 70 people on locations from Mysore to Udaipur. The climate posed its own challenges. Despite the intense heat, the "mad dogs and Englishmen" conceit took over, and

the actors ignored warnings to stay out of the noonday sun—until they began to pass out all over the place. After that they were issued black umbrellas and learned to stay under them, giving the filming sites the look of a funeral party gathered around a grave in rainy weather. The logistics of getting the 16mm film to England were so complicated that the cast and crew didn't see the rushes for weeks.

At the beginning of the filming an Indian holy man blessed the production. He marked everyone's forehead with sandalwood paste, gave cast and crew flowers to throw at his portable shrine, and had director Christopher Morahan tap a camera lens with a coconut. The four months of filming in India were indeed fortunate, but that luck changed when the crew returned to England for another 12 months of production based primarily in Manchester (where Granada's studios are located), as well as in Cheshire and Lancashire. The biggest spot of bad luck was a disastrous studio fire that burned a warehouse full of sets, costumes, and props (including Merrick's metal arm), all of which had to be replaced. Other delays were caused by the difficulty of matching the film shot in India with scenes filmed in England, such as the one where Barbie orders a cup of tea on the veranda of a house in Simla and finally drinks it on a set in the Manchester studio.

None of these problems, however, is apparent in this seamless production. As one reviewer fretted, "There is only one serious fault in *The Jewel in the Crown*. In two weeks it will all be over."

"The richness of Jewel *lies in the wonderful deliberation of its performances, in the watchfulness of Geraldine James' Sarah, the contained arrogance of Judy Parfitt's Mildred. So little seems to happen; so much actually does. When the tensions burst, the results can be terrifying."*
—Sean Day-Lewis, *The Daily Telegraph*

UPDATE

Several stars of *The Jewel in the Crown* had significant roles in other major films about India: Dame Peggy Ashcroft and Art Malik were both in *A Passage to India*, Malik was also in *The Far Pavilions*, and Geraldine James was in *Gandhi*.

BLEAK HOUSE

8 EPISODES
December 1, 1985–January 19, 1986
Produced by *BBC*
Producers *John Harris, Betty Willingale*
Based on the novel by *Charles Dickens*
Writer *Arthur Hopcraft*
Director *Ross Devenish*

CAST
John Jarndyce *Denholm Elliott*
Esther Summerson *Suzanne Burden*
Lady Dedlock *Diana Rigg*
Sir Leicester Dedlock *Robin Bailey*
Ada Clare *Lucy Hornak*
Allan Woodcourt *Brian Deacon*
Richard Carstone *Philip Franks*
Miss Barbary *Fiona Walker*
Jo *Chris Pitt*

IF WE CAN *believe the novels of the last century, middle-class English people were concerned with three things: a suitable marriage to someone richer, a bigger house, and a wealthy relative who would soon die and leave them a lot of money. The English, it seems, didn't go out and make money for themselves; they inherited it from someone who had stolen it from the poor and spent a lifetime hoarding it. As a consequence, wills were very important—the writing of them, the changing* of them, the hiding of them, and, particularly, the reading of them to a roomful of potential heirs who hate one another.

All of these activities appear in Charles Dickens' *Bleak House*, which follows the endless case of Jarndyce vs Jarndyce in Britain's Court of Chancery. It is there that the lives of several characters are stretched on the torture rack of a meaningless judicial system that drags out the settlement of a disputed will year after year, generation after generation, while the heirs and would-be heirs spend their lives waiting. Some are more impatient than others. Tom Jarndyce blows out his brains in between drinks at the neighborhood coffeehouse. Others, such as tiny Miss Flite, visit the court in daily anticipation of a judgment that will bring her the wealth she has dreamed of. For any viewers who await inheritances from older relatives, *Bleak House* is a horror story. And that's how the BBC played it in the eight-part series starring Diana Rigg as Lady Dedlock and Denholm Elliot as John Jarndyce.

*W*here There's a Will, There's Dickens

If there is one thing more fascinating to the English than a will, it is a *second* will—and the discovery of just such a document gives the final chapter of *Bleak House* its special twist. The Jarndyce testament that has been disputed for 80 years of the family's time, 625 pages of the reader's time, and seven hours of the viewer's time, is invalid. Dickens is at it again! A second will of a later date found among a dead junk dealer's personal possessions settles, forever, the question of the Jarndyce family inheritance. It goes to Richard and Ada, two nice cousins of John Jarndyce, the great nephew of the man who shot

"[Bleak House is] an unequivocal masterpiece, equal in quality, power, delicacy, and pure dramatic effect to some of the finest films ever made.... The reason for the success is, I think, basically twofold. First, the filmmakers took Dickens for what he was, a master of realism. Dickens had a camera eye, and so has the BBC's Bleak House. Second, the filmmakers recognized that the human beings in the drama could have lived at any time and anywhere in man's history. Bleak House therefore has a remarkable measure of universality.

"Nearly every character and almost every line of dialogue is vital. Nothing is casual or there just for the 'mood' or flavor of it. Bleak House is as compact— delightfully so—as those ancient stars that have collapsed in upon themselves by the force of their own, accelerated gravity. Look carefully at the images in the opening and closing of each episode: for example, the dull, gold pendulum of the clock in episode number one, or Richard Carstone's voice crying out at the outset of episode four, 'It's only a matter of time!' They are all fraught with meaning.

"Watching the eight episodes is like visiting a gallery of fabulous paintings, intricately linked yet able to stand on their own as individual works of art as striking as the caricatures of Daumier.... A number of scenes are so perfectly composed that you want to clip them from the film and frame them." —Thomas Hoving, *Connoisseur*

The complicated plot involving the loves and deceptions of the cold and haughty Lady Dedlock made the novel popular at the time it was written because several of the minor characters were caricatures of well-known people, now long forgotten.

himself in the coffeehouse. Unfortunately the entire fortune has been eaten up by lawyers and court costs, so the young heirs are left to face a lifetime of genteel poverty.

In between the anticipation of the Jarndyce will and the discovery of the second, Dickens unfolds another plot—that of Lady Dedlock and Esther. This gives readers yet another favorite theme of 19th-century novels: the reuniting of lost parents and children. Lady Dedlock visits poor Esther, whose beauty has been destroyed by a tragic illness, and tells her, at last, that they are mother and daughter.

The lasting appeal of the story is in its satire of the greed and insensitivity of lawyers. Combine that with Dickens' ability to mix characters with causes—a device popular in today's cause-conscious climate—and you have a winning ticket. And so *Bleak House* was, when it appeared on Masterpiece Theatre in 1985.

Dickens' Kind of Town

The look of the series contributed to its appeal. To simulate the grimy atmosphere of Victorian London, the producers dumped real mud and horse manure on streets where outdoor scenes were filmed. The omnipresent fog, simulated by noisy machines, was held in huge canvas flaps and silently released when needed so as not to interfere while cameras were rolling. One British critic commented: "Fog and mud are indeed everywhere, and the effect is immediately to

mark out this serial as far and away the most visually authentic Dickens yet brought to TV."

Dickens put so much of his own life in his novels that they can almost be regarded as autobiography. Considering his castigation of lawyers, it is interesting to learn that he first studied law but realized he would never be a good lawyer and turned to writing instead. A brief stint as court reporter gave him the firsthand knowledge of the labyrinthine procedures and jargon. At the same time he began to submit vignettes of London life to various literary magazines. He was a serialized writer whose novels reached readers a chapter at a time. It is a format that fits television like a glove and has made him the darling of TV writers and producers more than a century after his death. Other Dickens novels that have appeared on Masterpiece Theatre include *Our Mutual Friend, David Copperfield, A Tale of Two Cities, Hard Times,* and *Martin Chuzzlewit.*

Jewel of a Director

Christopher Morahan

CHRISTOPHER MORAHAN'S achievement as both producer and co-director of *The Jewel in the Crown* (1984) ranks as one of the most significant in the history of Masterpiece Theatre. Based on four novels by Paul Scott collectively known as *The Raj Quartet,* the 15-hour miniseries became a worldwide phenomenon, winning both the American Emmy award as the season's best limited series and an international Emmy.

The son of motion picture designer-producer Tom Morahan, Christopher Morahan began his career in theater at age 20, rising to become associate director at England's National Theatre. He also was head of plays at the BBC from 1972 to 1976 and continues to direct for stage, television, and movies. Among his other television dramas are *The Heat of the Day* (1990) for Masterpiece Theatre, and *The Bullion Boys* (1994), which won an international Emmy award. He recently completed a new TV movie, *Peacock Spring,* which took him back to India for the first time since *The Jewel in the Crown.*

Author Paul Scott often described The Raj Quartet *as "the story of a rape." Most critics believe he wasn't referring to the physical rape of Daphne Manners in the story, but to the "rape" of India by Imperial England. Was that your interpretation?*

Morahan That's right. I think Scott's books were a marvelous act of imagination. But more than that, they were honorable books that asked a whole lot of questions about a number of relationships between India and England that had been unquestioned up until that time.

Britain had a very close relationship with India for about 200 years. Lots of the very best young men and women went there with the intention of making a fortune. They saw it as their right to govern in the name of Queen Victoria. There was a desire to convert [the Indian people] to Christianity and to pass on the various parliamentary traditions and the rule of law. There was a great sense among British people that they had a divine right to rule and that the Indians were their children.

How did you wind up both producing and directing The Jewel in the Crown?

Morahan I was in the process of leaving the National Theatre in 1980 and was looking around for a project that would engage me. I wanted a large project. It was exactly what I was looking for. I hadn't considered producing it. I'd worked quite extensively with Granada in the early 1970s and I knew them all there. When they announced they were making *The Jewel in the Crown,* I just put my name forward as a person they might consider as one of the directors.

Sir Denis Forman, chairman of Granada, said he wanted you to produce as well as direct because you're "one of those unusual people equally suited to command an army corps in action or direct actors in the most intimate scenes." Would you agree with that assessment?

Morahan (Laughs) It wasn't exactly an army corps. I'm able to take on responsibility—and to delegate responsibility. Being a producer, as much as anything, means finding good people to work with. I was able to pick from among all the people working for Granada. The only freelancers I brought in were a designer and my fellow director, Jim O'Brien. Then it was a matter of talking to the people in the company and evolving a team. It was very important to do it from the ground up. I think the people who worked on it found it very rewarding indeed.

When you took over, had the decision already been made to rearrange the sequence of events in the four novels and put them in chronological order?

Morahan Yes. Six of the scripts already were written. There was another writer involved with Ken Taylor then. When I was asked to produce it, one condition of accepting was that Ken Taylor must write them all. I told Granada, you must write off six of those scripts and I want Ken to start again and write another six—and they agreed.

After getting Ken Taylor to start rewriting the scripts, what was the next step?

Morahan I took about a year to prepare the whole thing. Granada wanted to know that it was possible. The first job really was to go to India with the designer, the production manager, and a local contact man and come back with a proposal. At the time it was a very big financial outlay as far as Granada was concerned.

What turned out to be the biggest problem about filming there?

Morahan Finding the right places to film. If you start filming in India, you find yourself surrounded by a crowd of 500 to 1,000 before you can say Jack Robinson. India also had changed radically in the last 50 years and a lot of it had become industrial. We had to find places that matched the story. That's why it took us so long to prepare. We were shooting for about 14 months.

What did the local Indian people who worked with you think of the English style of filmmaking?

Morahan We have a work ethic, which is probably shared by Americans, that inspires us to work very, very hard in sometimes appalling circumstances. The Indians thought we were balmy, mad as hatters.

Why did you decide to hire a co-director?

Morahan I think it would have been impossible for one director to do it all and do it well. The crucial process was finding somebody who was willing to take on that mutual responsibility. Jim and I always worked with the same cameraman, the same editor, and the same designer. I might be working in the morning and Jim might be working in the afternoon. We were responsible to each other.

What rules did you make to guarantee your cinematic styles would match?

Morahan I said we'd use prime lenses, wouldn't use zoom lenses, and would use tracks if we needed to move the camera. I wanted a classic look to it. Secondly, I said we wouldn't take landscape shots. India was a part of what we were making, but I didn't want us to spend our time trying to make it pretty. I bet we'd be able to bring back the real India on the screen—and I was right.

How did the large cast react to such a long stay in a foreign land most had never seen before?

Morahan They found it amazingly stimulating, every single one of them. People can't help but be touched by India—its different pace, the depth of its religious faith, the complexity of the society, the great beauty of the landscape, and the extraordinary harshness in terms of climate.

One of the most praised performances in The Jewel in the Crown *was given by Tim Pigott-Smith as the villainous Ronald Merrick. How was he picked for the role?*

Morahan Tim was a friend. I hadn't worked with him, but when I read the books it seemed to me he was the right actor for it. He's a highly intelligent, passionate man from a lower-middle-class background himself. I'd seen his work in theater and television and found it amazingly vivid. He was not a leading man in a handsome way. He was just a remarkable young character actor. I asked him if he wanted to play it. He read it and said yes. It was as simple as that.

Another acclaimed performance was by Dame Peggy Ashcroft playing the elderly former missionary Barbie Batchelor. Some critics feel Barbie was meant to represent the decent soul of the British people in The Jewel in the Crown. *Is that how Peggy Ashcroft saw it?*

Morahan No, I don't think so. Peggy came from a very ordinary suburban background. I think she was brought up in Croydon and orphaned at a very early age. She found Barbie a celebration of that kind of ordinariness—with courage and dignity. She found that very touching and moving.

There is a persistent rumor that Peggy Ashcroft had something to do with the decision to add an extra episode to The Jewel in the Crown. *Is that true?*

Morahan Yes. We increased the number of hours we were doing just because of what Peggy was doing with the Barbie character.

You also directed Peggy Ashcroft in your next Masterpiece Theatre production, The Heat of the Day. *What was it like to direct her?*

Morahan Peggy was a friend and a very fine actress, who did everything with total dedication, care, and love. I admired her greatly. She worked in a very private way. She was not a person who theorized about her work or how she arrived at it. You know, the English pragmatic tradition. She was a marvelous exemplar of that. I was very fortunate to work with her a couple of times. She was old and had to conserve her energy, but she had the most marvelous concentration.

Right in the middle of production on The Jewel in the Crown, *the huge soundstage in Manchester, where you were filming most of the interiors, burned to the ground. How big a setback was that?*

Morahan It wasn't a setback at all because everybody responded to the crisis marvelously. We suspended production for eight days and built another studio within a few weeks. We took a warehouse and equipped it. It was a stimulating crisis.

You were in charge of one of the most expensive television dramas in English history. Did that mean you always had head-office types looking over your shoulder?

Morahan No, not really. There were the accountants back in Manchester who thought we were totally out of control, but they were absolutely incorrect. In fact, we came in under budget. We made it for £5.25 million, which was a ridiculous sum of money. You certainly wouldn't be able to do it for that now.

Were there any major surprises in the critical reaction to The Jewel in the Crown?

Morahan We received much more intelligent criticism in the United States than we did in England. American writers were unencumbered by this very extraordinary sense of paradox which seemed to infect the English.

Two opposing veins of criticism ran through British writing. On the one hand, there was a total dismissal of *The Jewel in the Crown* on the grounds that the author knew nothing about India and was an outsider.

I actually had quite a difference with my father-in-law on that issue. He wouldn't quite accept the fact that Paul Scott was at liberty to have an artist's view of the world to which my father-in-law had given the best part of his life. My father-in-law was [an officer in the] Indian Army. My mother-in-law had married him out there in Calcutta in 1941, and my wife was born in Bangalore in 1942. My wife's grandparents also lived and worked out there. Those two generations felt *The Jewel in the Crown* betrayed everything they stood for.

Another strand of criticism that was leveled at us was from the opposite spectrum. The radical writers—people like Salman Rushdie—accused us of just being nostalgic. Of course, the last thing in the world we wanted to do was make a nostalgic piece. But there's something in the British temperament that took to it in a nostalgic way.

The Asian radicals saw it as a reflection of Thatcherite Britain, that we were creatures of the jingoism Margaret Thatcher had generated by the Falklands War. What was absurd about it was that we had predated the Falklands War. As a matter of fact, we were filming in Kashmir when the Falklands War broke out. Nevertheless, there was an extraordinary wave of jingoism in Britain at the time, which I found repellent when I returned from India. I had seen the other side of the coin, you might say.

You've just returned from India, where you filmed Rumer Godden's Peacock Spring, *the story of a 16-year-old English girl who falls in love with an Indian boy. What changes did you find?*

Morahan The power of the middle class has grown, so there are many more cars on the road. There's a lot of pollution in Delhi and Bombay. Also, it's a country threatened by a number of insurgencies of one kind or another, so there's a greater concern for security than there was. It seems India is a more dangerous place for public figures.

Would it be much harder to film The Jewel in the Crown *there today?*

Morahan No, not really. India has become used to people making films there. I was shooting there for about nine weeks on *Peacock Spring* and had no problems whatsoever. I mean, it was very pleasant. It's still a vast democracy and it works, in its way. ❧

Paradise Postponed (Euston Films for
Thames Television)
October 19–December 28, 1986, 11 episodes

Goodbye Mr. Chips (BBC/MGM)
January 4–18, 1987, 3 episodes
Based on the novel by James Hilton

Lost Empires (Granada Television)
January 25–March 8, 1987, 7 episodes
Based on the novel by J. B. Priestley

Silas Marner (BBC)
March 15, 1987, single 2-hour episode
Based on the novel by George Eliot

Star Quality: Noel Coward Stories (BBC in associa-
tion with Quintet Films)
March 29–April 26, 1987, 5 episodes
Based on five short stories by Noel Coward

The Death of the Heart (Granada Television)
May 3, 1987, single two-hour episode
Based on the novel by Elizabeth Bowen

Love Song (Anglia Television)
May 10–May 17, 1987, 2 episodes
Based on the short story by Jeffrey Archer

The Bretts, Series 1 (Central Independent
Television)*
October 11–November 29, 1987, 8 episodes

Northanger Abbey (BBC)*
December 6, 1987, single 90-minute episode
Based on the novel by Jane Austen

Sorrell & Son (Yorkshire Television)
December 13, 1987–January 10, 1988, 5 episodes
Based on the novel by Warwick Deeping

Fortunes of War (BBC)*
January 17–February 28, 1988, 7 episodes
Based on the novels *The Balkan Trilogy* and
The Levant Trilogy by Olivia Manning

The Day After the Fair (BBC)
March 6–13, 1988, 2 episodes
Based on the short story "On the Western Circuit"
by Thomas Hardy

David Copperfield (BBC)
March 27–April 24, 1988, 5 episodes
Based on the novel by Charles Dickens

By the Sword Divided, Series 2 (BBC in association
with Consolidated Productions)
August 28–October 9, 1988, 10 episodes

A Perfect Spy (BBC)*
October 16–November 27, 1988, 7 episodes
Based on the novel by John le Carré

Heaven on Earth (Primedia Productions)*
December 4, 1988, single 2-hour episode

A Wreath of Roses (Granada Television)
January 8, 1989, single 90-minute episode
Based on the novel by Elizabeth Taylor

A Very British Coup (Skreba Films for Channel 4)§
January 15–16, 1989, 2 episodes
Based on the novel by Chris Mullen

All Passion Spent (BBC)
January 22–February 5, 1989, 4 episodes
Based on the novel by Vita Sackville-West

Talking Heads: Bed Among the Lentils (BBC)
February 12, 1989, 1 episode

Christabel (BBC)*
February 19–March 12, 1989, 4 episodes
Based on the autobiography *The Past Is Myself*
by Christabel Bielenberg

The Charmer (London Weekend Television)*
April 30–June 4, 1989, 6 episodes
Based on the novels by Patrick Hamilton

The Bretts, Series 2 (Central Independent
Television)*
June 11–August 13, 1989, 8 episodes

And a Nightingale Sang (Portman Productions)§
October 15, 1989, single 90-minute episode
Based on the play by C. P. Taylor

Precious Bane (BBC)
October 22–29, 1989, 2 episodes
Based on the novel by Mary Webb

Glory Enough for All (Gemstone Productions/
Primedia Productions)
November 5–12, 1989, 2 episodes
Based on the *The Discovery of Insulin* and
Banting: A Biography by Michael Bliss

A Tale of Two Cities (Granada Television/Dune
and Antenne II)§
November 19–December 10, 1989, 4 episodes
Based on the novel by Charles Dickens

The Yellow Wallpaper (BBC)
December 17, 1989, single 90-minute episode
Based on the short story by Charlotte Perkins
Gilman

After the War (Granada Television)
January 7–February 25, 1990, 8 episodes

The Real Charlotte (Granada Television/
Gandon Productions)§
March 25–April 8, 1990, 3 episodes
Based on the novel by Edith Somerville
and Martin Ross

The Dressmaker (Freeway Films and
Ronald Shedlo Productions)*
April 15, 1990, single 2-hour episode
Based on the novel by Beryl Bainbridge

Traffik (Carnival Films for Channel 4)§
April 22–May 20, 1990, 5 episodes

Piece of Cake (Holmes Associates with
London Weekend Television)*
July 8–August 12, 1990, 6 episodes
Based on the novel by Derek Robinson

The Heat of the Day (Granada Television)
September 30, 1990, single 2-hour episode
Based on the novel by Elizabeth Bowen

The Ginger Tree (BBC/NHK and WGBH/Boston
in association with Hallett Street Productions)
October 14–November 4, 1990, 4 episodes
Based on the novel by Oswald Wynd

Jeeves and Wooster, Series 1 (Carnival Films
for Granada Television)§
November 11–December 9, 1990, 5 episodes
Based on the stories of P. G. Wodehouse

Scoop (London Weekend Television)
December 30, 1990, single 2-hour episode
Based on the novel by Evelyn Waugh

A Room of One's Own (Oyster Television/
Thames Television)
January 6, 1991, 1 episode
Based on lectures by Virginia Woolf

**TWENTIETH ANNIVERSARY
FAVORITES**
January 13–March 10, 1991, 9 episodes

Upstairs, Downstairs
  "Guest of Honour"
  "Such a Lovely Man"
  "All the King's Horses"

The Flame Trees of Thika, Episode 1

On Approval

I, Claudius, Episode 9

All for Love: A Dedicated Man

Elizabeth R, Episode 1

The Jewel in the Crown, Episode 1

The Tale of Beatrix Potter

The Six Wives of Henry VIII, Episode 5

House of Cards (BBC)
March 31–April 21, 1991, 4 episodes
Based on the novel by Michael Dobbs

The Shiralee (Seven Network of Australia
and the BBC with the assistance of the
Australian Film Commission)
April 28, 1991, 1 episode
Based on the novel by D'Arcy Niland

Summer's Lease (BBC)
May 12–June 2, 1991, 4 episodes
Based on the novel by John Mortimer

---

*Available on video   §Video out of print
*Video cassettes of many Masterpiece Theatre programs are
available at public libraries and video rental stores. For
information about the availability of any program or about
purchasing videos, call VideoFinders, a service of public television station KCET, at 1-800-343-4727.*

Seasons 16–20

FORTUNES OF WAR

7 EPISODES
January 17–February 28, 1988
Produced by *BBC*
Producer *Betty Willingale*
**Based on the novels The Balkan Trilogy and
The Levant Trilogy by** *Olivia Manning*
Writer *Alan Plater*
Director *James Cellan Jones*

CAST
Guy Pringle *Kenneth Branagh*
Harriet Pringle *Emma Thompson*
Prince Yakimov *Ronald Pickup*
Sasha Drucker *Harry Burton*
Simon Boulderstone *Rupert Graves*
Dobson *Charles Kay*
Inchcape *James Villiers*

THE ENGLISH *seem to have staked out the dramatic rights to both world wars in such dramas as* TESTAMENT OF YOUTH, PRIVATE SCHULZ, *and* DANGER UXB. *The most recent of these to wash up on our shores is* FORTUNES OF WAR, *which is notable for abandoning Paris and London and using the refreshingly new locales of Bucharest, Athens, Alexandria, and Cairo. It tells of the war's effect on a small group of British citizens—most* especially a newly married couple, Guy and Harriet Pringle—caught in the terrifying backwash of Hitler's armies as they march across the eastern front, first in the Balkans and later in North Africa. "A love story with teeth and a war story with brains," is how one reviewer described this blockbuster.

Fortunes of War opens with a nice shot of the Orient Express speeding across the Balkans with the curiously mismatched Guy and Harriet aboard. Guy, a bespectacled young professor, is bringing his new wife to Bucharest with him as he resumes his university post as a guest lecturer in English literature. His friends are an eccentric collection of expatriates who gather in the English bar of the Hotel Athenee Palace: a drunken newspaper correspondent, several incoherent British embassy employees, an endangered Jewish family, and a scrounging, down-at-the-heels Russian prince named Yakimov (who is perilously close to Mischa Auer's Czarist playboy character seen in dozens of ancient Hollywood movies). They are all endangered species adrift in the Balkans. They know that the Germans have invaded Poland but seem blissfully unaware that Romania is about to be hacked to pieces by Germany, Russia, and Hungary. In the center of the approaching holocaust, they sip their tea, discuss John Donne, and stage amateur productions of *Troilus and Cressida.*

Viewers quickly learn that Guy is a foolishly optimistic liberal idealist who believes in the goodwill of the Russians to hold off the

"Yakimov has a wonderful quality of innocence, a desire to give people fun. He says that 'People are nice to me and they give me things. So I like to entertain them.'… He doesn't expect something for nothing, even though he is on the face of it a terrible old codger—totally selfish and shameless and blatant and all that, but somehow you cannot hate him."
—Ronald Pickup

"Thompson, a subtle beauty, is especially winning. She is so crisply intelligent, so saucily droll, so beguiling, that one wants to thump Guy Pringle over the head with a lead bar to make him realize what a cad he's being to this enchanting woman." —Ron Miller, *Knight-Ridder Newspapers*

"Harriet Pringle is tremendously admirable. She has mental fiber and muscle, with a sense of irony you need in this world to deal with its many blows. She's tough, intelligent, and independent. Until now I've rejected the idea of marriage, and it's been fascinating for me to explore what an extraordinary thing marriage is for a man and a woman."
—Emma Thompson

Nazis. He is totally wrapped up in his lectures and playlets and professes such a great love for mankind that he has none left for his wife. Harriet's growing displeasure with her marriage is summed up in a comment to her husband: "I love you, but I can't remember why." Or, as director James Cellan Jones explains it, "Harriet married a man who made her feel special and unique. Then she discovers that the trouble is he makes everyone else feel that way, too."

The Misfortunes of War

The group moves on to Greece, where the treacherous Yakimov meets his fate when he makes a final, careless gesture by lighting a cigarette during a blackout (curiously filmed in broad daylight), wisecracking, "Do I look

"The message is that even 30 or 40 years ago women longed for and needed independence and to be individuals in their own right. And now they are taking hold of that." —Director James Cellan Jones

"Guy is the golden youth, facing the slow realization of getting further away from achieving any of his political or professional aims.... And I became fascinated by the shift of power in the relationship [with his wife]." —Kenneth Branagh

like a military objective?" and is shot dead by the police. By the time they reach Cairo, scenes of international turmoil alternate with Harriet's inner turmoil over the attentions of a handsome officer played by Jeremy Brudenell, who had wooed her at the Parthenon and almost won her at the Hotel Grande Bretagne.

As the plot moves down the map, it is interesting to watch Kenneth Branagh and Emma Thompson, both well trained but young performers still in their twenties, grappling with their characterizations. Harriet was Thompson's first major dramatic role and she played it with great sensitivity to the character's vulnerability, uncertainty, humor, and unfolding strength. Particularly poignant is the sympathy she shows for a caged bear in the Cairo zoo. Thompson has since gone on to major film roles, including one in *Howards End* for which she won an Academy Award. Branagh was brilliant in a new production of *Henry V* and as actor-producer-director of *Much Ado About Nothing* (in which Thompson co-starred), both seen on Masterpiece Theatre. Despite a meteoric career, Branagh still

Not Quiet on the Eastern Front

Location filming presented a number of challenges. For the scene on the Egyptian pyramid, heavy equipment had to be carried up, and the actors had to climb up toting a change of costume for a second sequence. To dress the legions of extras (recruited from among local residents at each location, mostly through newspaper ads), the BBC transported nearly 2,000 costumes of the 1940s from place to place. Some 150 British residents of Cairo and British-looking Egyptians participated in the Cairo assassination scene, which was filmed in a very large lecture hall. "The people went crazy when we fired off the gun," director James Cellan Jones said. "It was quite frightening. Then we had to stop them and shout, 'Let's do another take.' In Egypt, a semi-independent republic, the people speak a variety of languages, and if you yell, 'Quiet!' in the wrong language, they turn funny."

"The feel throughout these seven hours is that of Durrell's overripe Alexandria *novels and Waugh's melancholy* Sword of Honor *trilogy, with all that Doris Lessing would later tell us about women and imperialism, plus some mischief. Brilliant images wed to witty words and actors lazing about like lions add up to a thoughtful delight."*

—John Leonard, *New York*

"I couldn't understand how a man so intelligent and sensitive could be so crass in his behavior to his wife. I began to warm to him later, partly because I began to see—a bit guiltily—elements of myself in him, the way he's always too busy to pay attention to her, saying, 'I love you, yes, but well, we'll talk later.'" —Kenneth Branagh

They Protest Too Much

"My busy schedule doesn't leave much time for a girl friend," Kenneth Branagh said during filming of *Fortunes of War*. "I'd never get married unless I was economically independent," said Emma Thompson. Shortly thereafter they both got married—to each other.

describes himself with remarkable modesty as "just a bright working-class lad from Belfast who got rid of his accent." But not his Irish sense of humor.

Rupert Graves, familiar to theatergoers as Freddy in *A Room With a View*, is particularly fine as Simon Boulderstone, the young officer who joins the group in Egypt and shares the final scene with Guy and Harriet atop the great pyramid of Cheops, peering into the sand far below and into the uncertain future ahead. Guy says, "You'll never leave me again, will you?" And Harriet answers, "Don't know. Can't promise. Probably not."

With a total cost of £6.5 million, *Fortunes of War* was, at the time, the most expensive BBC series ever filmed. It is based on 2,000 pages of six novels comprising *The Balkan Trilogy* and *The Levant Trilogy* which, Anthony Burgess once wrote, may "well appear to be the finest fictional record [of World War II] produced by a British writer." Written by Olivia Manning, they are close to autobiography. Like Harriet, Manning accompanied her lecturer-husband to Bucharest just before the war and fled from the approaching Nazis to Greece, Egypt, and eventually to Jerusalem, where her husband became the head of the Palestine Broadcasting Station. At the end of the war they returned to England, where she died in 1980. The extraordinary task of turning Manning's wealth of material into a seven-part serial fell to Alan Plater who, as one critic said, was "a perfect choice—witty, discreet, judicious in his juxtapositions, his elisions, his highlighting." His script, coupled with the excellent acting and superb location filming, which was the most expensive in BBC history, gave viewers the reassuring sensation of actually being there in the cafés, in the hotels, and on the streets of Bucharest, Athens, and Cairo, one step ahead of the Nazis.

A PERFECT SPY

7 EPISODES
October 16–November 27, 1988
Produced by *BBC*
Producer *Colin Rogers*
Based on the novel by *John le Carré*
Writer *Arthur Hopcraft*
Director *Peter Smith*

CAST
Magnus Pym *Peter Egan*
Rick Pym *Ray McAnally*
Mary Pym *Jane Booker*
Miss Dubber *Peggy Ashcroft*
Jack Brotherhood *Alan Howard*
Axel *Rudiger Weigang*
Magnus as a teen *Benedict Taylor*

I N RECENT YEARS *Americans have seen and read a lot about espionage, the job that dare not speak its name, from the G-string jocularity of James Bond to the investigative articles on the Central Intelligence Agency. But it is likely that the public comes closer to the truth in the miniseries* A PERFECT SPY, *because the John le Carré novel on which it is based isn't a who-done-it, it's a why-done-it, a cunning account of the subtle*

"It wasn't until three or four years ago… that it dawned on me that the only way I could tell this story and get the humor out of it that I wanted—and through the humor, the compassion—was to make the son, by extension, in many ways worse than the father. So there could be no question of self-pity…. There's a feeling I have very much…. I think many fathers have it, that somehow we are there not to pass on the things we inherited from our own fathers."

—John le Carré, *The New York Times Magazine*

influences that guide a man into a profession that often tempts its practitioners to betray their own country.

With a charismatic con man for a father and two masters of espionage as his tutors, Magnus Pym couldn't help becoming a spy. From the beginning he is destined for a life of duplicity and betrayal. Even as a child he shows a natural talent for deceit that delights his father, Rick Pym, a jolly and unflappable minor crook and major con man, who is as charming in a jail cell as he is in a Rolls-Royce—and he is familiar with both, bouncing from fat times to lean. As a result, young Pym has a Dickensian childhood, watching the police take his father to prison, seeing his mother go mad, and ending up in the care of an abusive uncle. Because the facts of his own existence are hidden from him, he becomes a listener at doors, trying to break the subtle codes used to deceive him. He loses his innocence at an early age. He trusts no one. He is trained to lie. He is a perfect spy.

While Magnus is at school in Switzerland, a British agent sees him as a likely candidate for Intelligence, and he is recruited to report on politically active students. After Oxford he joins the service officially and marries a woman who is considered suitably safe for the life he has chosen. In Czechoslovakia he is reunited with a German friend from his Swiss schooldays who is spying for the Czechs and discovers that his attachment to him is stronger than his loyalty to England, and so they become spying partners, exchanging secrets. After a lifetime as a double agent, when both sides are becoming suspicious of him, his manipulating father dies.

"It's not really a spy story—it's about the way one's parents and childhood make one the kind of person one is. Because Magnus is deprived of love as a child—because the people he loves are suddenly taken away from him without his knowing why—he grows up having to steal it, to cheat people out of love in the same way his father cheats him out of money. And although he spends his life trying to escape from his father, Rick goes on being the motive force in his life—when Rick dies there's nothing left to keep him going; he's an empty man."

—Director Peter Smith, *The New York Times*

The marionette still has strings, but now there is no one to pull them, and Pym goes into hiding from everyone, even his wife, in a small Victorian boardinghouse in Dawlish where he has hidden before and is known under a different name. The old landlady (Dame Peggy Ashcroft) scolds him in motherly fashion: "Oh, Mr. Canterbury, isn't it just like you to disappear for months and then come back in the middle of the night!"

Magnus has returned to the seaside where he had once spent an out-of-season holiday with his father, the only really happy memory he has of his childhood. When the police find him and surround the old house, a single shot is heard. The perfect spy has come to a perfect end.

"A Perfect Spy, the John le Carré opus described by one critic as A Perfect Novel, is now A Perfect Television Serial." —The Sunday Times

"Our fictional spies are different from yours.... Perhaps our spies are more elegant, more cerebral, less given to car chases and shootouts and extreme violence.

"What le Carré offers is an inside view of a particular kind of English society that not only Americans, but continental Europeans, are fascinated by. Americans see our fictional spies as rather like David Niven, someone with an aura of intellectual and social excellence. Well, what le Carré does is not to deglamorize the people; he deglamorizes the job. He sets the spy in a much more realistic context."

—Writer Arthur Hopcraft, Los Angeles Times

By the time the series reached Masterpiece Theatre in 1988, American viewers had become well acquainted with le Carré's brand of espionage in BBC adaptations of *Smiley's People* and *Tinker, Tailor, Soldier, Spy.* It's a territory le Carré knows very well, and in *A Perfect Spy* he places himself in the middle of the story. David Cornwell worked for British Intelligence and has hidden behind the pen name of John le Carré ever since. His father, Ronald Cornwell, was a credit shark who, like Magnus' father, served time as a parliamentary candidate and a convict. Other similarities between novelist and hero are stamped all over the book.

Le Carré is a master of plot by nuance and of character by innuendo. His spy novels are not for readers who nod off at long passages of laborious prose, and who find it difficult to follow a story that jumps around. Television viewers were spared the flashbacks and flashforwards by BBC scriptwriter Arthur Hopcraft, who pulled the book apart and rearranged the story in chronological order—all with the author's approval based on their previous collaboration on *Tinker, Tailor, Soldier, Spy*. By terms of his contract, le Carré had the right to disapprove any casting but never exercised it and visited the set only once, in Switzerland.

Apart from the American scenes, the film was shot entirely on location in 216 spots in England, Austria, Wales, Berlin, and the Greek island of Corfu. Some preliminary still-photography in pre-glasnost Czechoslovakia proved that filming there would be impossible, and the Czech scenes were filmed in Austria.

A Perfect Spy carries its central character from age 6 to age 53. A pair of identical twins rotate in the role of Magnus at six, followed by Benedict Taylor in his teens, and Peter Egan from 21 to the end. Egan is familiar to Masterpiece Theatre viewers as Oscar Wilde in *Lillie*. But Irish actor Ray McAnally (who has appeared in some 200 film and television shows and 250 plays) steals the show as the charismatic father whose moods turn in the blink of an eye. In one scene, Rick Pym is campaigning for office in a dreary town in East Anglia and sees that the audience is responding favorably to his speech. His eyes fill with genuine tears, but a moment later we see in those same eyes the calculating con man who knows that his victims have taken the bait, suggesting, perhaps, that the closest profession to spying may be acting.

"Every single person Magnus Pym meets is betrayed by him. But that is done not to be destructive but because he is a chameleon; he becomes what other people want him to become, and he tries to give people what they want. Because of his childhood, the negative input of his father, he has no moral standpoint of his own, no moral basis.... He is the perfect spy basically because he has no inner feelings about anything."
—Peter Egan

"There is something about his writing that makes it particularly suitable for television adaption—perhaps its innerness, its feeling of privacy, its introversion. Watching it alone, at home on a small screen, perhaps is the right way to see a drama of personal confusion, personal betrayals, and personal understanding."
—Minnette Marrin, *Daily Telegraph*

"They sheared the top of my head, and I put on a different toupee practically every morning so that I could be 55 on Monday, 25 on Tuesday, and 35 the next day." —Ray McAnally

Traffik

5 EPISODES

April 22–May 20, 1990

Produced by *Carnival Films for Channel 4*

Producer *Brian Eastman*

Writer *Simon Moore*

Director *Alastair Reid*

CAST

Jack Lithgow *Bill Paterson*

Helen *Lindsay Duncan*

Fazal *Jamal Shah*

Caroline *Julia Ormond*

Tariq Butt *Talat Hussein*

Ulli *Fritz Müller-Scherz*

Dieter *Tilo Prückner*

*T*RAFFIK *(the German spelling of the word) is a breathless international tour of the world of heroin, the narcotic made from opium poppies that have been grown in the dry heat of Pakistan ever since they were brought there from Sumeria some 4,000 years before Christ. Viewers are familiar with countless dramas about drugs told from the sordid standpoint of addicts or the hazardous viewpoint of the police.* TRAFFIK *takes a different look at heroin—as a well-organized, high-profit business.*

Drug running is not a business to get into if you like to sleep at night. Its cold cruelty as well as its dangers are enhanced in this drama by a riveting musical score and fast-cut photography that keep the viewer's adrenaline pumping. The script by British writer Simon Moore sprints across the screen without pause. Only at the end of each episode, when the TV screen goes dark and the credits run, is the viewer allowed to relax.

Moore chose what he calls "a tapestry style" to tell his story, weaving the threads of his plot from three stops on the heroin trail: Pakistan, where the poppies are grown and the heroin is made; Hamburg, where it comes in by ship; and London, where the government has a plan to destroy it. And he hangs his plot around the necks of three characters.

*T*aking the Poppy Trail

Fazal is a small poppy grower in Pakistan, where opium is a highly socialized drug and its production is deeply rooted in the local culture and economy; in Pakistan it is alcohol that is illegal. When Pakistani reformers burn his poppy fields, Fazal moves to Karachi and works for the city's big heroin trafficker to support his family.

"Traffik is terrifik.... It's about drugs, shooting up, shooting at. It's got killings, fast cars, explosives, music you can't dance the gavotte to. It makes A Very British Coup *look like* Little Women."
—Marvin Kitman, Newsday

"The series has a rich, authentic look to it, the Pakistani scenes, especially, with their hot, steaming streets and wall-to-wall people. Alastair Reid's direction is outstanding. He both involves you and, with use of long-lens shots, makes you an observer, offering what's akin to a satellite view of the international scene. It's mind-boggling ..."
—Kay Gardella, New York Daily News

The Political Realities of Filming

Shooting on location is always a logistical challenge, but shooting in Pakistan in spring 1989 entailed unforeseeable difficulties. According to producer Brian Eastman: "The mujahidin rebels who wanted to take over Afghanistan were massing on the northwest frontier precisely where we wanted to film. Coincidentally, Salman Rushdie had just published his book *The Satanic Verses* and there was an enormous amount of anti-British feeling in Muslim countries. So we found ourselves in the middle of Karachi with demonstrations going on around us against Rushdie, and we found ourselves on the northwest frontier with the mujahidin army behind us marching on Afghanistan. But I have to say that despite both of those we were extremely warmly welcomed in Pakistan."

In Germany the heroin is smuggled into the free port of Hamburg on a French ship, where it is to be picked up by the agents of a rich and respectable German, Karl Rosshalde, whose role as a drug tycoon is camouflaged by a company that supplies pipe to Pakistan. When he is caught and imprisoned awaiting trial, Helen, his innocent English wife, is shocked to learn her husband's secret. But in an effort to save their property from confiscation and to pay old debts and new court costs, she rebuilds her husband's business. She moves quickly and confidently and soon becomes a murderous druglord who arranges the death of a witness expected to testify against her husband.

The third city of the triangle is London, where Jack Lithgow is a Home Office minister assigned to a project that encourages Pakistani farmers to replace their poppy fields with sugar cane, which takes longer to grow, requires expensive fertilizers and irrigation, but pays only a fraction of what they have been getting from heroin. Lithgow's problems are doubled by the discovery that his daughter is an addict. Director Alastair Reid holds the trio in tight rein like a three-horse charioteer, keeping their parallel stories racing alongside one another though never intersecting.

"What we wanted to do," said producer Brian Eastman, "is to treat the drug business like the car business; not show it in the usual black-and-white morality, but put in perspective of how the world of drug trade looks, and force people to think a little more closely about it as a world industry.... There is a tremendous amount of vested interest in pursuing the drug trade. And I think that again is something a lot of conventional series have shied away from—having one character who is quite high up in government being allowed to deal with some of those contradictions and hypocrisies."

A production of England's Channel Four, *Traffik* took two years to research, five months to film, and had a budget of £4 million. It was filmed in the three countries with actors from those countries speaking four languages. (Fortunately, subtitles let viewers know what's being said, though the director was never certain during filming when dialogue was flying past in German, Pashto,

"Traffik is a thoroughly satisfying thriller, but it's also researched so well that anyone watching will come away with an understanding of the drug problem that far exceeds the cops-and-robbers scenario preferred by most Western governments.... Traffik is mercifully free of American TV moralizing. The sight of a pretty young girl sticking a syringe in her foot is ugly enough; she doesn't have to die hideously to drive the lesson home. Similarly, when Lithgow finds himself on the Khyber Pass with a tribesman who offers him some opium to smoke, he resists but then tries it. This would be unlikely in an American docudrama, but what follows would surely be impossible: the drug relaxes him and affords him a flash of insight into his family problems. 'I'm frightened that I've forgotten how to love people,' he says." —Emily Prager, *Mirabella*

"Jack Lithgow is pragmatic, driven by ambition, obviously careless of his own family life—until his daughter's involvement with heroin makes him realize the world is really more complex than he'd believed. At the end of the story, he becomes more sympathetic." —Bill Paterson

"You realize that with someone like Helen Rosshalde, who's spent her youth training at that level [to become an Olympic swimmer], she's got steel in her somewhere, enormous discipline. So when her husband is arrested and she's threatened with the loss of her family and her whole way of life, she doesn't give in." —Lindsay Duncan

"Traffik doesn't sanitize or oversimplify any element of the narcotics business. When Lithgow's daughter shoots up, you can feel the needle. Her nose runs. She vomits. When her father finds her, you can feel his despair. And you can see him change from a man with a mission who thought he knew the answers to a man who thinks he knows nothing."

—Gordon Walek, *Daily Herald*

and Urdu). "In Pakistan we got quite a lot of feedback and did a lot of rewriting the closer we got to actual production," said Eastman in *City Limits.* "People would come and say, 'This isn't quite the way it would be,' and we'd change incidents and dialogue accordingly. The government approved the project and made some comments, which helped us make it more authentic."

The scenes of heroin manufacture were real and the cause of some backstage derision. The original script explained a very complex method of heroin manufacture, which the Pakistanis scoffed at. "Oh, no," they said. "You don't do it like that. All you need is a tin bucket, some water, a few stones, and a cloth to drain it through." Moore and Eastman worked with drug enforcement agencies in Pakistan who arranged access to heroin-processing facilities. The drugs seen on camera were destroyed immediately after the shooting was completed. The scenes where Fazal wanders through a field of poppies were the only parts that had to be faked, as poppy farmers wouldn't allow more than one camera in their fields. So plastic plants were made by the thousands in Karachi and transported to the Afghan border, where the scene was filmed.

During his extensive research for this bang-up thriller, screenwriter Moore reached a sobering conclusion about the war on drugs: "The best way to reduce drug taking is to reduce the demand rather than destroy the supply. If drugs ever were wiped out of Asia, Africa would be set up and ready to take its place just a few years later." Moore didn't interpose his views on the script, but has a British politician reach a similar verdict on supply and demand: "We cannot police the world. We cannot stop [heroin] supplies. We can only limit the demand for it by producing a decent society that people want to live in, not escape from."

Some Memorable Quotes from Traffik

🌿 "It doesn't need much water, it doesn't need much in the way of nutrients. They are just weeds—the richest weeds in the world."—A poppy grower to Jack Lithgow

🌿 "Do you know that people in the West are dying from the heroin you make?" Lithgow asks Fazal. "Sir, I grow opium, not heroin. You deal with the heroin problem," Fazal replies.

🌿 "The CIA helps us, the DEA tries to destroy us. America is never a problem when it is fighting itself."—An Afghan rebel–drug dealer

🌿 "Nothing that grows from the ground is evil. There are only evil men."—A Pakistani speaking with Lithgow

🌿 "There's always a way. If people can shoot the Pope and the president, you can get to anybody."—Helen Rosshalde, plotting the murder of a witness against her husband—excerpted from the *Washington Post*

The GINGER TREE

4 EPISODES

October 14–November 4, 1990

Produced by *BBC/NHK and WGBH/Boston*
in association with Hallett Street Productions

Producer *Tim Ironside-Wood*

Based on the novel by *Oswald Wynd*

Writer *Christopher Hampton*

Directors *Anthony Garner, Morimasa Matsumoto*

CAST

Mary Mackenzie *Samantha Bond*

Count Kurihama *Daisuke Ryu*

Richard Collingsworth *Adrian Rawlins*

Baroness Aiko Onodera *Fumi Dan*

Alicia *Joanna McCallum*

ESTERNERS *have been trying to figure out the Japanese ever since Portuguese explorers and missionaries went ashore in the 1540s. Japan's polished elegance and delicate beauty stun any visitor, but underneath the canopy of pink cherry blossoms and brocaded kimonos is a society whose complex rules of conduct are never fully grasped by outsiders.*

In 1902 Japan entered into an alliance with Great Britain, and THE GINGER TREE, *based on a novel by Oswald Wynd, maps the*

cultural divide by telling the story of a bright young Scots woman, Mary Mackenzie, who travels solo to Manchuria to surprise her fiancé, Richard Collingsworth, a British military officer posted there. The six-hour drama was co-produced by the BBC with NHK and WGBH, filmed entirely on location in Japan, Taiwan, and Britain, and shown on Masterpiece Theatre in the autumn of 1990.

Mary's fiancé is a handsome, plumed, and beribboned officer of her majesty's overseas corps who has just been appointed British military attaché. On their wedding night he reveals himself to be a cold, self-centered man, as insensitive in bed as he is out of it. Before long he is sent away and becomes enmeshed in the Russo-Japanese War. Deserted and desperately unhappy, Mary accepts an invitation to tea from Count Kentaro Kurihama, the charismatic Japanese military attaché who is everything her husband is not—a sympathetic, beautifully mannered aristocrat. They become lovers,

and she finds in Kentaro the passion that her husband has denied her.

Their idyllic affair is shattered months later when Richard returns and finds Mary pregnant. Infuriated, and knowing the child is not his, he throws her out. She has no alternative but to accept Kentaro's gift of a house, where she will live as his concubine, a status governed by a strict etiquette quite unlike any Mary has

"As a Western woman, I had mixed feelings about wearing [a kimono]. On the one hand they are very beautiful. But all the bowing and nodding to men that goes with it was difficult for me emotionally. They were also hard to walk in." —Samantha Bond, *Today*

"The interplay of Western and Eastern cultures is portrayed with glorious location shots in Japan and Taiwan. The series displays the same sense of style and period as the TV dramatisation of Paul Scott's The Jewel in the Crown."
—Compton Miller, *Daily Express*

The Downside of High Definition

The Ginger Tree was the first high-definition television (HDTV) drama to air in the United States. HDTV offers a super-real clarity, but the medium presents a new set of problems, as *Ginger Tree* producer Tim Ironside-Wood discovered when noticing that dust on the set and props or layers of makeup were glaringly visible. "Where in the past you could get away with using a fake brick wall, with HDTV you need a real brick wall," Ironside-Wood said. HDTV was invented by NHK.

known. Through a sympathetic woman friend of Kentaro's, she learns that her lover is married with four children. As a final blow, her son, Taro, is taken from her and placed with a Japanese family because a nobleman's son cannot be raised by a concubine. She is forbidden to ever see her son or even be told of his whereabouts. Determined to be independent of Kentaro and hoping to find Taro, Mary moves out of Kentaro's house. She eventually sets up a salon designing and selling European fashions to rich Japanese women and becomes rich herself. Kentaro visits her occasionally and professes his love, but still Taro is kept from her.

Decades later, on the eve of World War II, as Mary is being evacuated with other foreigners, Kentaro commits suicide after a failed diplomatic mission. But before he takes his life, he arranges for a handsome young Japanese soldier to meet Mary on the dock and ease her departure. In a scene of tender recognition Mary and the soldier silently acknowledge with their eyes that they are mother and son. It is a sweet moment in television storytelling.

Samantha Bond (who's on screen for all but three minutes of the four-hour show) is perfect as the plucky Scottish import, and Japanese film idol Daisuke Ryu gives a performance that is as smooth as the sliding paper screens of his native land. Language differences were just one of the difficulties they encountered. "I speak a lot of Japanese in episode 4 and a bit in episode 2, and I had to learn all that in 17 hours," says Bond. "It was a bit daunting. It's a terribly difficult language and I still don't know what my words mean—I just got terribly good at saying them phonetically. About all Daisuke and I could say in the other's language at first was 'Hello,' 'How are you?' and 'Are you happy?' We communicated by asking each other those three questions. We did a lot of looking deep into each other's eyes and trying to understand. We learned to trust each other very quickly."

They also learned how to be comfortable playing sensitive scenes. "I realized that the love scenes between us were going to be a problem," Bond said in *Today.* "With an English actor, you'd have a small kiss in the morning and have tea together in the afternoons and so by the time you have to get into bed together and do anything embarrassing, you both understand how each of you feels.

"I realized early on that bowing every morning to Daisuke wasn't going to get us anywhere. So whenever we met, I'd walk up to him and put my arms around him and hug him. And he loved it. But he said he would never do that at home." The cultural divide portrayed in *The Ginger Tree* was very present even in the making of the series.

"I was very much aware of the parallels between [Mary and me]. There I was, a single foreign woman abroad, frightened and homesick. I couldn't communicate with anyone, and no one could communicate with me. It was as though I was living through Mary's eyes.... Mary's courage and her ability to cope against very grim odds are aspects of her character that I admire as a modern woman.

"If her story was set in modern times, I don't think it would be much different. While other women talk about feminism, she is living it." —Samantha Bond, *Today*

Produced by *Carnival Films for Granada Television*
Producer *Brian Eastman*
Based on the stories of *P. G. Wodehouse*
Writer *Clive Exton*
Directors *Robert Young (Series 1);*
Ferdinand Fairfax (Series 2 and 3);
Simon Langton (Series 4)

CAST
Jeeves *Stephen Fry*
Bertie Wooster *Hugh Laurie*
Aunt Agatha *Mary Wimbush*
Aunt Dahlia *Brenda Bruce (Series 1);*
Patricia Lawrence (Series 2 and 3);
Vivian Pickles (Series 4)
Honoria Glossop *Elizabeth Kettle*
Tuppy Glossop *Robert Daws*
Gussie Fink-Nottle *Richard Garnett (Series 1 and 4);*
Richard Braine (Series 2)
Madeline Bassett *Francesca Folan (Series 1);*
Elizabeth Morton (Series 2 and 3);
Diana Blackburn (Series 4)
Angela Travers *Amanda Elwes*
Barmy Fotheringay-Phipps *Adam Blackwood*
Bingo Little *Michael Siberry*
Sir Watkyn Bassett *John Woodnutt*
Roderick Spoke *John Turner*
Lady Florence *Fiona Gillies (Series 2);*
Francesca Folan (Series 3)
Stiffy Byng *Amanda Harris*
Stinky Pinker *Simon Treves*
Biffy Biffen *Philip Shelley*
Chuffy Chufnell *Matthew Solon*
Mabel *Charlotte Avery*
Bobbie Wickham *Niahm Cusack*

Jeeves and Wooster

*L*ITERATURE *is full of blissfully contented male couples, joined together in companionship that no woman can put asunder. Sherlock had Watson, Hawkeye had Chingachgook, Don Quixote had Sancho, and Robinson Crusoe was the first person in history to say "Thank God It's Friday."*

But only in England could we find such a satisfactory male duet as Jeeves and Bertie Wooster, the give-and-take pair who share the same quarters and care for each other—Jeeves with a manservant's devotion to his master, and Wooster with his family's money. It could be called a match made in heaven if it weren't for the fact that the match was made by writer P. G. Wodehouse, consummated by Britain's Granada TV, and brought to full flower on Masterpiece Theatre for richer or for poorer, in sickness and in health.

American audiences were both delighted and puzzled by the series of man-and-master situations. While Jeeves and Wooster may be perfectly understandable to the English, they often appeared to defy the laws of social gravity on this side of the Atlantic. Jeeves, with his mannered reserve and calm rationality, frequently takes charge of Wooster, whose impetuousness needs tempering and whose muddleheadedness needs guidance. The distance between the two men was created by class distinctions based on an unwritten code of the superiority of inherited status, wealth, and education, which has dictated the behavior of the British for hundreds of years, regardless of whether they are at home or on a rubber plantation in Malaysia. But any viewers who worry too much about credibility are missing the point: Jeeves and Wooster are good fun, and

"Wodehouse describes Jeeves' cough as 'like a sheep clearing its throat of a blade of grass on a distant hillside.' I tried practicing that but sounded more like a goat clearing its throat of a piece of cheese on a nearby hillside. These things are difficult." —Stephen Fry

"Bertie, it is young men like you who make a person with the future of the race at heart despair." —Aunt Agatha

their silly predicaments are designed to entertain without intellectual distractions of any nature. As Stephen Fry (Jeeves) says, "Theirs is a wonderful world, that one just wants to dive into it, like being able to dive into a soufflé."

The Odd Couple

Wodehouse begins their partnership when Bertram Wooster, the young man-about-Mayfair, is suffering from the effects of Boat Race Night. Bertie staggers home to find on his doorstep a grave-looking, rather portly man impeccably dressed in morning coat and striped trousers.

"I was sent by the agency, Sir. I was given to understand that you need a valet. My name is Jeeves …"

And so Jeeves dutifully awaits his master's beck and call from wherever it might come—the back of Wooster's car, his bed, his club, a country estate of one of his school chums. The one great menace that lurks in the background of many episodes is Honoria Glossop, Bertie's predatory girl friend. She is determined to marry Bertie and bring an end to his happy bachelorhood, which would also be a threat to Jeeves, as well, because it would mean that Mrs. Wooster would run the household. Like Bertie and Honoria, all

Early Wodehouse Fans

As a precocious 11-year-old, Stephen Fry was enchanted by the works of comic novelist P. G. Wodehouse. At 15, he wrote Wodehouse a fan letter and received an autographed photo in return. During the filming of *Jeeves and Wooster*, the photo stood on his dressing-room table as a good-luck charm. Hugh Laurie also caught the Wodehouse bug early on. When assigned to write a school essay about some period in which he would like to have lived, Laurie chose the gentle era of Wodehouse's 1920s and '30s. "I was crestfallen afterwards to be taken aside and told that none of that ever existed," Laurie said. "Being told there was no such world was like that ghastly moment when you're told there is no Father Christmas."

the characters in each episode generally work at cross-purposes, whether they are attempting to repair the plumbing in a grand country house or trying to locate a stolen necklace. Through it all, Jeeves remains steadfastly in control.

The unflappable Jeeves and his overwrought employer were familiar to an older generation of Americans who had grown up with the Wodehouse characters in books as well as countless *Saturday Evening Post* stories in the twenties and thirties, but they were new faces to younger viewers who hadn't yet discovered the laugh-out-loud pleasure to be found in the Wodehouse books. There's an innocence about the characters that is particularly appealing, as Evelyn Waugh so beautifully explained: "Wodehouse characters never have tasted the forbidden fruit. They are still in Eden, the Gardens of Blandings Castle, from which we are all exiled." Wodehouse created the characters in 1915, when they were already relics of the Edwardian age, and continued to write about them for six decades just as if their world hadn't even lost a cuff link. "There's always the feel of Never-Never Land in the settings where Wodehouse plunks poor Bertie down," explained Russell Baker. "These are fairy tales for grown-ups. Worrying about authenticity will spoil them."

The difficult task of translating the stories from the printed page to a television script fell to writer Clive Exton, who succeeded in beautifully capturing the charm and humor. Each episode is

"Bertie is such a good soul. His whole aim in life is to help his idiot friends out of trouble, and he really has no thought of self. You can imagine that he'd be very good company. His use of language is so fabulous that just asking you if you'd like a cup of tea would become an event." —Hugh Laurie

"[Wodehouse's world is] quite *sui generis* and prelapsarian." —Stephen Fry

"One day when Wodehouse was just in his eighties, he told me that his books had taken a new lease on life in the Soviet Union. For the same reason, he said, that the Russians were gobbling up the grimmer works of Charles Dickens—Oliver Twist, Little Dorrit, Hard Times. *Dickens, he explained, showed the Russians how the faces of the English laboring poor (never mind the date) were being ground down. And Wodehouse's Bertie Wooster and his friends of the Drones Club revealed the heartless types who were doing the grinding."* —Alistair Cooke

"There is this extraordinary goodwill that exists between Jeeves and Wooster, though people do tend to think of Jeeves as being incredibly snooty and haughty, which he isn't, and of Bertie Wooster as some kind of yammering ass, which he isn't. He is very intelligent. After all, *Bertie* wrote these books. The extraordinary language in them is *Bertie's* language." —Stephen Fry

"In creating Jeeves, Wodehouse has done something which may respectfully be compared to the work of the Almighty in Michelangelo's painting. He has formed a man filled with the breath of life … If, in say 50 years, Jeeves shall have faded, then what we have so long called England will no longer be." —Hilaire Belloc

The Two Classes of Gentlemen's Clubs

The gentlemens' clubs of London were a very important part of the genteel world of the twenties, and Wodehouse's satire of them is continuous and hilarious. While American club life tends to be business-oriented, the British clubs are elegant clandestine establishments designed to serve as escapes from the responsibilities—and often the drabness—of their members' home lives. Wooster's club is The Drones, whose exclusively upper-class members are invariably shown in their beautifully furnished clubrooms jumping on sofas, playing catch with cricket balls, or throwing dinner rolls at one another. Jeeves' club is The Ganymede, whose equally exclusive membership is composed of butlers, valets, gentlemen's gentlemen, and others in the upper reaches of London's servant class. The Ganymede clubrooms are as elegant as The Drones', but the behavior of Ganymede members is impeccable. The club names themselves are a deft malicious touch. Drones, of course, are the stingless male bees that make no honey and live off the work of other bees. Ganymede, in classic mythology, is the cup-bearer to the gods.

actually an amalgam drawn from several stories. The next task, moving from printed script to dramatic action, required performers capable of acting lighthearted without being silly or teetering into camp. If performers don't have that special timing that comedy requires, they aren't likely to acquire it. That's the reason why many otherwise fine actors never even attempt comedy. Jeremy Brett, TV's Sherlock Holmes, says, "The trick of playing light comedy is to swallow a secret smile, then babble on." By a stroke of good fortune, producer Robert Young and director Brian Eastman found just the right pair of swallowing performers—Stephen Fry, who smiles secretly, and Hugh Laurie, who babbles on.

A Bit of Fry and Laurie

The first meeting of Fry and Laurie was quite different from that between Jeeves and Wooster. They were introduced by Emma Thompson *(Fortunes of War, Much Ado About Nothing)* when they were undergraduates at Cambridge, and the two men have remained best friends ever since. In 1981 the trio appeared in the university's Footlights Revue. During the 1980s *A Bit of Fry and Laurie* had a successful run on British television.

When they were offered the roles of Jeeves and Wooster, these two admirers of Wodehouse thought it best to decline because they were afraid of antagonizing the millions of other fans all over the world, each of whom already knew precisely how the characters should look. They needn't have worried. Once viewers see them, it is difficult to imagine anyone else in the roles.

It is equally difficult imagining anyone other than Wodehouse as the creator of these characters. Due in part to the lasting public affection for Jeeves, Bertie, and his other characters, Wodehouse was knighted by Queen Elizabeth in 1975, though he had exiled himself from England since the 1940s. (During World War II British authorities had denounced Wodehouse for having made five radio broadcasts of Nazi propaganda to then-neutral America during his imprisonment—reportedly a comfortable one—in a German camp in France.)

Sir Pelham Grenville Wodehouse died on Long Island, New York, in 1975 at the age of 93. But he is still very much alive as simply "P. G." on Masterpiece Theatre.

"The typical Wodehouse story was a genial assault on the British class system. His targets were Britain's well-heeled, well-born, empty-headed upper-class twits. It was the sweetest satire ever written. Wodehouse was blessed with a power that's very rare in this kind of writing. He could make the swells look silly without being mean about it." —Russell Baker

It has been reported that the Queen Mother said she reads the Jeeves and Wooster stories every night so she can go to bed "with a smile on my face despite the strains of the day."

HOUSE
OF CARDS,
TO PLAY THE KING,
THE FINAL CUT

House of Cards
4 EPISODES
March 31–April 21, 1991

To Play the King
4 EPISODES
January 16–February 6, 1994

The Final Cut
3 EPISODES
February 4–6, 1996

Produced by *BBC*
Producer *Ken Riddington*
Based on the novels by *Michael Dobbs*
Writer *Andrew Davies*
Director *Paul Seed, Mike Vardy (The Final Cut)*

CAST
Francis Urquhart *Ian Richardson*
Mattie Storin *Susannah Harker*
Roger O'Neill *Miles Anderson*
Elizabeth Urquhart *Diane Fletcher*
Tim Stamper *Colin Jeavons*
Henry Collingridge *David Lyon*
Charles Collingridge *James Villiers*
The King *Michael Kitchen*
Sarah Harding *Kitty Aldridge*
Chloe Carmichael *Rowena King*
Princess Charlotte *Bernice Stegers*
Lord Quillington *Frederick Treves*
Emmy Award *1990–1991*
Best writer for a Limited Series *Andrew Davies*

OUSE OF CARDS *and its sequels* TO PLAY THE KING *and* THE FINAL CUT *are terrifying dramas focused on Francis Urquhart, a British prime minister who stops at nothing to stay prime. The terror lies in the grim truth that the villains win, while the nobler souls are destroyed one by one. That the series is so beautifully and effectively produced makes them all the more chilling.*

"Richardson's performance remains a marvel. There is a great balancing act going on here—he takes us inside the beast, but cushions our journey with such droll urbanity that we want the ride to go on and on. The soliloquies to camera seal this delicious complicity ('I think now it's gloves-off time at the Palace, don't you?'). Beneath the show's high gaiety, signalled by the theme tune, there is satire of the blackest order." —Alison Pearson, *Independent on Sunday*

Viewers may recognize a similarity between Urquhart and the aristocrat in the Rolls-Royce who tries to borrow a jar of mustard in those Grey Poupon commercials—that's because they're both Ian Richardson.

Urquhart doesn't stand alone in this political tale of treachery, blackmail, and murder at the top of the English political heap. He is backed by someone equally ambitious—his wife Elizabeth (expertly played by Diane Fletcher) who plans her deadly schemes with the quiet assurance of a suburban housewife arranging a luncheon party. They are a contemporary Macbeth and Lady Macbeth, but far more deadly because they have at their disposal all the devilish tools of modern-day cowards: wiretaps, car bombs, and personal scandals planted in the London newspapers which have always been among the dirtiest on the globe. The prime minister and his wife use these weapons with virtuosity for their own insidious purposes. The tone of the BBC dramas surprised those Americans who had assumed, incorrectly, that the British Broadcasting Corporation is a coin-operated business enterprise of the Royal Family instead of the publicly financed independent corporation that it is.

"There's something about Urquhart you like. He has refined ruthlessness to an art.... The film draws the viewer into Urquhart's Machiavellian high jinks, partly because, as in House of Cards, *Richardson stops every now and then to speak directly into the camera. He takes us into his confidence and thereby makes us complicit."*
—Tom Shales, *Washington Post*

"It's four hours of the best political drama, involving what the British do best—sex, blackmail, power, and intrigue—you've ever seen. Why can't more American television dramas equal BBC's?" —Ed Koch, *New York Post*

Elizabeth Urquhart plans her deadly schemes with the quiet assurance of a suburban housewife arranging a luncheon party.

A Nation of Fierce Bad Rabbits

Ian Richardson's Urquhart is a remarkable creation of menacing charm and world-weary evil. All the important scenes are accompanied by his running commentary on the proceedings, spoken directly to the camera and delivered with a raised eyebrow. When everything else about these dramas may be forgotten, Richardson's face, with its watery eyes and faint Mona Lisa smile, will be remembered. There is something almost infantile in his cruelty as he arranges murders and justifies them by quoting from the children's books of Beatrix Potter, saying, "We are a nation of very fierce bad rabbits."

Urquhart thinks he has removed the last obstacle to his absolute power when he murders an inquiring young journalist who had become his mistress and confidant, by throwing her from the roof of

the House of Commons. But the succession of a new king, who is opposed to Urquhart's materialistic policies, poses a new threat. The honorable king tries to reach out to his people, but he is severely hampered by English law, which prohibits a monarch from directly interfering in politics.

The drama's royal players bear striking resemblances to figures at the highest level of the English court today: The idealistic new king, who is interested in architecture, has just replaced his mother as head of state after a long waiting period as Prince of Wales; his divorced wife is a tall, slender blond who is willing to help Urquhart destroy the king so that her young son can replace his father on the throne; and there's the frolicsome, vulgar Princess Charlotte, an embarrassment to the Royal Family, which pays her to stay out of the public eye.

In response to questions about the similarities between the real royals and the reel royals, Ian Richardson, while acknowledging several of the similarities, said, "I've been very stern in my protestations that it is a work of fiction." The actor revealed nonetheless

Free Publicity

Two days after the BBC began airing *House of Cards,* balloting began in the Conservative Party's leadership battle, which led to Prime Minister Thatcher's resignation. "It was pure coincidence," Ian Richardson said. "You have to understand that the BBC, like American networks, schedule their programs at least six months in advance. I was afraid the British public might think that the BBC, in some cheap, snide way, was cashing in on Mrs. Thatcher's sad demise. Fortunately, people are more knowledgeable about TV nowadays. We didn't get that kind of comeback. People would stop me in the street and say with a laugh, 'What a wonderful piece of publicity, and all thanks to Mrs. Thatcher.'"

"For Washington audiences, the fact that all this takes place in England becomes almost irrelevant, since the political terrain includes many a familiar fixture: purloined documents, spin doctors, opinion polls, a charge of insider trading, leaks to the press, a witch hunt for the leakers and an obsessive media-mindedness about how things will play in the morning papers and the evening news." —Tom Shales, *Washington Post*

Upshot

The producers were criticized by members of the Conservative Party for having shot a scene at the Grand Hotel in Brighton, for it was there that Prime Minister Thatcher and other Tories were staying during the 1984 party conference, when IRA bombers killed three and injured 30. "It was just coincidence," said producer Ken Riddington. "It was the only hotel that could accommodate us and they offered a good deal."

that the cast and crew were filming one day in a country house, which represents Buckingham Palace. "We did not know that the Prince of Wales was a luncheon guest there that day. You can imagine my astonishment when I had finished the scene and was marching down the corridor to come face to face with the real prince. 'What are you doing here?' he asked. 'It's all about me, isn't it?' And I answered, 'No, sir, not at all.' And he walked on." "Most of the characters are sort of composite bits," said author Michael Dobbs. "What you do is take reality and water it down a lot."

Another central character in *To Play the King* is Sarah Harding, a bright young political analyst selected by Urquhart's accommodating wife to be a consultant and mistress to her husband. Sarah (Kitty Aldridge) excels in both roles, playing a willing Trilby to the PM's hypnotic Svengali, until she becomes suspicious of the circumstances surrounding the death of her predecessor in the prime minister's office and bedroom. When Sarah is dispatched by a car bomb, we, of course, are surprised by only the method not by the murder.

As the Cat's Eyelids Flicker

Urquhart instructs his hatchetmen to place the blame for Sarah's death and another murder on Irish terrorists, providing an excuse to gun down a few of them as well. The ease with which these arrangements are made is chilling enough, but when they are followed by the PM's remarks, delivered with a smile to the camera, they are devastating:

"Well, what would you have? These things happen all over the world. Believe me. It's all for the best. What's the matter? You do trust me, don't you? Of course you do ... They all betray us eventually so you can never quite entirely sleep. As the cat's eyelids flicker, some part of us must stay awake always, ready as the coiled spring is ready."

The grim litany of political treachery is relieved on a few memorable occasions, however, such as the scene in which the lecherous Princess Charlotte gets it on with a chubby London newspaper publisher. She pauses occasionally to dictate her scandalous royal memoirs, which are expected to sink the monarchy, while her obese husband is downstairs watching a wildlife program on the telly showing two fat sea lions cavorting on the rocks. Viewers are also taught a good lesson in steam-room diplomacy when the leaders of the establishment, wrapped in

the anonymity of bath towels, meet privately on wooden benches in white tiled rooms—to blackmail one another.

The two short serials are part of a trilogy adapted from the novels of Michael Dobbs, who had worked for ten years at the heart of the Tory government as an advisor to Margaret Thatcher and others, and as Chief of Staff at Conservative Party headquarters during an election. They leave viewers with a tease to watch the third, *The Final Cut,* shown on Masterpiece Theatre in the 1996–97 season. Urquhart has been re-elected, the king has abdicated, and his son is on the throne. The prime minister seems to have everything he desired, but the cat's eyelids are still flickering.

Tory Tit-for-Tat

England's majority Conservative party refused to permit filming at the actual sites where much of the series' action takes place—the prime minister's residence at 10 Downing Street and inside Parliament's debating chambers. Even though Conservative party leaders cited security as their chief reason for refusing the actors and crew access to the locations, some political observers suggested the Conservatives were incensed at the way *House of Cards* treats them and their party.

A Classic Producer

Louis Marks

BBC producer LOUIS MARKS is the person you want if the task is bringing a classic novel to television in the classic manner. Starting with George Eliot's *Silas Marner,* he has given Masterpiece Theatre a series of immensely popular and stunningly beautiful literary adaptations, including Jane Austen's *Northanger Abbey,* Thomas Hardy's *The Day After the Fair,* Mary Webb's *Precious Bane,* Muriel Spark's *Memento Mori,* and—the most wildly popular of them all—George Eliot's *Middlemarch,* which won the English Broadcasting Guild award as best television serial and a British Academy Award for cast member Julia Aubrey. Marks most recently completed a television adaptation of *Loving,* Henry Green's novel, on location in Ireland.

A former schoolmaster whose academic specialty was history, Marks also worked as a film critic and ran the English literary magazine *Books and Bookmen* before breaking into television as a writer for the British *Robin Hood* series. He also wrote for the original *Dr. Who* series and *Honey Lane,* a soap that ran for three years on British television.

He made an auspicious debut as a BBC producer in the late 1970s with a pair of acclaimed biographical dramas: *Eleanor Marx,* the tragic story of Karl Marx's youngest daughter, and *The Lost Boys,* about J. M. Barrie's real-life inspiration for *Peter Pan.*

How important is it to point up contemporary issues in the TV films you make from classic novels, such as the child custody dispute at the heart of Silas Marner?

Marks I think it's vital. The very word "classic" makes my flesh crawl a bit. They're just wonderful works by great writers that had a lot of truth in them for that time. One of the great movements happening today is that we're rediscovering these authors as real flesh-and-blood people like ourselves, rather than stuffy Victorians who churned out these books with tiny unreadable print. If you think of them as just like us, but wearing different clothes, you can see the life that's in them.

Silas Marner was a very conscious effort to break with tradition. I remember wanting to make it something that would reach out emotionally to an audience rather than simply be a Classics Illustrated version of the book. I had this feeling you could make a rather stirring drama out of it for an adult audience.

How did you get Ben Kingsley to play Silas Marner so soon after he became an international star in Gandhi?

Marks Ben was with the project from a very early stage, before the script was written. He loved the book and was very committed to doing it. Ben was paid virtually nothing compared to what he was getting from the movies. I don't remember it even being a serious issue. He just did it.

Do you remember anything unique about Kingsley's approach to the role?

Marks There was something about the relationship between him and that loom that was quite uncanny. It wasn't just an actor's prop. He felt he couldn't play the role without becoming a weaver. Over a period of weeks, he spent many hours with a teacher, actually learning to weave.

Your next Masterpiece Theatre production probably was your most offbeat—the 1987 version of Jane Austen's satirical novel Northanger Abbey. *Where did that idea come from?*

Marks It actually began in after-dinner chats between myself and director Giles Foster while we were making *Silas Marner.* We both knew the book, and he had this idea of doing it as a sort of sendup on the Hammer horror films. Austen wrote it as a satire on Gothic novels, so we thought that could work. I think it's actually in the spirit of Jane Austen. I flatter myself to think she might even have got the joke in a way and enjoyed it. The book has a sort of joke at the heart of it—that this girl's mind has been turned by these books she's been reading to think there are villains round every corner. So we got Maggie Wadey as the writer, who was also warm to the idea, and it kind of took off from that point.

Your next Masterpiece Theatre project, The Day After the Fair, *was based on a short story, not a classic novel. How did that come about?*

Marks That was from a marvelous story by Thomas Hardy, "On the Western Circuit," which was about a circuit lawyer who meets a servant girl at a fair in a town very much like Salisbury, where we filmed it, and has a thing with her. It was made into a stage play by a theatrical producer, who brought it to the BBC as a vehicle for an actress he knew, Hannah Gordon. We made it together and she played the mistress. A young actress, Sammi Davis, played the servant girl. It's a very romantic story, and it's my wife's favorite of all the things I've done.

You next tackled Mary Webb's novel Precious Bane, *another classic that had not been filmed before. How did you get involved with that project?*

Marks I'd wanted to work with Christopher Menaul, who was really coming on as a director at the time. He went on to do the original *Prime Suspect,* you know. He'd read the book and was keen to do it, but everybody thought it was impossible to film because the heroine has a harelip.

Jonathan Powell, who was then the head of BBC drama, said he was doubtful you could sustain public interest in a girl with a harelip. Everyone thought that it was the ultimate turnoff. But we convinced them that was what made it a great story: a girl who has this deformity and manages to turn it into a positive thing in her life.

How did you deal with her deformity?

Marks We didn't make any attempt not to show it—it was on camera quite a lot of the time. The astonishing thing was that Janet McTeer, who played the part, managed to incorporate it into her character, so that you really didn't notice it.

She had this incredibly painful makeup, which consisted of a kind of hook to hold up her lip and a prosthesis over that to conceal it. It took about three hours every morning to put it on. Then it would disintegrate during the day, so she'd have to have another makeup session in the mid-afternoon. She lost all feeling in her upper lip, and it even got a bit infected at one point. It was absolute agony for her, yet she appeared beautiful, which was an extraordinary thing. Nobody felt it was distasteful or wanted to look away from it. She just wrapped her personality around it and went with the positive nature of the character, whose courage was so strong that you just accepted it as a part of her, like green eyes or something.

What challenges did you face recreating rural England of the 19th century?

Marks I had to convince the BBC to invest in a wheatfield, which is a rather amusing story. You see, *Precious Bane* revolves around a harvest, but the designer told me the only way we could get it right was to sow seeds in January so the wheat would be ready for harvest when we filmed in August and September. Wheatfields today stand about 18 inches high because they've done away with all the straw part. But, in the period of *Precious Bane,* the wheat was much taller. We had to get the original kind of seed from an agricultural museum, which keeps it for experimentation. Then I had to beg the BBC to let us have about £5,000 to rent this field for a year and sow this wheat in it. At that point, they weren't even sure they wanted to do *Precious Bane,* but they gave us the money anyway. The actual field turned out wonderful because the wheat stood about shoulder high and looked like something out of a period painting.

Why did you break from your pattern of costume dramas to make your next Masterpiece Theatre, Memento Mori, *which was set in the 1950s?*

Marks The chance to work with Jack Clayton, who was one of the great film directors *[Room at the Top, The Innocents, The Great Gatsby],* but had never done television. I asked him if he'd ever consider directing for television, and he came up with this project, which he'd never been able to interest anyone in doing as a feature film. From the start, Dame Maggie Smith, who played the leading role, was part of the deal we made.

How did Clayton adjust to television?

Marks He came into it feeling very nervous. He was very dedicated to it as a project and knew exactly what he wanted to do, but he felt the people and conditions wouldn't be as good as he was used to having. He ended up being absolutely taken with everybody. It turned out to be his final film.

Your next project was the elaborate serial drama Middlemarch, *from George Eliot's classic novel. How did* Middlemarch *get started?*

Marks It had been sitting at the BBC for several years as one of those great books that had to be done sooner or later. Another producer was involved at first, and Andrew Davies' script was commissioned and partly written before the other producer decided to leave.

I read the book first, then Andrew's scripts, which I felt were very good in terms of structure, but needed to be enriched with more from George Eliot. I felt more could be drawn out of the book. In fact, we added about an hour's worth of material to what was already there.

How do you manage to get such rich production values into a program like Middlemarch *on a television budget?*

Marks *Middlemarch* cost about £6.5 million, which seems a lot until you compare it with a period feature film like *The Age of Innocence,* which cost about $40 million. Our budget was about 20 percent over the standard budget.

But we still needed to be economical, so the focus was always on the characters and the story. We were very lucky in finding Stamford, a town in England that was virtually unchanged from the time it was built, a couple of hundred years ago. The streets were unchanged, apart from a few modern lampposts. We had an extremely ingenious and clever production designer, Gerry Scott, who has been part of my team for many years. She makes a little money go a long way.

Can you give an example of how Gerry Scott created such an authentic look and saved you money at the same time?

Marks The road surface she made for us to use in Stamford. It would have cost a fortune to lay down plastic cobblestones. So she created her own mix of sand and various ingredients—150 tons of it all laid on a plastic sheet over the existing road. She went for a surface that might have been there at the time. It was her invention.

Peter Featherstone in Middlemarch *was the last great role for Michael Hordern, who performed in many Masterpiece Theatre productions, including your own* Memento Mori. *Do you have any special memories of working with him that last time?*

Marks He was just enormously brave. I had worked with him two or three times in the past. He had been very ill. He had picked up some infection on holiday in the Caribbean and his kidneys collapsed. He was on dialysis, and we thought he wouldn't make it. He found his concentration had gone completely, so it was an enormous effort of will to master those lines and deliver them. He got so angry with himself because he knew he wasn't giving his best work. All the other character actors stood around and dabbed at tears because they knew what he was going through.

What was your roughest time as a producer while filming Middlemarch?

Marks Rome was a catastrophe because we arrived for ten days of location shooting at the height of a crisis in which government fraud investigations were under way. Everybody was waiting for the ax to fall, including city councilors and the mayor of Rome. We had to film in various public facilities, but everybody got cold feet at the last minute, and all permission was withdrawn about a week before we started filming. It was a potential nightmare.

We were supposed to film Dorothea and Casaubon at the Capitoline Museum, but we lost that. We finally found another museum through our Italian contacts—a privately owned palazzo with a gallery. We had to shoot on Monday, so on Saturday I went with the director and our Italian contact to see the family. Fortunately, the daughter had gone to school in England and studied *Middlemarch.* She persuaded her mother this was a good thing to support, and we were able to film the sequence where they walk through a gallery. It was just a miracle that we found that place.

What's behind the resurgence of big, expensive multipart literary adaptations like Middlemarch?

Marks There are lots of possible explanations. The cynical one is that we're making them because there's a taste for them in America and, in particular, at Masterpiece Theatre, and that we're driven by pure economic reasons. But I don't think that's totally the truth. There's an artistic truth behind it, which is a growing impatience with a lot of contemporary writing. It seems to have lost touch with any kind of tradition, so there's a sort of need to plug back into it. I think people need to breathe that sort of oxygen, which they get from these great works. ❦

A Murder of Quality (Portobello Films for Thames Television)
October 13–20, 1991, 2 episodes
Based on the novel by John le Carré

Sleepers (Cinema Verity Production for BBC)
October 27–November 17, 1991, 4 episodes

She's Been Away (BBC)
December 1, 1991, 1 episode

Parnell and the Englishwoman (BBC)
December 29, 1991–January 19, 1992, 4 episodes

Titmuss Regained (New Penny Production for Thames Television in association with WGBH/Boston)
February 9–February 23, 1992, 3 episodes
Based on the novel by John Mortimer

Adam Bede (BBC)
March 1–8, 1992, 2 episodes
Based on the novel by George Eliot

A Doll's House (BBC)
March 29, 1992, single 2½-hour episode
Based on the play by Henrik Ibsen

Clarissa (BBC in association with WGBH/Boston)
April 5–19, 1992, 3 episodes
Based on the novel by Samuel Richardson

Henry V (Renaissance Films in association with BBC)*
April 26, 1992, single 2-hour episode
Based on the play by William Shakespeare

A Perfect Hero (London Weekend Television)
May 3–24, 1992, 4 episodes
Based on the book by Christopher Matthew

Portrait of a Marriage (BBC in association with WGBH/Boston, NZTV)
July 19–August 2, 1992, 3 episodes
Based on the book by Nigel Nicolson

A Question of Attribution (BBC)*
October 4, 1992, single 90-minute episode
Based on the play by Alan Bennett

The Best of Friends (London Films)
October 18, 1992, single 90-minute episode
Based on the play by Hugh Whitemore

Memento Mori (BBC)
October 25–November 1, 1992, 2 episodes
Based on the novel by Muriel Spark

Two Monologues (Oyster Productions, BBC)
November 8, 1992, single 90-minute episode

The Secret Agent (BBC)
November 15–29, 1992, 3 episodes
Based on the novel by Joseph Conrad

Jeeves and Wooster, Series 2 (Carnival Films for Granada Television)
December 27, 1992–January 17, 1993, 4 episodes
Based on the stories of P. G. Wodehouse

The Countess Alice (BBC)
January 24, 1993, single 90-minute episode

Impromptu (Sovereign Pictures in association with Governor Productions and Les Films Ariane)§
February 7, 1993, single 2-hour episode

The Blackheath Poisonings (Central Television in association with WGBH/Boston)
February 14–28, 1993, 3 episodes
Based on the novel by Julian Symonds

Hedda Gabler (BBC)
March 28, 1993, single 2-hour episode
Based on the play by Henrik Ibsen

The Black Velvet Gown (Worldwide International Television and Tyne Tees Television in association with Portman Entertainment)
April 4–11, 1993, 2 episodes
Based on the novel by Catherine Cookson

Calling the Shots (BBC in association with WGBH/Boston)
April 18–May 2, 1993, 3 episodes

Doctor Finlay, Series 1 (Scottish Television)
May 9–June 13, 1993, 6 episodes
Based on characters created by A. J. Cronin

Selected Exits (BBC)
October 3, 1993, single 90-minute episode

Jeeves and Wooster, Series 3 (Carnival Films for Granada Television)
October 10–31, 1993, 4 episodes
Based on the stories of P. G. Wodehouse

Where Angels Fear to Tread (Sovereign Pictures in association with London Weekend Television)§
November 7, 1993, single 2-hour episode
Based on the novel by E. M. Forster

Sharpe (Celtic/Picture Palace Production for Central Television)*
November 14–December 5, 1993, 4 episodes
Based on the novels by Bernard Cornwell

To Play the King (BBC)
January 16–February 6, 1994, 4 episodes
Based on the novel by Michael Dobbs

Body and Soul (Red Rooster Films and TV Entertainment for Carlton Television)
February 13–March 6, 1994, 4 episodes
Based on the novel by Marcelle Bernstein

Middlemarch (BBC in association with WGBH/Boston)*
April 10–May 15, 1994, 6 episodes
Based on the novel by George Eliot

A Foreign Field (A Fingertip Film Production for BBC)
May 22, 1994, single 90-minute episode

The Best Intentions (SVT 1)§
July 10–24, 1994, 3 episodes

The Blue Boy (BBC/Scotland in association with WGBH/Boston)
October 2, 1994, 1 episode

The Rector's Wife (Talisman Production for Channel 4)*
October 9–23, 1994, 3 episodes
Based on the novel by Joanna Trollope

Dandelion Dead (London Weekend Television)
October 30–November 6, 1994, 2 episodes

Doctor Finlay, Series 2 (Scottish Television)
November 13–December 18, 1994, 6 episodes
Based on characters created by A. J. Cronin

Jeeves and Wooster, Series 4 (Carnival Films for Granada Television)
January 8–February 5, 1995, 5 episodes
Based on the stories of P. G. Wodehouse

The Cinder Path (World Wide International Television/Festival Films for Tyne Tees Television)*
February 12–March 5, 1995, 3 episodes
Based on the novel by Catherine Cookson

Martin Chuzzlewit (BBC)*
March 26–April 23, 1995, 5 episodes
Based on the novel by Charles Dickens

Hard Times (BBC)*
April 30, 1995, single 2-hour episode
Based on the novel by Charles Dickens

Much Ado About Nothing (Samuel Goldwyn Co.)*
May 7, 1995, single 2-hour episode
Based on the play by William Shakespeare

Sharpe, Series 2 (Celtic/Picture Palace Production for Central Independent Television)*
May 14–28, 1995, 3 2-hour episodes
Based on the novels by Bernard Cornwell

The Buccaneers (BBC)
October 8–10, 1995, 3 episodes
Based on the novel by Edith Wharton

The Great Kandinsky (BBC)
October 15, 1995, single 90-minute episode

Prime Suspect: The Lost Child (Granada Television)
October 22, 1995, single 2-hour episode

The Choir (BBC)
October 29–November 19, 1995, 4 episodes
Based on the novel by Joanna Trollope

The Politician's Wife (Channel 4)
January 6–21, 1996, 3 episodes

The Final Cut (BBC)
February 4–6, 1996, 3 episodes
Based on the novel by Michael Dobbs

Prime Suspect: Inner Circles (Granada Television)
Single 2-hour episode

Peacock Spring (BBC)
2 episodes
Based on the novel by Rumer Godden

Prime Suspect: Scent of Darkness (Granada Television)
Single 2-hour episode

---

*Available on video   §Video out of print
Video cassettes of many Masterpiece Theatre programs are available at public libraries and video rental stores. For information about the availability of any program or about purchasing videos, call VideoFinders, a service of public television station KCET, at 1-800-343-4727.

Seasons 21–25

PORTRAIT OF A MARRIAGE

3 EPISODES

July 19–August 2, 1992

Produced by *BBC in association with WGBH/Boston, NZTV*

Producer *Colin Tucker*

Based on the book by *Nigel Nicolson*

Writer *Penelope Mortimer*

Director *Stephen Whittaker*

CAST

Vita Sackville-West *Janet McTeer*

Violet Keppel Trefusis *Cathryn Harrison*

Harold Nicolson *David Haig*

Denys Trefusis *Peter Birch*

Lady Sackville *Diana Fairfax*

MERICANS *have not been accustomed to thinking of the English in terms of their sexuality, but* PORTRAIT OF A MARRIAGE *changed that misconception forever with a remarkable honesty and explicit eroticism rarely seen on television. The miniseries was based on a scandalous love triangle that raised eyebrows as high as Nelson's Monument when it first became* public. Love triangles have been common since the Garden of Eden, but this one was unusual because the women were the lovers and the man was left out in the cold.

The participants in this triangle were famous in England between the wars and shortly afterward. Vita Sackville-West was a talented writer, who had written more than 50 books of poetry, short stories, and novels (among her books is *All Passion Spent,* which was adapted for Masterpiece Theatre). She was a member of the famed Bloomsbury group, a well-known horticulturist, and the descendant of a noble English family whose mansion in Kent was the gift of Queen Elizabeth I. Her husband, Harold Nicolson, was an aristocrat by nature if not by blood and a second-generation

diplomat in the top layer of the British Foreign Office, that hallowed sanctuary of international skullduggery. He too was an author, of biographies, historical works, and novels. The other woman in the triangle was Violet Keppel Trefusis, a childhood friend of Vita's and the daughter of Mrs. George Keppel, who was

"The Nicolsons are the kind of TV couple who could make Dan Quayle drop to his knees and pray for more Murphy Browns." —Charles Leerhsen, Newsweek

"Vita is driven by a rage against male privilege. As they lie on a hill overlooking Knole, the Sackville-West family estate, Violet says to Vita that 'I love this place. If you'd been a man, I'd have married you for it.' But because she's a woman, Vita has no property rights; she's supposed to resign herself to being treated as property, and that she refuses to do. Instead, she develops a fiercely proprietary relationship to Violet, engendering endless scenes, break-ups, and reunions." —Amy Taubin, *Village Voice*

the last mistress of Edward VII. (Masterpiece Theatre viewers may remember Mom from *Upstairs, Downstairs;* she accompanied the King the night he had dinner at the Bellamy's—presumably after she had tucked little Violet in bed.)

Sacking-Out with Vita

Vita and Harold's marriage was one of considerable comfort and convenience—she could have her girl friends and he could have his boy friends, as long as the third party was of no importance and did not disrupt the household or the raising of their two children. That's where Violet becomes troublesome. Her love for Vita is so strong that Harold and the children are pushed aside while the women take a long holiday.

Portrait of a Marriage is adapted from the 1973 bestseller by Nigel Nicolson, which is based on his mother's diary and tells the story that she wished to have made public after her death. Although not everyone feels comfortable with adultery and homosexuality, no one can criticize the tastefulness with which the love scenes between the two women are presented—

"Getting into the head of a lesbian character [was not the problem but] getting into the head of novelist Vita Sackville-West was…. What I did was go down where Vita lived, stayed there for a bit, talked to her son, and then I read her biographies—the one that Nigel wrote and a brilliant one, *Vita,* by Victoria Glendinning—plus listened to her voice on tape, and visited places she went."

—Janet McTeer, *New York Daily News*

they're tame compared to the heterosexual bumps and grinds on shows that get family ratings. As one reviewer said, "Forget the fact that no television movies have treated gay or lesbian love as well as *Portrait of a Marriage.* Few TV movies have treated any kind of romantic or obsessive love as movingly." The most unappetizing aspect of the film is Vita's cruel determination to destroy Violet's marriage, even if it means the destruction of her own. The viewer may be tempted to say aloud, "For heaven's sake Vita, stop making everyone miserable and take Violet to Greece. That's where it all began anyway."

Despite producer Colin Tucker's admission that he was "taken aback" at the initial kiss, the BBC televised *Portrait of a Marriage* with very little editing (Nicolson requested that a scene in which Vita emerges naked from bed with Violet be dropped because he felt it incorrectly emphasized the physical aspects of the affair.) For the American showing on PBS two years later, 34 minutes—including a scene in which Vita rapes Violet—were "cut for length" by Boston's WGBH, co-producer of the BBC series along with New Zealand TV. Tucker's reply to complaints about the brief violence of the rape was wholly on point: "Shocking? It's *meant* to be shocking."

All Passion Spent

Nigel Nicolson expressed his dissatisfaction with the production at the other extreme, saying that the portrait of his parents ended on too kindly a note, claiming that his father never forgave Violet and died believing, as he himself does, that she was an evil force in their lives. As the book tells but the film does not, the Nicolsons' marriage lasted 50 years,

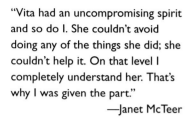

"Vita had an uncompromising spirit and so do I. She couldn't avoid doing any of the things she did; she couldn't help it. On that level I completely understand her. That's why I was given the part."
—Janet McTeer

during which time both Harold and Vita each had many homosexual affairs of a more tranquil nature, such as the one where Vita showed that she was not afraid of Virginia Woolf.

"It is the story of two people who married for love and whose love deepened with every passing year, although each was constantly and by mutual consent unfaithful to the other," Nicolson says in his book. "Both loved people of their own sex, but not exclusively. Their marriage not only survived infidelity, sexual incompatibility and long absences, but became stronger as a result."

Reviewers raved about the production. As Susan Stewart of Knight-Ridder Newspapers said, "Nicolson, played by David Haig, is … gentle, fine-featured, radiating kindness as well as prissiness; he makes you understand both why Vita loves him and why she could never be in love with him. He's wonderful. Janet McTeer as Vita is equally wonderful. Big and gawky, her face recalling the young Vanessa Redgrave, she is

"I admire women who have the courage to be different in a time when it was so difficult. I admire people who have the courage to break molds. … West, a gifted gardener, was terribly kind toward friends, and at the same time she was an incredible snob. She could be very rude. She was also very shy, and got shyer as she got older. Consequently, she appeared to be rather aloof, and kind of strange and eccentric." —Janet McTeer, *New York Daily News*

equal parts misery and cruelty. You can't stop watching her. Cathryn Harrison (Rex's granddaughter) plays Violet as a sort of Edwardian Catwoman. 'I have no morals,' she says. 'It's why I always get my way.' When Nicolson finally gets mad and calls her a 'fungus,' you want to cheer.… This three-part Masterpiece Theatre is riveting, intelligent and sleazy, all at once. It's almost too entertaining to believe."

Middlemarch

*G*EORGE ELIOT'S MIDDLEMARCH *has been showered with praise as one of the greatest English novels, and one of the few to be written for adults, according to Virginia Woolf. One of its unique features is its focus on the condition of marriage, a subtle but important aspect that most Victorian novelists either took for granted or ignored entirely. But* MIDDLEMARCH *is about more than marriage. It shows how idealistic*

6 EPISODES

April 10–May 15, 1994

Produced by *BBC in association with WGBH/Boston*

Producer *Louis Marks*

Based on the novel by *George Eliot*

Writer *Andrew Davies*

Director *Anthony Page*

CAST

Dorothea Brooke *Juliet Aubrey*
Rev. Edward Casaubon *Patrick Malahide*
Dr. Tertius Lydgate *Douglas Hodge*
Will Ladislaw *Rufus Sewell*
Rosamond Vincy *Trevyn McDowell*
Fred Vincy *Jonathan Firth*
Arthur Brooke *Robert Hardy*
Peter Featherstone *Michael Hordern*
Nicholas Bulstrode *Peter Jeffrey*
Sir James Chettam *Julian Wadham*

"Like any afternoon soap, this greatest of English novels is full of the huffing and puffing of youthful idealism, lofty hopes, blind pride, bad luck, oppressive society, sublime art, sexual dysfunction, sudden death, money problems, hypocrisy, and vindictiveness—everything, in fact, except amnesia and an evil twin. That Eliot was also writing about politics (the nineteenth-century Reform movement, to which she subscribed even though it omitted suffrage for women), science (about which she was well informed and enthusiastic), religion (she had her doubts), class and gender (my favorite character is Mary Garth, too good for Fred Vincy), and the obdurate cross-purposes of intellect and emotion (mating for life is probably a mistake) is almost incidental to this handsome, indeed gaudy, production." —John Leonard, New York

men and women of good will are towed into mediocrity by provincial society and the dead hand of the past. This BBC dramatic adaptation was selected by the producers of Masterpiece Theatre to mark a return to the classics following a concentration on contemporary works.

Eliot sets her story in the fictitious small town of Middlemarch in Lincolnshire in the 1830s at the start of the Industrial Revolution, when a predominantly agricultural society was becoming a manufacturing society, and the spirit of reform was in the air. Middlemarch is a microcosm of English provincial life at a time when the landed gentry lived on large estates outside of town, while their retainers lived in hovels and worked for potatoes.

The series opens with a coach-and-four rolling up the road and into the camera, scattering a herd of sheep and swaying precariously on the turns. Viewers are quickly introduced to a trio of single young women, different in nature, but striving to begin their adult lives in ways that are compatible with their personalities and desires. The manner in which they win or lose the game will keep viewers tuned in for six weeks. Central among them is Dorothea Brooke (Juliet Aubrey), a sensitive young woman with strong ideals. She is bright and dedicated but trapped in a society that expects little of women except a talent for embroidery, the piano, and aimless chatter. She longs for something more substantial in a husband than does her sister Celia (Caroline Harker), who has no intellectual aspirations and is happy to sink into comfortable domesticity. The third in the trio is Rosamond (Trevyn McDowell) the mayor's daughter, a pretty coquette who has been to charm

school and can play the piano, sing, and dance, but is otherwise irresponsible and thoughtless.

Arrayed opposite them are: Sir James, a typical country squire who pats his tummy jovially at home, hunts small animals on weekends, and staunchly opposes the Reform Bill; Casaubon (Patrick Malahide), an aging religious scholar and social bore who is writing a history of mythology; Will Ladislaw (Rufus Sewell), Casaubon's artistic young nephew with seductive eyes and political aspirations; and Tertius Lydgate (Douglas Hodge), an idealistic young doctor who is trying to pull his colleagues into the modern world of medical science.

Celia marries Sir James, the country squire, as one might expect. Dr. Lydgate, the one person in Middlemarch who appears to be right for Dorothea, falls instead for the lovely but manipulative Rosamond, who always looks as if she has just come from the hairdresser—and probably has. Her passion for possessions eventually runs her husband into bankruptcy, forcing him to abandon his dreams for a hospital that would combine research and service to the poor.

Dorothea, the soul of the novel, marries Casaubon, the old scholar who is twice her age, and looks to him to teach her foreign languages and initiate her into other scholarly pursuits closed to women. She longs for "some great purpose in life which will give it shape and meaning." She has plans to help the poor of Middlemarch by developing a system of welfare and a desire to help Dr. Lydgate in establishing his hospital. Instead of encouraging Dorothea's altruism, Casaubon crushes it and eventually shuts her out of his love and his life, then dies—mercifully for her and everyone else in the cast, particularly the young Will Ladislaw, who has been attracted to Dorothea from the beginning.

"To my amazement and delight, after years of ignorant prejudice against Middlemarch, *I was absolutely and hopelessly hooked. It was a page-turner."*

—Russell Baker

"What strikes me now is not the entrapment and frustrated dreams of her heroines, but [Eliot's] own wit, and her sharp eye for social comedy.... The most striking quality of the dramatic adaptation by Andrew Davies is precisely this sense of humour."

—Janet Barron, *Middlemarch Guide*

"Casaubon's a fearful man. He has great ideas of his own destiny, but when he comes face to face with it, he's overcome by fear. The fear leads to suspicion and then the suspicion leads to bitterness. And he dies an embittered man. What I found so interesting was that George Eliot never condemns him, never pillories him even though he behaves so appallingly." —Patrick Malahide

That Dorothea has feelings for Will is also apparent to her husband, who stipulates in his will that Dorothea must forfeit her inheritance if she ever marries Ladislaw. In the end, Dorothea gives up her estate, marries Will, and abandons her nobler plans, devoting herself to helping him win a seat in Parliament.

Eliot has filled Middlemarch with interesting characters who are skillfully brought to life by an excellent cast. Among them are Squire Arthur Brooke (Robert Hardy), Dorothea's uncle and guardian—a big bumbler who mouths the words of reform but treats his farm laborers like serfs—and Peter Featherstone (the late Michael Hordern), the cantankerous invalid whose greedy relatives anxiously await his death and the reading of his will, that familiar but durable Victorian literary device. In addition there is Mary Garth, an honest, down-to-earth young woman whose family circumstances have forced her to seek employment. She is in love with Fred Vincy, the mayor's feckless son, but realizes his shortcomings. He is pressured by his family to marry well, which excludes Mary, but eventually he proves his independence and they are united at the garden gate.

The real woman behind the novel is as interesting as any character in it. She was born with one of the most prosaic names imaginable—Mary Ann Evans—at a time when it was considered improper for women to write novels. To be taken seriously, she chose the name George Eliot. She was almost excessively well educated, having translated a large German work on the life of Christ at the age of 26. In the early part of her life she was very pious, but after her father's death she left her home town of Coventry, the model for Middlemarch, to become a successful journalist in London, where she fell in with some of the best minds of the time, and quickly turned from God to Man. She entered into a relationship with a highly respected journalist and literary critic who was separated from his insane wife, and they lived together until his death. Such a relationship was very daring for the time, but all the people in their circle of friends understood—and outsiders be damned. When she finally married, in the last year of her life, it was to an American banker 20 years younger than herself. Obviously Mary Ann Evans was determined to live her life as she wished and that spirit spilled over into her novels.

Eliot's admirers note that she moved the real action of her novels *inside* her people. She was the first to create characters from the intellectual class, the sort who are absent from the works of Austen, Fielding, and Dickens. Her early books *Adam Bede* and *Silas Marner* established her reputation. While Eliot never enjoyed the enormous popularity of Dickens, she had a large following by the time she wrote *Middlemarch* at 52 years of age. Clearly, it is the work of a serious intellectual who could, at times, be amusing. But there is a sadness here too because we see the early idealism of Dorothea Brooke and young Dr. Lydgate stifled by the establishment of Middlemarch as well as by the "spots of commonness" in their own character, which keep them from being the distinguished men and women they had dreamed of becoming.

BBC dramatist Andrew Davies has been remarkably faithful to the novel. There are many nice moments, beautifully framed, such as the scenes filmed in Rome when Will gets the opportunity to see Dorothea while her old husband is fussing around at

"The book is disturbing rather than comforting. It reflects the question that occupies people's minds today: Where did it all go wrong, this society that we all thought was so fine?" —Producer Louis Marks, *Boston Globe*

Middlemarch-keteers?

According to director Anthony Page, quoted in *The Register,* "The [residents of Stamford] can't adjust to not being Middlemarch anymore. There are Middlemarch tea shops and Middlemarch tours. It's turned into a kind of Middlemarch Disneyland."

"He's got a kind heart but absolutely no brain, and he just lets people down.... Nothing's connected properly. All the circuits are wrong."—Robert Hardy

"George Eliot said she was like Casaubon because she was very lonely and she translated very heavy books from German. She understood this thing of being smothered by research and books, and not being able to live. There's a lot of George Eliot's common sense in Mary Garth, and I think this whole sense of disappointment in life—that it never gives you this wonderful answer you want. Eliot's sister married a doctor—Lydgate was based largely on what happened to her brother-in-law. There's obviously a lot of her in many characters." —Director Anthony Page

Signs of the Success of Middlemarch *in Britain*

- Bingo clubs closed down at 8:30 so people could see it

- More than 7 million people—one eighth of the population—watched each of the six episodes

- More than 105,000 paperback copies of the novel were sold since the show aired

—excerpted from *Naples Daily News*

the Vatican. There are some hilarious ones also, such as the reading of Featherstone's will, which bypasses his greedy relatives to endow a home for old men—the ultimate deathbed revenge.

Filming took 30 weeks, with a cast of 73 and a crew of 80 shooting on location in Rome, Stamford, Dorset, and Somerset. Production designer Gerry Scott had the difficult task of turning the city of Stamford in Lincolnshire into Middlemarch, which called for slipcovering parts of the town. High Street had to be closed to traffic and the double yellow lines hidden underneath a surface of peat and stone chips—Scott's own invention—that turned the paved road into a muddy 19th-century byway but could be removed without harming the concrete underneath. Houses that were in the right location for the camera were often wrong for the period, which meant their facades had to be boarded up, historically correct architectural details added, and old doors in muted colors hung to replace the contemporary ones. Twentieth-century artifacts such as telephone wires, TV antennas, mailboxes, and phone booths had to be concealed. As designer Scott observes, "Nobody ever notices what you've done, but they would notice it if you *hadn't*."

The novel was written in 1870 as the author's backward look at the 1830s, but the problems of *Middlemarch* often ring true today, which is a reliable test of the lasting appeal of any classic. Public health and welfare services are still inadequate and, as Dr. Lydgate found, social services are thwarted by political corruption and personal gain. Enormous amounts of money are spent on parliamentary campaigns while poor people are homeless and hungry, and worthy politicians cannot afford to represent them. Even the marital difficulties of the couples in *Middlemarch* are familiar to us, and today's women still struggle to bring meaning to their lives. Eliot is either a remarkably reliable prophet or a writer who knows that human nature usually remains the same. Only the bonnets and the top hats change.

THE
Buccaneers

3 EPISODES
October 8–10, 1995
(shown on three consecutive nights)
Produced by *BBC*
Producer *Philip Saville*
Based on the novel by *Edith Wharton*
Writer *Maggie Wadey*
Director *Philip Saville*

CAST
Laura Testvalley *Cherie Lunghi*
Virginia St. George *Alison Elliott*
Nan St. George *Carla Gugino*
Lizzy Elmsworth *Rya Kihlstedt*
Conchita Closson *Mira Sorvino*
Idina Hatton *Jenny Agutter*
Julius, Duke of Trevenick *James Frain*
Sir Helmsley Thwaite *Michael Kitchen*
Lord Brightlingsea *Dinsdale Landen*
Lady Brightlingsea *Rosemary Leach*
Lord Seadown *Mark Tandy*
Lord Richard Marable *Ronan Vibert*
Guy Thwaite *Greg Wise*

*T*HE BUCCANEERS *may sound like an faction drama, but the series, like the book, has been slyly mistitled because it has no pirates, no brawling marauders, no Errol Flynns, and no hero. It is a woman's show: based on an unfinished novel by a woman, adapted for television by a woman, produced by a woman, packaged by women on both sides of the Atlantic, and telling the story of four young*

American women who go to England to buy titled husbands with their families' money.

The young women are lively, attractive, and rich, but their money and their lineage are too new. They are snubbed by East Coast society leaders and denied invitations to winter balls in Manhattan and summer parties in Newport, the major watering holes for eligible bachelors. So they decide to take their revenge in a noble way by going to England and marrying into British aristocracy. In this manner they become the buccaneers of the title, marching into the stately homes of England like pirates from abroad. Conchita marries Lord Marable, Virginia gets Lord Seadown, Nan becomes the Duchess of Trevenick, and Lizzie settles for a member of Parliament.

Cupid does not play a major role in these marriages, and viewers who listen carefully can hear that the ring of the cash register is louder and more melodic than the church bells. Aside from this, the buccaneers appear to have negotiated splendid bargains. The Americans get the English titles, the Englishmen get the American

The production required more than 1,000 period costumes with often ten costume changes a day for the major characters.

"Marriages were arranged and women struck a deal that they would be domesticated pets. There was usually a mistress or two for the husband. Laura preferred control of her own life. She's ahead of her time. Today she'd be a writer, a painter or an academic. She'd definitely have a career and family."
—Cherie Lunghi, *Radio Times*

money, and Virginia's mother gets even with the dowagers of New York's high-society circuit.

Unfortunately contentment never lasts long in the novels of Edith Wharton. Her four young Americans have barely learned the words to "Rule Britannia" before the crumpets hit the fan. Lords Marable and Seadown turn out to be unfaithful spendthrifts, and the duke sleeps with men instead of his duchess. Only Lizzie is happy with her man, though, alas, poor.

Completing the Unfinished Novel

Wharton died in her seventies, leaving one-fifth of *The Buccaneers* unfinished but with a detailed outline for its completion. BBC screenwriter Maggie Wadey followed Wharton's wishes for Nan. She runs away from her husband, the rich but selfish Duke of Trevenick, and makes a new life for herself in South Africa with Guy Thwaite, the man she really loves. But screenwriters are seldom content to follow precisely the original text, much less an outline. So Wadey added two items that Wharton did not mention and which would have been unprintable in 1938, when the book was published: She turned the duke into a homosexual and had him rape his wife. "I think Wharton would have liked it," Wadey said in an article in *The Scotsman*. "Everyone who works in this vein takes a certain liberty with another author's work, and remember this novel was unfinished and unrevised.... As I read the material there were tremendous gaps, sometimes I was left not knowing what a character thought or did. It was quite clear though that the young Duke of Trevenick was under enormous pressure to produce an heir and does force himself on his wife."

Wadey's additions spiced up the plot but also fueled the ongoing critical bonfire set under the BBC for juicing the original texts of two other Masterpiece Theatre productions: *Middlemarch* and *Martin Chuzzlewit*. This is nothing new. The English have been

"Finding locations wasn't always easy. The story is set in Saratoga, which has fallen prey to the developer since 1870. 'Just multi-storey car parks and supermarkets now,' says [director and producer] Philip Saville. 'So we went to Newport, Rhode Island, where the Astors had their summer season, and convened for balls and soirees.'... Filming in the greatest country houses in Britain wasn't much easier. The owner of Grimsthorpe Castle had luxurious white shag pile in the state rooms. Days before filming was due to begin, she decided the carpets weren't to be removed, forcing the production team to lay fake floors."—Radio Times

From the Pages of Titled Heiresses

The transatlantic marriage market pictured in *The Buccaneers* has a solid basis in fact. At the time of Wharton's story the English peerage had become a stud farm for rich American families with daughters baying for titles. Peers willing to trade their coat of arms for cash were listed in an American publication, *Titled Heiresses.* Records show that more than 100 such marriages took place between 1870 and 1914, including some impressive names: Jennie Jerome, daughter of a New York newspaper tycoon, who married Lord Randolph Churchill and gave birth to Winston; American railroad heiress Consuelo Vanderbilt, who became the Duchess of Marlborough; and Consuelo Yznaga, daughter of a rich Cuban-American, who became the Duchess of Manchester.

updating classics to fit the times ever since play doctors in the late 17th century gave King Lear a happy ending.

Wharton gives her novel one heroine—Nan St. George, who is skillfully portrayed by Carla Gugino, an Irish-Italian actress from Florida with a refreshingly different face that sets her apart from her professional sisterhood on both sides of the Atlantic. Equally sympathetic is Nan's ally Laura, her plucky but unlucky governess, played with endearing sensitivity by Cherie Lunghi.

*W*harton Like Her Characters

Wharton's real life spills into the plots of her novels quite naturally. She came from a wealthy New York family and knew the top layers of the Manhattan-Newport social set in the 1870s, which was as corseted as London's but newer, richer, and more arrogantly insecure. Like Nan, Wharton had an awkward childhood and wore the wrong color dress to a debutante party. Her own marriage, to Teddy Wharton, was as confusing and demoralizing as Nan's, and her autobiography reveals that she did not have a satisfying relationship with a man until several years before her divorce at 46, when she moved to France and became the lover of an expatriate American journalist.

Wharton had seen her share of Europe during some 30 trips across the Atlantic, which caused Henry James, her close friend and fellow writer, to call her "the pendulum woman." She had carefully observed the natives and how they treated foreigners. Thus the outspoken American buccaneers are constantly being reminded that they are outsiders, even when they are eager to learn the customs of the older society into which they have married. Their unwitting breaches of protocol—calling servants by their given names, for example—cause many British eyebrows to rise. The English are equally ignorant of America, but refuse to acknowledge it, which gives the series some of its rare moments of humor, such as Lady Brightlingsea's insistence that Brazil is part of the United States. When she hears that archery is popular in America she says, "I suppose the Indians taught you."

In several of her other novels, Wharton wrote about women such as the "buccaneers" and herself, who were entrapped in doomed and dismal marriages. It is as though by writing about them, she gave

vent to the extreme frustration she felt over her own stifling domestic circumstances.

Wharton would have been delighted with the beauty and variety of the gardens and interiors shown in the television series because she had built and remodeled a great number of homes, including a mansion in the Berkshire hills of Massachusetts and a monastery converted into a chateau overlooking Hyères on the French Riviera. Surely she would have enjoyed the delightful room-to-room romp through the duke's magnificent country house at Christmastime. (Viewers probably recognize the place as "Brideshead," but the English know it as Castle Howard, the Yorkshire home of the late Lord Howard, former chairman of the BBC.) Wharton once remarked that she had a "photographic memory of rooms and houses," and the novel provided the production designer with a working blueprint for the frequent scene changes: a hotel veranda in Saratoga, New York—which becomes Rhode Island in the series—a charming cottage on the bank of the Thames, a country house in the Cotswolds, the ballroom of a New York town house, and the magnificent ruins of a 13th-century castle overlooking the sea at the tip of Cornwall. This glorious scenic authenticity more than makes up for the scenic anomaly of fox hunting in the summer; faithful Masterpiece Theatre viewers know that the hunting season is from October to March.

"The novel is not Wharton's best although, written at the end of her life in the 1930s, it is a winning blend of 20th-century sense and 19th-century sensibility. The in-house anthropologist of a tribe whose prime commodity remained the bartered bride, Wharton understood that though it was the fathers who imposed the life sentences, the mothers made all too eager jailers. After a grim marriage of her own to a chump who said approvingly of Edith that to look at her waist you would never have thought she'd written a book, Wharton spent her artistic life trying to unpick the lock. In Age of Innocence, House of Mirth, *and* Ethan Frome, *the impulse to break out and live in truth was crushed by duty, death, and horrible disfigurement respectively. Her last book would be the first to release its heroine into happiness."*

—Allison Pearson, *Independent on Sunday*

A Transatlantic First

Boston PBS station WGBH, which co-funded the production, proposed *The Buccaneers* to the BBC, a first in their 25-year relationship. Normally WGBH picks up productions made in England or co-finances programs already in development there.

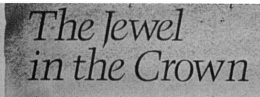

The Jewel in the Crown

Based on Paul Scott's
The Raj Quartet

Starring Dame Peggy Ashcroft,
Eric Porter, Tim Pigott-Smith
and Art Malik

A 14-part series
Begins Sunday Dec. 16
9PM Channel 13 PBS
Host: Alistair Cooke

"The Jewel in the Crown is the best
sustained television I've seen
in more than 30 years of watching."
John Leonard, New York Magazine

The Raj Quartet, published by Avon Books, available wherever books are sold.

The Ensemble

PBS' MASTERPIECE THEATRE is television's great showcase for actors—a treasure chest of polished performances that seems to display more riches each time it opens for a new TV season. Because the series is devoted to presenting programs of unrivaled quality, it has been able to attract the very best performers even when their services are at peak demand.

That's why Masterpiece Theatre viewers saw Glenda Jackson in *Elizabeth R* the year before she won her second Oscar for *A Touch of Class;* Ben Cross as white hunter Ian Crawfurd in *The Flame Trees of Thika* immediately after his sensational movie debut as Olympic runner Harold Abrahams in *Chariots of Fire;* Dame Peggy Ashcroft in *The Jewel in the Crown* the same year as her Oscar-winning performance in *A Passage to India;* Emma Thompson in *The Blue Boy* just a year after her Academy Award for *Howards End;* Paul Scofield in *Martin Chuzzlewit* while moviegoers still cheered his Oscar-nominated performance in *Quiz Show.*

For a quarter of a century, Masterpiece Theatre has also provided American television viewers with a rare chance to see England's acting "royalty" give dazzling performances in the twilight years of great careers. Some classic examples: Lord Laurence Olivier playing a confused old stage actor in *Lost Empires;* Sir John Mills as Jarvis Lorry in *A Tale of Two Cities;* Dame Edith Evans as a spirited grandmama in Dostoyevsky's *The Gambler;* Dame Wendy Hiller as the haunted Alice von Holzendorf in *The Countess Alice;* Sir John Gielgud as a randy old repro-

bate in *A Summer's Lease;* Sir Alec Guinness playing a shell-shocked war veteran in *A Foreign Field.*

Masterpiece Theatre has been the ideal venue for actors seeking to stretch their talents with new and challenging roles: Roy Marsden shedding his spy-master mask from his 1970s series *The Sandbaggers* by playing the gentle schoolmaster in *Goodbye, Mr. Chips;* Bob Hoskins shaking his Cockney thug persona from *The Long Good Friday* by playing a comical film impresario in *Flickers;* Dame Diana Rigg ditching her sexy Emma Peel image from *The Avengers* to play the austere Lady Dedlock in *Bleak House.*

The series also is a legendary launching pad for great careers, bringing us stars of tomorrow in their formative years: future Oscar-winner Jeremy Irons (*Reversal of Fortune*) testing his appeal as a recklessly romantic leading man in *Notorious Woman* and *Love for Lydia;* Pierce Brosnan in *Nancy Astor* a decade before becoming the movies' James Bond; Kenneth Branagh playing the neglectful husband of Emma Thompson in *Fortunes of War,* a year before his feature film *Henry V* made him an international sensation and their marriage made them England's new first couple of acting.

In this section, some great stars from the series' first 25 years share their memories of Masterpiece Theatre, telling what it has meant to their careers and why it remains an oasis for ambitious actors in the often arid landscape of television.

Susan Hampshire

SUSAN HAMPSHIRE was the first great star of Masterpiece Theatre—and the first in the series' long string of award winners. Hampshire won an Emmy as best dramatic actress of the 1970–71 television season for her portrayal of Sarah Churchill in *The First Churchills,* the 12-episode drama that opened Masterpiece Theatre for business on January 10, 1971.

The First Churchills

Still a very busy stage actress in her native England, Hampshire looks back with awe at the success of *The First Churchills* in America and her earlier success as one of the stars of *The Forsyte Saga,* the phenomenally popular serial drama that inspired the creation of Masterpiece Theatre.

"At the time, I don't think anyone thought a black-and-white series with a lot of English people in tight bodices and full skirts with not even their toes showing would be so compelling to an American audience," says Hampshire of *The Forsyte Saga.*

But it was, earning Hampshire her first Emmy and creating a demand among American viewers for a chance to see her again soon. In fact, her appeal to American viewers is cited by Christopher Sarson, the first executive producer of Masterpiece Theatre, as one of the reasons he picked *The First Churchills* to launch his new venture.

Hampshire hasn't forgotten the imposing challenge of filming that series, which traced the early achievements and assorted troubles of Prime Minister Winston Churchill's 17th-century ancestors, John Churchill (John Neville) and the spirited Sarah Jennings, a lady-in-waiting who married him and became the first Duchess of Marlborough. For one thing, the filming kept falling behind schedule, no matter how hard the cast worked.

"They had tremendous trouble writing the scripts," says Hampshire. "The pages would arrive as we rehearsed. We'd do a scene, then the pages would be whipped away from us to be rewritten. We were working under a tremendous amount of pressure."

For Hampshire, the pressure was extraordinarily intense. At 31, she was an undiagnosed dyslexic, and her learning disability made it even harder for her to keep up with the new lines. Her only hope was that director David Giles wouldn't give up on her.

"He was just naturally patient, naturally kind," she says. "If you do a first reading and you can't get through it, it knocks your confidence down for the rest of rehearsal. If you came to a bit and weren't going to be able to read it, he'd read it and we'd just carry on."

Giles' patience with her had already been amply rewarded. He had directed her in her Emmy-winning performance as Fleur in *The Forsyte Saga.* So he helped her over the difficult words—Hampshire says "apothecary" was one of the worst—and elicited another magnificent performance from her.

Ironically, Hampshire says she wasn't the first choice to play Sarah Churchill and got the part only after Judi Dench turned it down. The fire she brought to the character of the legendary "torpedo in skirts" convinced the producers they hadn't made a mistake.

Sarah Churchill is regarded by many historians as a headstrong, willful, and ambitious woman. Hampshire researched her background feverishly and decided she must have been a "very, very strong woman with a brilliant brain." Not long ago, Hampshire met the present Duke of Marlborough and his family and she began talking "very enthusiastically" about Sarah until she realized the family had "a very unpositive view" of their ancestor and considered her an "awful, interfering woman" best not discussed.

"As I'd played her, I almost took it personally," Hampshire says. "So, I reminded them Blenheim Palace never would have been built if it hadn't been for her tremendous hard work, and her husband wouldn't be remembered in the glorious way he is today if she hadn't badgered the queen about giving him honors and such."

The following year, Hampshire tackled another high-spirited character under Giles' direction: Becky Sharp in the BBC's first color serial, *Vanity Fair.* Hampshire won another

Vanity Fair

The Forsyte Saga

American Emmy, her third in five years—setting a record still unsurpassed by any foreign actress.

"We didn't realize they were so inexperienced at doing color television," Hampshire recalls. "We had to paint our faces green in order to look a normal color, and dye our hair carrot-red for it to look brown. You couldn't cut the videotape, so we had to perform it like a live show in just two hours. We had to run off the set, rush into a dressing room, change costumes, then run back on to the set to play the next scene, panting, with maybe your tiara half-crooked. It was the most extraordinary experience."

For Hampshire, Becky Sharp was an irresistible character, even if most readers of Thackeray's novel consider her a vain, self-serving person. "When you're playing a character, you always have to believe she's in the right," Hampshire explains, "even if she's the biggest monster known to mankind."

Hampshire took one of Becky's lines from Thackeray's novel as the key to her character: "If I had 5,000 [pounds] a year, I could have been a good woman." To her, that meant Becky's behavior was motivated not by malice or selfishness but by an overwhelming urge to avoid poverty.

"She was scheming," says Hampshire, "but it was for survival."

Hampshire steeped herself in everything that she could learn about the way women lived in the early part of the 19th century, the setting for the novel. She insisted on wearing the most uncomfortable of authentic costumes and undergarments, so that she would move exactly like a woman in Becky's social class. She even asked Giles to have someone find one of the marble eggs that British ladies used to carry to cool their hands.

"One tiny little detail that's true to the period can help an actress find her own historical truth for the character," says Hampshire.

For *Barchester Chronicles* (1984), Hampshire put on an "unspeakable" corset to get in touch with the historical truth of her character, the flirtatious and meddlesome Signora Madeline Vesey-Neroni, a mostly bedridden busybody of irresistible charm. Though some critics likened this role to the other historical schemers she'd played on Masterpiece Theatre, Hampshire saw the signora as an unselfish sort of Machiavellian socialite.

Today, Hampshire works mainly in theater, doing yearlong runs in popular shows such as *The King and I, A Little Night Music,* and Noel Coward's *Relative Values.* She has written three books: *Susan's Story,* about her struggle with dyslexia; *Maternal Instinct,* about the problems some women face during childbirth; and a children's book about ballet.

Though there have been no formal reunions for cast and crew from the first Masterpiece Theatre production, Hampshire says her friends from *The First Churchills* frequently meet for what one might call "accidental reunions."

"Very often four or five of us will get together because we all happen to be going to the same event," she says. "We'll gravitate to each other, then sit and talk. I see a lot of Maggie Tyzack, a lot of David Giles, and I write a long letter each Christmas to Donald Wilson, who wrote and produced *The First Churchills.*"

Acting Credits

Theater credits include: *Blithe Spirit, The King and I, A Little Night Music, Miss Julie, Expresso Bongo,* and *Night Must Fall.*

Television credits include: *My Secret Garden (Gardening Theories), Don't Tell Father, David Copperfield, Barchester Chronicles, The Pallisers, Vanity Fair, The First Churchills,* and *The Forsyte Saga.*

Film credits include: *The Three Lives of Thomasina, Fighting Prince of Donegal, Night Must Fall,* and *Living Free.*

Jean Marsh

JEAN MARSH'S career-making ride on the longest-running dramatic series in the history of Masterpiece Theatre—the 55-episode *Upstairs, Downstairs*—began as a casual exercise in writing by two old friends.

"We thought writing together would be a discipline, a kind of responsibility to each other," Marsh recalls. "And we wanted to use our backgrounds."

Her friend was actress Eileen Atkins. Both had been raised in working-class households in London, and both could trace their lineage back to servants. Both had considerable stage experience and Marsh already had begun to play small roles in some big international films such as *The Eagle Has Landed* and Alfred Hitchcock's *Frenzy.*

The two imagined writing parts for themselves in a television series that would open each week with the same photograph of a group of servants about to go on an outing together. "We thought it would be a good idea to zoom in on different servants each week, then tell their story," says Marsh. "Eventually, after much talk, we decided it should be about life in a London house, upstairs and down."

Marsh had two goals: to use the mythical household to portray, in microcosm, the class struggle in Edwardian England and, in the process, to write herself a juicy role as an outspoken parlor maid named Rose.

"When I wrote the idea down, I described Rose with me in mind," Marsh recalls. "I even wrote a bit of dialogue to make it clear she was a tough Cockney girl."

Marsh didn't model Rose after any of her ancestors, although she put a few traces of her mother here and there. Rose was too politically conservative to resemble Marsh, but they did share one trait.

"I'm a little like Rose inasmuch as I'm a very hard worker," says Marsh. "If I commit myself to something, I really do it properly. I liked it that Rose was a rounded character. She wasn't always nice or sympathetic, you know."

Upstairs, Downstairs quickly became the rage of England, then crossed the Atlantic to take America by storm in the 1973–74 season of

Upstairs, Downstairs

Masterpiece Theatre with the first of four batches of episodes that made the folks of the Bellamy digs at 165 Eaton Place household names everywhere.

Jean Marsh's Rose immediately leapt out of the pack as the best-loved character in the much-loved series, and her visage, complete with frilly maid's cap, became the logo for the show. Her fellow players celebrated her good fortune along with their own.

"They were very, very loving when I became a success and was chosen to promote it," Marsh recalls. "When I first went to America for the launch, everybody gave me little gifts for the journey. There wasn't one smidgeon of jealousy."

That spirit of family among the members of the large *Upstairs, Downstairs* ensemble became the show's trademark. Marsh says it was an unwritten rule among the players that their closeness should be maintained at all costs—and the exemplar of that rule was Gordon Jackson, who played Hudson, the head of the downstairs staff.

"Gordon Jackson set a very good example," she recalls. "He'd put out the hand of friendship even to guest actors who only spoke one or two lines."

Marsh says friendships among the cast tended to divide along the "class lines" of their roles, mostly because the downstairs people played most of their scenes together and the upstairs actors did the same. Every once in a while they found themselves taking it all too seriously.

Marsh remembers having a "tiny tiff" with the studio because Rachel Gurney, who played high-toned Lady Marjorie, was given a posh corner dressing room with windows and free

Return to Oz

Kleenex while she was assigned to a drab, windowless one with no tissues.

"Everybody thought it was frightfully funny because I was automatically being treated like a maid," says Marsh. "Nobody resented me saying anything because it was so funny, but I could see how ridiculous I'd been as well."

Among the cast, Marsh's closest friends were Jackson, Angela Baddeley, who played elderly Mrs. Bridges, and, closest of all, Simon Williams, who played James.

"Simon always looked after the women very well," she says. "He took care of Angela, who was very old, and he also watched over me. I remember coming back to work after a horrible operation one time. Simon stopped rehearsals, told everybody I must be sent home, then called me a taxi."

Jackson and Baddeley both passed away, but Marsh and Williams remain close friends—and country neighbors—to this day.

"We're both incredibly keen walkers," she says, "and we're both writers. I sometimes call him up and whine that I can't write anything. He once told me to put a sign above my desk, saying 'Don't get it right; just write!'"

Those warm friendships made working on *Upstairs, Downstairs* a constant pleasure, but they also made leaving the show a sorrowful ordeal. When the time came to film the final episode—"Whither Shall I Wander"—in 1977, Marsh found herself in a trying situation. She was booked to appear in a Broadway play before the final season was complete, so the producers agreed to film the final episode out of sequence, then do another three later, without Marsh.

"I didn't have the catharsis of the last night's party," says Marsh. "I was desperately sad and upset, and people were sad to see me go, but I was the only one going."

Marsh gave everyone farewell gifts—she had glasses made up at Harrods with little staircases on them, along with each player's initials—and they pressed her with gifts. But the rest of the cast would experience the real finale without her.

"I didn't have the tears, the hugs, and the kisses like everybody else did," she says.

Since *Upstairs, Downstairs* ended with the closing down of the Bellamy household, various

Upstairs, Downstairs

attempts have been made to revive the series, including a stage version for London's West End and a TV spinoff proposed by American producer Jack *(Dragnet)* Webb, who wanted Marsh and Jackson to bring Hudson and Rose to the United States to open a domestic service agency. Marsh turned down all such offers.

Instead, she went on to a wide variety of other projects, including the American TV series *Nine to Five* and *The House of Eliott*, another episodic television series she created with Atkins. Marsh wrote the novelization of that show and recently completed her first novel.

"It's gone, it's done," Marsh says of *Upstairs, Downstairs.* "I think we were right to end it." Her memories of *Upstairs, Downstairs* are still warm—and she believes that avoiding offers to revive the show will keep them that way.

Acting Credits

Theater credits include: *Much Ado About Nothing, The Importance of Being Earnest, Habeas Corpus, Whose Life Is It Anyway?,* and *You and I.*

Television credits include: *The Moon and Sixpence, Upstairs, Downstairs, Nine to Five, Master of the Game, Adam Bede,* and *Fatherland.*

Film credits include: *Cleopatra, Frenzy, The Eagle Has Landed, Return to Oz, Rock-a-Bye, Willow,* and *Danny Champion of the World.*

Ian Carmichael

IAN CARMICHAEL's rendition of Lord Peter Wimsey, Dorothy L. Sayers' aristocratic sleuth, remains the most popular detective in the first 25 years of Masterpiece Theatre, lasting through 21 hours of complex crime-solving over five television seasons. Yet Carmichael practically had to beg for the chance to bring Wimsey to television.

"I took the idea to the BBC in the mid-1960s, and they wouldn't have it," Carmichael recalls. "They said sales to the United States were a very important factor for them, and they felt there would be no market for an effete English detective in America."

Carmichael then presented the concept to virtually every commercial station in England, but they all turned him down. When the BBC finally reconsidered the idea five years later and assigned a producer to develop a sample program, Carmichael was still left out in the cold.

"The producer didn't want me to play Lord Peter Wimsey," says Carmichael. "He wanted another actor, John Neville."

Carmichael persisted, though. His association with Wimsey had begun in his youth when he read a couple of Sayers' novels and loved them. Many years later, when he was firmly established as one of England's most popular stage and screen actors, his agent's brother wrote a memo suggesting Wimsey would be an ideal character for Carmichael to play.

"All that memo did was jog my memory," Carmichael recalls. "I rang up the book department at Harrods and asked them to send me the entire line of books. I sat down and read them all in chronological order without interruption. By the time I had read them all, I was very much into the gentleman."

But Carmichael had a considerable obstacle to overcome before anyone else could picture him playing Wimsey: his popular image as a light comedy star, forged in numerous British classic movie comedies, from *Private's Progress* (1956) and *Lucky Jim* (1957) through *I'm All Right, Jack* (1959) and *Heavens Above!* (1963). Worse yet, he was coming off the tremendous success of the TV series *The World of Wooster* (the earlier non-Masterpiece Theatre version), in which he played the silly, monocled upper-class twit, Bertie Wooster (this predates the Masterpiece Theatre series *Jeeves and Wooster*).

"I had an awful job selling myself as Peter Wimsey," he explains. "They could only see me as Bertie Wooster and thought I'd make Wimsey into a silly ass."

Yet the fates finally smiled on Carmichael when the proposed BBC project fell apart and a new producer was brought in—Australian Richard Beynon, who thought Carmichael was much better suited to play Wimsey than anyone the BBC had in mind.

Once he had the part, Carmichael pushed for all the Wimsey mysteries to be filmed in chronological order. Instead, the BBC insisted on trying just one to see how it worked. So production began on *Clouds of Witness*. The five-hour mystery was first telecast in England in 1972, where it was an immense popular success. The following year, it was the opening attraction of the 1973–74 Masterpiece Theatre season. Again, it was a smash with viewers, proving there was indeed a hunger in America for at least this one literate English detective.

"After that, we did four more," says Carmichael. "But they never would risk a whole lot. Whenever I finished one, I never knew when—or if—they'd ever do another."

A four-part mystery, *The Unpleasantness at the Bellona Club,* was rushed into production and came to Masterpiece Theatre in late 1973. That was followed by three more four-hour mysteries: *Murder Must Advertise* (1974), *The Nine Tailors* (1975)—Carmichael's personal favorite—and *Five Red Herrings* (1976).

Carmichael's Wimsey was universally acclaimed on both sides of the Atlantic. London's *Daily Express* suggested his "immaculately constructed" performance was so good that Sayers might have created Lord Peter just so Carmichael could play him.

Actually, Carmichael wasn't the first actor to

Five Red Herrings

The Great Kandinsky

bring Wimsey to life. Sayers' *Busman's Honeymoon* had been turned into a stage play in the 1930s. MGM bought the rights, and in 1940 Robert Montgomery played Wimsey in the film, rechristened *Haunted Honeymoon.* The critics—and Wimsey readers—were not kind.

Though Carmichael never met Sayers, who died in 1957, he believes he knew what her beloved character was really like and insisted on playing him as she created him.

"He was a character I dearly wanted to play, and I was very, very anxious that we be as true as possible to the original stories," he says.

By the time Carmichael finally stepped in front of a camera as Lord Peter Wimsey, he needed little additional preparation to assume the character. In fact, the actor says, he might well have been Wimsey if he'd been born into the same milieu—and with the same bank balance.

"I identified with so much of him," he explains. "He was a great music lover, a great wine lover, and loved good food and drink. He also was a great exponent of cricket. All these are things I enjoy. I think I just fell into the role."

Carmichael believes Wimsey's enduring popularity comes from the fact that he is brilliant and thoughtful, yet he can play the fool when that's necessary to solve a case.

A chain of disasters brought the series to a premature end. The producers had prepared to film *Strong Poison,* in which Wimsey first meets Harriet Vane, the woman he eventually marries, when a strike shut down all production at the BBC. After the strike ended, no studio space was immediately available, and the project was abandoned.

To save the series, the BBC commissioned a rushed adaptation of *Five Red Herrings,* which could be filmed largely on location in Scotland, where the story takes place, and at the BBC studios in Glasgow. Beynon wasn't available, so a new producer, Bill Sellars, was assigned.

"It was entirely the wrong time of year to shoot *Five Red Herrings,*" Carmichael recalls. "It

Murder Must Advertise

was a summer subject. One of the vital clues in the mystery was a picture painted in the open air that, because of the summer sunshine, had dried too quickly. But we had to shoot it in terrible winter weather."

Carmichael believes the script was inadequate and the production was below par. He thinks it's the worst of the lot, and feels his constant complaining about it may have clinched the BBC's decision to kill the series.

"I think I made myself pretty unpopular," he says. "I kept trying to lay down the law because I was the only one left who knew what had been done before. They thought I was throwing my weight around a bit, so I think they probably tired of both me and the series."

Much later, the Wimsey character was revived for another series of television mysteries without Carmichael, but the public continues to associate him with the role. In addition to the five projects for Masterpiece Theatre, Carmichael also has performed all the original Wimsey mysteries as BBC radio dramas and has finished recording all but one of them for a series of audio books.

No matter what else he does in his long career, Carmichael knows there always will be a large group of fans in England and America who will think of him only as Wimsey. And that's just fine with him because, after more than 20 years of living with the character, Carmichael still feels Lord Peter Wimsey fits him like a very classy suit from the best Bond Street tailor.

Acting Credits

Theater credits include: *The Gazebo, Overheard, Pride and Prejudice,* and *The School for Scoundrels.*

Television credits include: *The World of Wooster, Bachelor Father, Clouds of Witness, The Unpleasantness at the Bellona Club, Murder Must Advertise, The Nine Tailors, Five Red Herrings,* and *The Great Kandinsky,* also for Masterpiece Theatre.

Film credits include: *Lucky Jim, I'm All Right Jack, Heavens Above!, The Lady Vanishes,* and *Diamond Skulls.*

Sian Phillips

Crime amd Punishment

NO PERFORMER has played more rich and colorful characters over the first 25 years of Masterpiece Theatre than has Welsh actress Sian Phillips. Though probably best remembered as the grotesque Livia in *I, Claudius* (1977–78), she has also created indelible portraits of suffragette Emmeline Pankhurst in *Shoulder to Shoulder* (1975), Beth Morgan in *How Green Was My Valley* (1976), Katerina Ivanova in *Crime and Punishment* (1980), and Clementine Churchill in *Winston Churchill—The Wilderness Years* (1983).

Phillips earned British Academy awards for *I, Claudius* and *How Green Was My Valley*, and drew a nomination for *Shoulder to Shoulder*. She finds them all unforgettable roles, for one reason or another. In *Shoulder to Shoulder*, for example, Phillips found herself involved with a truly feminist ensemble for the first time in her career.

"There were about 50 actresses, a woman producer [Verity Lambert], a woman director [Moira Armstrong] for about half the episodes,

I, Claudius

and even a woman camera-person," says Phillips. "I thought it might be ghastly with all these women, but it went on for about seven months, and I don't think anyone spoke a cross word during the whole time."

One reason the women became such a tight group was that they all were caught up in telling the story of how women won the vote in England in 1918. Many, like Phillips, knew little about the original women's movement and found themselves swept up in the spirit of it.

"I think it affected everybody," Phillips recalls, especially during the filming of sequences in which militant suffragists were imprisoned, went on hunger strikes, and were force-fed by authorities. "We were shocked by the idea of force-feeding. Until you know the details, you don't know how painful, horrible, and humiliating it is." That's why a group of the players, including Phillips, decided to organize protests against the force-feeding of two Irish women—

the Price sisters—who were imprisoned for offenses against British security while the series was being filmed.

"It was incredible this was still taking place in 1974," says Phillips. "We went to Holloway Prison to protest, went to the House of Commons, and I even had dinner with two members of Parliament. We had a moderate effect, because the force-feeding was stopped."

For all her militancy in favor of universal suffrage, Phillips' character, Emmeline Pankhurst, believed women belonged at home. "I finally had to settle for the fact she wasn't a completely sympathetic character," says Phillips, who found playing the role a valuable experience.

How Green Was My Valley, Phillips' favorite Masterpiece Theatre project, was a distinct contrast—a nostalgic return to her own Welsh roots, playing the hardworking mother in a coal-mining family that might have been her own.

"I spent a lot of the series cooking," she recalls. "We had a working range and I actually cooked the food. We ate it in between takes. A lot of the things I cooked were specifically Welsh dishes I remember my grandmother cooking."

Phillips says the Masterpiece Theatre version was much more accurate than John Ford's famous 1941 movie version of *How Green Was My Valley*, which used mostly Irish actors because Germany's wartime blockades of England prevented Welsh actors from coming to Hollywood. The new version had an all-Welsh cast and was filmed in a Welsh mining town.

"Beth was a limited woman, not stupid," Phillips says of her character. "She had no experience of the world outside her little world. I patterned her very much after my aunts. She wasn't sophisticated, but she was very strong and good."

Phillips has another very bittersweet memory about that show. She remembers going to dinner with co-star Stanley Baker shortly after they finished filming. He had been to the doctor that day—and learned he had terminal cancer.

"Stanley always played a tough guy in the movies—and he really was a very brave man," she says. "He told me he'd done everything he'd ever wanted to do, had provided for his family, and had had a better life than he'd ever hoped to have. He said he wasn't complaining—and he

How Green Was My Valley

never did." Baker never worked again. Knighted shortly after finishing *How Green Was My Valley,* he died within six months.

From the beloved Beth Morgan, Phillips went on to Livia, the darkly evil wife of the emperor Augustus Caesar in *I, Claudius.* Livia poisoned a slew of family members so that her son, Tiberius, could rise to the throne. Then she ran the empire through him.

"I found her fascinating," says Phillips. "I enjoyed that part, although it was difficult, initially, to play the sort of person who literally governs all the known world." In the course of *I, Claudius,* Phillips, who was barely 40, had to age nearly 50 years into the wizened crone Livia becomes. "It took five hours every day to do that makeup," she recalls with distaste. "You've got to get used to how awful you look."

Phillips couldn't find much to like about Livia, but the humor in the script made it bearable. She also relished the nasty scenes between Livia and her grandson, the vile Caligula, played by her good friend John Hurt. They kept themselves in good humor between scenes by joking about all the debauchery. "We were able to do quite daring things in those scenes," she recalls, especially a grossly incestuous kiss, "because we were friends and knew each other so well. We could do things it would have taken strangers weeks and weeks to get around to doing."

Phillips was completely bowled over by the worldwide success of *I, Claudius,* which she knew was good but doubted would become a mass audience hit. She still sees many dear friends from the cast, including George Baker (Tiberius), Brian Blessed (Augustus), and Patricia Quinn (Livilla).

Her next Masterpiece Theatre production, the four-part *Crime and Punishment,* was mostly punishment, Phillips recalls, especially those scenes filmed at the Naval College in Greenwich, where temperatures fell well below zero. "It was so cold!" she says. "It was eleven below when we did the barefoot dancing scene in the snow. The

Vanity Fair

weather was so incredibly awful that very little acting was required."

After that, she played Winston Churchill's long-suffering wife, Clementine, in *Winston Churchill—The Wilderness Years,* which was filmed partly at Chartwell, Churchill's family home. "There wasn't time to tell her story at all," says Phillips. "I'm afraid we didn't reveal much about Clementine Churchill." What Phillips remembers most about that popular production, which starred Robert Hardy as Churchill, was the incredible ordeal it represented for her. During the day, she filmed in Kent, then had to dash over icy roads to London's West End each night to play Vera in the musical *Pal Joey.* "It was a terrible time because I only got about five hours of sleep a night," she recalls.

Though she did lots of research into Clementine's life, she didn't get to use much of it. What she took away from that experience was her eternal gratitude she didn't have to put up with all that the real Clementine had to endure, especially husband Winston. "I think she found him intolerable," says Phillips. "It would be very hard to live with a man like that. He was so depressed all the time. He had an ungovernable temper and these terribly black, black moods when he couldn't be spoken to at all."

Clearly, Phillips rates Churchill low among the husbands she's had on Masterpiece Theatre. Her favorite: Stanley Baker's rough-hewn Gwilym Morgan in *How Green Was My Valley.*

"But I had a soft spot for Augustus Caesar. He was rather nice," she says, though her character ended up poisoning him.

Acting Credits

Theater credits include: *The Glass Menagerie, Man and Superman, Hedda Gabler, Painting Churches, Ghosts,* and *An Inspector Calls.*

Television credits include: *Winston Churchill— The Wilderness Years, Crime and Punishment, Smiley's People, Tinker, Tailor, Soldier, Spy, I, Claudius, How Green Was My Valley, Shoulder to Shoulder,* and *The Borrowers.*

Film credits include: *Dune, Goodbye Mr. Chips, Valmont, A Mind to Kill,* and *The Age of Innocence.*

Jeremy Irons

JEREMY IRONS believes his early experience as a leading man on Masterpiece Theatre helped him find the right path for an acting career that has taken him to an Academy Award and enduring international stardom. In fact, Irons often wonders what track his career would have taken if he hadn't been chosen for Masterpiece Theatre's *Love for Lydia* (1979).

In that 12-episode series, Irons played hard-drinking, fast-driving playboy Alex Sanderson, one of the ardent suitors of the rich, beautiful, but sheltered Lydia Aspen (Mel Martin). He was so memorable in that tragic role that two years later he was the leading choice to play the equally reckless playboy Sebastian Flyte in another long and handsomely mounted British television series, *Brideshead Revisited*.

"Having seen me play Alex Sanderson, they thought I was perfect for Sebastian," Irons recalls. "But because I'd already played that sort of guy before, I rooted for the role of Charles. Had I been perceived as more like the flamboyant Sebastian, my career might have gone in a different direction."

Love for Lydia

Irons' other reason for wanting to play the part of the quiet, introverted Charles Ryder was that he thought he could do more with that role. Indeed, his performance as Charles is now generally considered to be the one that lifted him to stardom and made him one of the most keenly sought-after of all English actors, acclaimed internationally for his performances in such films as *The French Lieutenant's Woman* (1981), *Dead Ringers* (1988), *Damage* (1992), and *Reversal of Fortune* (1990), for which he won an Oscar.

Love for Lydia was actually Irons' second Masterpiece Theatre role. His first was as the great composer and pianist Franz Liszt, one of the lovers of writer George Sand, in the seven-part series *Notorious Woman* (1975).

Then in his mid-twenties, Irons already had been landing stage roles in London's West End theaters and was hoping to become a little more widely known by doing some television work in quality productions. The role of the charismatic Liszt, a notorious womanizer, was a big step up for him because it cast him opposite one of England's most respected leading ladies, Rosemary Harris, who played George Sand.

Though Irons is a competent blues pianist, he needed expert help to convince viewers he was the sort of mesmerizing stylist Liszt was reputed to be. Liszt was one of the first to play on the large new pianos of his era, Irons learned, and the "big" sound he created made him a sort of phenomenon comparable to Vangelis *(Chariots of Fire)* during the early stages of electronic music.

"The ladies just went wild over the sounds Liszt made," says Irons, who was rehearsed intensively in the master's keyboard techniques. "I remember sitting at a wooden keyboard for a long, long time, working with an expert they brought in to give me a bit of style. I also remember I had a wig, which kept falling in front of my face whenever I was supposed to be playing."

Irons remembers *Notorious Woman* with considerable affection. Even though they had no scenes together, it gave him the chance to work on the same production with his future wife, actress Sinead Cusack, who played Marie Dorval in the series. It also gave him the chance to make a permanent friend, Rosemary Harris.

"Though we haven't worked together that much since, we became great friends," says Irons. "I'm a huge admirer of her. She's really one of our best, but we don't see her enough here. She's always working in America."

Irons also retains pleasant memories of *Love for Lydia*, which remains one of the most lyrically beautiful series in the history of Masterpiece Theatre. The adaptation of H. E. Bates' novel—about a carefree young heiress who enchants and ruins several young men—had a rather rocky beginning. The firing of the original director necessitated reshooting the first two episodes.

"He was a great director, but he didn't like close-ups," Irons recalls. "The powers-that-be felt they were paying an awful lot of money to have Rachel Kempson, Beatrix Lehman, and Michael Aldridge, and the audience ought to be able to

Brideshead Revisited

see who they were. So he left, and various other directors took over."

The filming itself was bucolic. "We were always out on location in the countryside," he says. "I don't remember ever being in a studio for that. It was a beautiful summer. The weather was very hot, and after work each day we'd all go find a bit of water and swim in it. I remember swimming in more English rivers than I've ever swum in before or since."

He also made a distinct impression on the entire *Love for Lydia* ensemble because of his mongrel dog, Speed, which he had rescued from the Battersea Dogs' Home shortly before starting the series. In those days, Irons rode a small motorcycle and had mounted a large box on the back of it to carry Speed.

"Our long-suffering producer was Tony Wharmby," Irons recalls. "I thought I was really taking advantage of him by having my dog on the set." To illustrate his point, Irons tells about the time Speed ruined an elaborate sequence in which Irons led a long procession of vintage cars up the roadway of an estate where a party was in progress and unloaded a bevy of pretty young women. As soon as Irons stepped out of the car, his faithful traveling companion, Speed, dashed out of the dark and jumped into the driver's seat—in full view of the camera.

Speed's screen debut died on the cutting room floor that time, but Irons says his pet can be seen briefly in *The French Lieutenant's Woman* and in *Moonlighting* (1982), "looking extremely unhappy" about being walked on a leash by a stranger.

Irons also recalls with some humiliation the time that one of the *Love for Lydia* directors asked him to drive by the camera as close as he could at very high speed. He got that part right, but just missed hitting the soundman and ran over the mike boom.

"The soundman got very good gravel noises out of it," Irons says.

As far as his role was concerned, Irons thoroughly enjoyed playing the part of Alex, a handsome young man who "drove too fast, drank too much, loved his mother, and drove off a bridge in episode eight" after it became clear he couldn't have Lydia.

"Was he drunk or was it suicide? I don't think even he knew," says Irons. "He just came off the bridge and didn't care. He was a tragic figure. I was quite attracted to him."

In retrospect, Irons suggests he probably wasn't very good in either *Notorious Woman* or *Love for Lydia,* though his reviews for those two series were uniformly flattering.

"Both series helped my career," he says. "But what you saw in them really was me learning how to work on camera." What Irons began developing then and has subsequently perfected is his restrained and subtle acting style, in which less always seems more. It's a style he even carried into his tongue-in-cheek performance as Simon, the riddling terrorist, in his 1995 box office hit, *Die Hard With a Vengeance.*

"That comes from my distaste for the obvious," says Irons, "a feeling that acting out large emotions is somewhat vulgar. I tend to believe real people are more interesting than acted people, so when I play someone I try to make them real by minimizing what I show."

Acting Credits

Theater credits include: *Godspell, The Taming of the Shrew, The Rear Column, The Real Thing, The Rover,* and *Richard II.*

Television credits include: *The Pallisers, Notorious Woman, Love for Lydia, Brideshead Revisited, Tales from Hollywood, The Dream,* and *The Captain's Doll.*

Film credits include: *The French Lieutenant's Woman, Dead Ringers, Reversal of Fortune, Kafka, Damage, M. Butterfly, The Lion King,* and *Die Hard With a Vengeance.*

Notorious Woman

Francesca Annis

Lillie

FRANCESCA ANNIS may never run out of fresh compliments from ardent admirers of her performance as legendary stage star Lillie Langtry on Masterpiece Theatre in 1979.

"People are still talking about it, even though it was all those years ago," says Annis, reflecting on the magic that happened between her and the international television audience when she played the person known in her day simply as "the most beautiful woman on earth."

Langtry was surely a woman ahead of her time. She repeatedly defied the Victorian code of behavior for women, first by becoming the mistress of Bertie, the future King Edward VII, then by having a child out of wedlock by Prince Louis of Battenberg, and finally by launching a phenomenally successful career on the stage.

"I think she would have gotten along quite well with the tabloid press," says Annis. "She always reminded me a little bit of Elizabeth Taylor."

Annis is also aware that many fans see her as a modern kindred spirit of Lillie and believe she was born to play the part.

Widely known for her independent ways and pungent views on marriage—she doesn't believe in it—Annis was single and pregnant with her first child while filming *Lillie,* and she made no effort to keep it a secret. She had already shocked moviegoers by playing the first nude Lady Macbeth in Roman Polanski's *Macbeth* (1971) while carrying on a stormy affair with the film's star, Jon Finch.

"I suppose I've mellowed over time," says Annis, who no longer carries her opinions like picket signs. She and photographer Patrick Wiseman have three children, but the couple never married. "We're still together after all this time. That's a real commitment to someone, as far as I can see."

Annis seems amused, but not bothered, by the comparisons people draw between her and Lillie Langtry. While preparing for the role, she learned a great deal about Langtry and wound up liking her a lot.

"I really admired her turning every situation

Parnell and the Englishwoman

to her advantage," she says. "She had a great sense of humor, was very down to earth, and everybody liked her."

Before playing Langtry, Annis had portrayed a very different type of woman, Flaubert's Emma Bovary, in the Masterpiece Theatre series *Madame Bovary* (1976). Playing Emma made Annis appreciate the independent spirit of Lillie even more.

"She was not afraid of her society at all," says Annis, "whereas Emma Bovary was provincial and so afraid of her society that she thought suicide was the only way out."

Annis' own upbringing seems to have prepared her for both of her best-known parts. Her mother, actress Mara Purcell, is half-Brazilian, and gave Francesca a convent education, traditional rules to live by, and a duenna who chaperoned her until she was 18 years old. Yet her parents encouraged her to develop an independent mind.

Sent to ballet training as a girl, Annis was spotted by a TV producer at a charity show and made her professional acting debut at 14. By 16, she was playing a handmaiden to Elizabeth Taylor in the historical epic *Cleopatra,* studying closely the female superstar she admires as "a true survivor."

By the time Annis won the role of Emma Bovary, she was an experienced Shakespearean actress and had played major roles in several television shows and feature films. She also had been swept up in the sexual and social revolution of the late 1960s and early 1970s and was in exactly the right frame of mind to play Flaubert's tragic heroine, a young woman trapped in a loveless marriage, then destroyed by a provincial society that condemned her for seeking love elsewhere.

"I could relate to Emma Bovary because I was part of a very romantic movement myself," she says. "We were benefiting from the changes that had come since her time. Women could make choices about their life, which was exactly the opposite situation Emma was coming from."

Annis still chuckles over her most indelible memory of filming *Madame Bovary.* It came during an outdoor love scene, set in a gazebo.

"I had to be in a nightdress, but it was winter and I was freezing," she says. "I had these hot-water bottles attached to me and whenever I moved, it sounded like my stomach was gurgling. I'm afraid love just wasn't enough for me that night."

Though the four-part *Madame Bovary* was a popular success, it's believed Annis won her next great Masterpiece Theatre role over a host of other actresses because she played a cameo part as Lillie Langtry in another popular television serial, *Edward the King,* just before casting decisions were made for *Lillie.* Early in the production, though, Annis nearly lost the role for which she's best remembered. Several horseback scenes were scheduled to be filmed along a beach, and Annis, an experienced rider, wanted to meet the horse she'd be riding in the film, so they could get used to each other. Nobody told her the mount was a retired racehorse, so she was startled when the horse suddenly bolted as another rider drew up close behind them.

"Suddenly, it took off like a formula-one racing car," she recalls. "I totally lost control, but I held on. I wasn't thrown, but in pulling myself together I tore all the muscles on the inside of my legs and hurt my back."

Annis did not tell anyone about her torn muscles, assuming that she'd be fine when time came to film her horseback sequence. But when the day arrived, she was stiff, sore, and in miserable shape.

"I was riding along by the sea when a wave

Madame Bovary

dashed a rock and sprayed up on us. The horse reared back," she says. "I tried to hold on, but none of my leg muscles worked."

Annis was thrown that time and landed, painfully, on a rock. Only because of her superb physical condition and determination was she able to go on with the filming.

That was an unforgettable moment, but not the one Annis still remembers most vividly. That came much later, when they were filming the final episode. For that Annis was made up as the 70-year-old Langtry, playing a scene with a 40-year-old lover.

"I had to sit for hours while they were applying the prosthetics to age me," she says. "Once you've got it all on, you definitely start to lose sight of yourself, and you start imagining yourself as everybody else sees you. Here I was playing a woman of 70 with a man of 40, while I was seven months pregnant and had this baby bouncing around in my stomach. I remember thinking how glad I was this was the last episode because I felt so perverse."

Since *Lillie,* Annis has continued to enhance her reputation as a serious dramatic actress, primarily on stage. Having played Ophelia to Nicol Williamson's Hamlet in the acclaimed 1969 London and New York productions, she has recently wowed a new generation of critics as Gertrude opposite Ralph Fiennes' Hamlet in London and New York.

For all the critical raves, though, Annis believes most people still think of her as either Emma Bovary or Lillie Langtry because those Masterpiece Theatre roles remain "the two most successful things I've ever done for television."

Acting Credits

Theater credits include: *The Heretic, Troilus and Cressida, Month in the Country, Three Sisters, Lady Windemere's Fan,* and *Hamlet.*

Television credits include: *Schumann, Madame Bovary, Lillie, Partners in Crime, Parnell and the Englishwoman,* and *Between the Lines.*

Film credits include: *The Walking Stick, Macbeth, Coming out of the Ice, Krull, Dune,* and *Under the Cherry Moon.*

John Hurt

JOHN HURT looks back on *I, Claudius*—his first Masterpiece Theatre production—as a creative milestone in his career, even if it was something of a financial embarrassment.

"I think I was paid about £1,500 pounds an episode for that," he recalls. "In those days you didn't get a lot of money for British television. But those are the things that actually make your career, aren't they?"

That was certainly true in Hurt's case. Though over the course of 15 years, the actor had been in many feature films, including the 1966 Oscar-winner *A Man for All Seasons,* he hadn't become an international star until the epic TV series about the decadent Roman emperors became the rage of America early in the 1977–78 television season.

"I don't think anyone thought it would be that successful," he says, "I was certain we had good stuff, that it definitely was going to be good, but that's no guarantee something's going to be a success."

Now that *I, Claudius* is a perennial video attraction that keeps winning new audiences year after year, Hurt can laugh off the small amount he was paid to act a major role in it. Not only did that series help build his career, but it allowed for more freedom. "You can take a lot more risks with small budgets than you can with bigger budgets," he explains.

Hurt knew he was taking a big risk in playing the dissolute and insane emperor Caligula. But an earlier daring career move—the role of outspoken homosexual Quentin Crisp in the low-budget TV production *The Naked Civil Servant*—paid off well with a British Academy Award.

Hurt knew neither he nor viewers would be able to identify or empathize with Caligula. Caligula had, after all, declared himself a god, ordered a baby's head cut off to cure its cough, disemboweled his own sister, and, in one of the series' most amazing scenes, had his horse appointed to the Roman senate. ("At least the horse had the good grace to wink in that shot," Hurt chuckles.)

Hurt soon found the key that opened the historical character for him: He had to play the man straight because, he realized, Caligula, for all his excesses, was taken seriously by all those around him.

"I mean, they had to accept him," Hurt explains. "It was a ghastly era to put yourself into. All your conditioning had to be rethought."

Unlike most actors, Hurt is not a great believer in research. He did not read the two Robert Graves novels that *I, Claudius* was adapted from, nor did he bone up at all on ancient Rome.

"As far as I'm concerned, what I'm acting is the script," he says. "Whether I'm playing a real person or a fictitious one, I approach it exactly the same way. I use the script as a springboard for an imaginative leap."

What Hurt didn't count on, though, was the challenge of keeping a straight face.

"It was just so outrageous," he recalls. "I had one scene with Derek Jacobi [who played Claudius] that we never managed to get through in rehearsal without bursting into laughter."

In that scene, Caligula asks Claudius, "Do you think I'm mad?" and Claudius, who has a terrible stammer, replies, "I think you're the m-m-model for s-s-sanity t-t-throughout the whole world." Hurt cracks up nearly 20 years later, just remembering it.

Hurt says the *I, Claudius* ensemble was one of the finest he's ever worked with, all of them

Crime and Punishment

Crime and Punishment

theater-trained actors capable of improvising, which they often did. He remembers proposing to director Herbert Wise that Caligula ought to crawl in bed with his grandmother, Livia, who was played by Hurt's good friend, Sian Phillips.

"He wasn't exactly sure about that, but I told him it would be a wonderful image—and it was," Hurt recalls.

Hurt also had no fear of hamming things up too broadly. For one thing, director Wise was there to monitor his performance. But Hurt also knew it would be "very difficult to go over the top with Caligula."

Critics acclaimed Hurt's performance in *I, Claudius,* and he quickly received offers that led him to the very top rank of the world's motion picture character players. He earned his first Oscar nomination for his role as a drug-addicted convict in *Midnight Express* (1978); he played a doomed astronaut in the original *Alien* (1979)—that was his chest the alien creature popped out of—and earned a second Oscar nomination for *The Elephant Man* (1980).

In between, Hurt returned to Masterpiece Theatre to sandwich in another riveting performance, this time in the four-part version of Dostoyevsky's *Crime and Punishment,* adapted for television by Jack Pulman, who also had dramatized *I, Claudius.*

Hurt played the tormented Raskolnikov, the brilliant, starving student who murders a pawnbroker and her sister for money in order to survive. Raskolnikov justifies his crimes by explaining that extraordinary men should be above the law. Hurt doesn't believe that grand rationalization, but he was nevertheless able to bond with the Raskolnikov character.

"I don't know how to describe the state you get in when you're playing someone like that," Hurt says. "I only know you have to love them to make them come to life."

In the novel and screenplay, Raskolnikov's inner torment is finally silenced by the redemption he discovers through his punishment. But Hurt believes the character's initial self-centered philosophy retains an attraction for some: "I think there are people very much around today who still believe it."

Hurt's career continues to include work for television. He has just completed *Saigon Baby,* a BBC television drama about adoption in the Far East. Like his earlier Masterpiece Theatre projects, he didn't go into it for the money, but because the role fascinated him as an actor.

"You don't get that kind of material anywhere else," he says.

Acting Credits

Theater credits include: *The Dwarfs, Man and Superman, Travesties, The Seagull, London Vertigo,* and *A Month in the Country.*

Television credits include: *The Naked Civil Servant, I, Claudius, Crime and Punishment, King Lear, Red Fox, Prisoners in Time,* and *Saigon Baby.*

Film credits include: *Midnight Express, Alien, The Elephant Man, 1984, Rob Roy, Dead Man,* and *Two Nudes Bathing.*

I, Claudius

Rachel Kempson

RACHEL KEMPSON is a seasoned veteran of Masterpiece Theatre, starting with her performance as Glenda Jackson's governess in *Elizabeth R* during the first season and continuing with her roles as Julianna, the maiden aunt who watched over frisky Mel Martin in *Love for Lydia* (1979), another rustic H. E. Bates character in the "Breeze Anstey" episode of *Country Matters* (1979) and, finally, two productions with close friend Dame Peggy Ashcroft *The Jewel in the Crown* (1984) and *She's Been Away* (1991).

Her work in these and many other acclaimed television series—including *Jennie* (1974), in which she played the Duchess of Marlborough, and *The Shadow of the Tower* (1972), in which she was Margaret of Burgundy—capped a long career mainly devoted to the stage in England, punctuated by appearances in the Academy Award–winning films *Out of Africa* (1985) and *Tom Jones* (1963).

The Jewel in the Crown

Kempson is the matriarch of one of England's most renowned acting dynasties: She's the widow of Sir Michael Redgrave, the mother of actors Vanessa, Lynn, and Corin Redgrave, and grandmother of actors Jemma Redgrave, Kelly Clark, and Natasha and Joely Richardson.

"They don't often come to me for advice," she relates, "but they do come to take me out."

For Kempson, making the various Masterpiece Theatre series was not only artistically challenging but also great fun because of the actors with whom she worked, many of them dear friends from her theater days.

She remembers the actors in *Elizabeth R* as having been a cheerful company, full of high spirits—especially after actor Robert Hardy, who played the romantic Lord Robert Dudley, helped top them up.

"We were never supposed to have wine on the set, but Robert Hardy used to bring it anyway, and we'd gulp it down," she recalls. "I don't think it did us any harm. We had terrific fun. I loved being in it." She also remembers, still with great awe, Glenda Jackson's performance as the queen in *Elizabeth R* and feels Jackson was then at the top of her form.

A decade later, Kempson was cast in the 12-episode *Love for Lydia,* playing one of the two dotty spinster aunts charged with the guardianship of their flirtatious niece, Lydia Aspen (Mel Martin). Kempson was delighted to learn her companion in spinsterhood, Aunt Bertie, would be played by an old friend, Beatrix Lehman, a veteran stage actress who was president of British Actors' Equity from 1945 to 1948.

"I was awfully fond of Beatrix," says Kempson. "Mike and I used to have a cottage in the country and she used to come and stay with us. She was enormous fun—and a very good actress." For a good many weeks, it was like another country outing for Kempson and Lehman, because much of *Love for Lydia* was filmed on location in the English countryside.

Kempson also remembers with great affection a young actor she became acquainted with while filming *Love for Lydia*—Jeremy Irons, who played one of Lydia's suitors, Alex Sanderson. Still two years away from the fame he would earn in another TV serial, *Brideshead Revisited,* Irons already was a respected actor. But Kempson says nobody really suspected he'd soon become a major international star.

A few years later, Kempson made her first trip to India to play Lady Manners in the 15-hour production of *The Jewel in the Crown.* Not knowing exactly what to expect, she was delighted to find the people of India warm and friendly. The company of actors and crew became as close as a second family.

"It was hot, very hot," she recalls. "We wore very thin things everywhere, except, of course, when we were in costume. But when we filmed at Lake Srinigar, it was always very cool and lovely."

Adding to her enjoyment of the long location shoot was the fact that two of her oldest friends from her theater days were also in the cast: Fabia Drake, who played Mabel Layton, and Dame Peggy Ashcroft, who played Mabel's houseguest and intimate friend, ex-missionary Barbie Batchelor.

Drake had begun her career at age nine when she became the youngest student ever accepted into the Royal Academy of Dramatic Art. She was a leading lady at Stratford-upon-Avon in 1932 when Kempson was dazzling audiences there as Shakespeare's Juliet (this is still her favorite role).

"Fabia was a wonderful actress," says Kempson. "A funny thing was that, while we were making *The Jewel in the Crown,* a friend wrote warning me not to let Fabia try to tell me how to play my part, which she was inclined to do."

Ashcroft, on the other hand, seldom talked shop with Kempson, though the two had worked together many times and had been best friends for more than 30 years. In their youth, both had toured Europe in *Hedda Gabler,* traveling alone in a rented car for a long series of one-night stands from France to Scandinavia. They were inseparable filming *The Jewel in the Crown* in India.

Elizabeth R

"Peggy was very special to me for years," says Kempson. "I admired her very much and we did a lot together."

Many critics feel that Kempson's Lady Manners represented the very best side of the British colonial presence in India—she was strong and resourceful, retaining her equilibrium even in the face of tragic events. Though Kempson didn't know any women who had experienced what Lady Manners had, she had prepared herself to play the part by reading as much as she could about similar India veterans.

"People who used to go out there in earlier periods were like that," she says.

These days Kempson no longer acts on the stage, but she is willing to consider the occasional good film or television role. With her son

Love for Lydia

Corin, she performs an evening of poetry readings from Oscar Wilde and she gives an occasional reading for her church.

Many of her close friends from the old days are gone, but she continues to see John Gielgud, another veteran of several Masterpiece Theatre productions, whenever possible.

"Of course, he's getting on at 90-odd years, but he's still marvelous," she says. "I think he'll never die. Unfortunately, I think we all have to, otherwise this place would be too crowded."

Looking back on all her Masterpiece Theatre performances, Kempson remembers *The Jewel in the Crown* most fondly, considering it one of the great adventures of her career. She came back with many souvenirs—"I think I've lost them all by now," she says—and with many more memories she'll never lose.

Acting Credits

Theater credits include: *Women and Their Lives, The Old Country, A Family and Its Fortune, The Cocktail Party, The Father, Coriolanus,* and *Uncle Vanya.*

Television credits include: *The Jewel in the Crown, The Black Tower, Country Matters II, Love for Lydia, Elizabeth R, Jennie,* and *She's Been Away.*

Film credits include: *The Captive Heart, Tom Jones, The Charge of the Light Brigade, The Virgin Soldiers, Camille,* and *Out of Africa.*

Ian Richardson

IAN RICHARDSON is the latest in a long line of respected British actors whose first taste of international stardom came through their exposure on Masterpiece Theatre. Regarded for years as one of England's finest Shakespearean actors, Richardson was merely a familiar face to television viewers and didn't become a household name in England and abroad until he played the sinister Francis Urquhart in the Masterpiece Theatre series *House of Cards* (1991), *To Play the King* (1994), and *The Final Cut* (1996).

House of Cards

"Suddenly I was being treated as a celebrity, after years as an ordinary actor people only vaguely knew," says Richardson.

Fame sneaked up on Richardson so quickly that it took him completely by surprise. He remembers when he first realized how much the role of Francis Urquhart had changed his life. He and his wife, Marousia, were on holiday in Italy shortly after *House of Cards* was first telecast. They had climbed to the top of Mt. Vesuvius and had stopped to rest on the rim of the crater, when a tourist approached them up the slope, shouting, "Hey, I loved you in that series!"

"My God, we've come to the top of Mt. Vesuvius and there's still no peace from it!" he remembers saying.

Richardson began his long association with Masterpiece Theatre in 1983 with the five-episode comedy *Private Schulz,* which was inspired by a bungled Nazi attempt to destroy the British economy by flooding the market with counterfeit English currency. He was signed to play Nazi SS Major Neuheim, but ended up playing, under heavy makeup, three other roles as well: a British double agent, a Glasgow crook, and a waiter.

"It went so successfully," chuckles Richardson, "that Alistair Cooke saw the tapes, did his introductions, and never noticed it was me playing those other roles. It was his wife who finally told him."

Richardson decided the key to playing Major

Neuheim was to play him straight, but as if he "hadn't a brain in his head." He also suspected there might be many Jewish viewers who wouldn't find anything funny about Nazis and their concentration camps. So he and co-star Michael Elphick, who played Private Schulz, routinely rehearsed their comic scenes in front of Cyril Shaps, a devout Jew who played Solly, the Jewish counterfeiter.

"We dropped a couple of things because Shaps thought they were just a little too tasteless," Richardson recalls. "We didn't want to offend."

For his next Masterpiece Theatre production, Richardson appeared in *Lord Mountbatten—The Last Viceroy* (1986). He had sought the role of Mountbatten without great hope—he's only 5 foot 9, and Mountbatten was over 6 feet tall. He wound up being cast as Pandit Nehru because producer Judith de Paul, who had unsuccessfully auditioned 400 actors for the part, came across a poor photocopy of a photograph of Richardson that struck her as bearing a resemblance to the legendary Indian leader.

"When the offer came through," says Richardson, "I told them I would play the part only if they'd fly me out to India for a period of time—so I could go around the places where Nehru had lived and meet the people who knew him."

The company agreed, and Richardson spent a week in India, absorbing all he could about Nehru's idiosyncrasies and watching him on newsreels he screened over and over again in a small stuffy theater in Delhi.

"I came back with the man very much inside me," he says.

Still, Richardson nearly pulled out after British Prime Minister Margaret Thatcher approached him at a cocktail party at No. 10 Downing Street and warned him that he'd better do a good job or "my friend Mrs. Gandhi will be very upset."

Richardson later met Indira Gandhi, who was not only prime minister of India but also Pandit Nehru's granddaughter. She greeted him very cordially and posed for a picture with him. A week later, she was assassinated while standing in the very spot where she had chatted with him.

Private Schulz

After a pause, Richardson's spirits rise again when he turns to the details of his craft. "I had a marvelous makeup woman," he recalls. "I wore soft-brown contact lenses and had the top half of my head shaved. From the forehead to the bottom of my nose, I was very convincing. In fact, the Indian extras used to crouch in front of me to touch the hem of my garment."

The reception wasn't quite so reverent in England, where some scenes involving Nehru were filmed. After doing the first take of a famous Nehru speech, Richardson was startled when hundreds of Indian extras suddenly began shouting, "No white actors with black faces!" They pulled out placards and signs and rushed him. He escaped when husky crew members surrounded him and hustled him out of danger.

"I couldn't do that today," he says of an Englishman playing one of India's national heroes. "You couldn't get away with it."

After the Mountbatten series, Richardson's next Masterpiece Theatre stint was the first episode in the 1987 *Star Quality* series of stories by Noel Coward. In it he played a British stage director who constantly fought with his star, played by Susannah York. As it turned out, the two actors feuded as much off camera as they did on, which Richardson attributes to their competitive zeal to outdo each other. "Although she never actually struck me, I'll bet she wanted to." he says.

Lord Mountbatten—The Last Viceroy

By 1990, when Richardson finally landed what he considers the role of a lifetime—Chief Party Whip Francis Urquhart in *House of Cards*—he had become a specialist at playing spies and sinister plotters in such television dramas as *Tinker, Tailor, Soldier, Spy* and *Blunt*. Learning the "stillness and physical economy" he feels is necessary for such roles, Richardson had mastered the technique of letting "your eyes hold back their secrets."

The eyes of Francis Urquhart had many secrets to hold back. In his bid to take over as prime minister in *House of Cards,* he becomes involved in all sorts of political treachery. Egged on by his Lady Macbeth of a wife, he engages in a kinky love affair with an ambitious young journalist, and he finally resorts to murder to preserve his hold on power.

"The culmination of all these rather sinister gentlemen I've played was Francis Urquhart," says Richardson. Playing Urquhart also gave Richardson his chance to play steamy love scenes. He recalls it wasn't always enjoyable because of his abject embarrassment. "I remember lying in a very suggestive manner on top of Susannah Harker," Richardson explains. "We had absolutely nothing on except around our vital parts. I was lying there talking my head off about Stratford and things like that, while trying to keep my mind off the fact I was stark naked in the closest clinch imaginable with this beautiful woman. I don't know how those chaps in blue movies maintain their equilibrium."

Since filming the final series as Urquhart—Richardson wouldn't have done the third series had the producers not agreed to kill Urquhart off—he has returned to the stage after more than a decade's absence. Praise for his performance as Urquhart has been effusive, but he figures that the Royal Family may not have appreciated the drubbing the royals took at Urquhart's hands in *To Play the King.*

"I was invited to a reception at the palace before *To Play the King* went out," says Richardson, "but I have a funny feeling I may not darken their door again."

Acting Credits

Theater credits include: *The Duchess of Malfi, A Midsummer Night's Dream, Marat/Sade, My Fair Lady,* and *Lolita.*

Television credits include: *Tinker, Tailor, Soldier, Spy, Private Schulz, Lord Mountbatten—The Last Viceroy, Star Quality, House of Cards, To Play the King,* and *The Final Cut.*

Film credits include: *Brazil, The Fourth Protocol, Cry Freedom, M. Butterfly,* and *Savage Play.*

Pete Postlethwaite

PETE POSTLETHWAITE will be remembered for playing one of the most loathsome villains in the history of Masterpiece Theatre, the sinister, vengeful Sgt. Obediah Hakeswill of *Sharpe's Company* and *Sharpe's Enemy.*

Those were chapters in Masterpiece Theatre's *Sharpe* saga, based on Bernard Cornwell's novels about Richard Sharpe (Sean Bean), an English military officer during the Napoleonic Wars of 1812–13. In those two episodes, the villainy of Hakeswill changed Sharpe's life forever.

In *Sharpe's Company* Hakeswill threatens to rape Sharpe's wife, the Spanish guerrilla fighter Teresa (Assumpta Serna), then murder both her and her baby daughter. In *Sharpe's Enemy* the disgraced Hakeswill, by then a deserter from Wellington's British Army, finally kills Teresa before being executed himself.

For Postlethwaite, who earned a 1993 Academy Award nomination for playing the quietly courageous father (to a son played by Daniel Day-Lewis) in the feature film *In the Name of the Father,* the challenge of warming up to the character of Hakeswill was daunting. Yet he felt he had to do it to play him convincingly.

"I really have to like the guys I play," says Postlethwaite. "I had to love him dearly and believe nobody else existed but him." Looking for some kind of psychological link with Hakeswill, Postlethwaite finally decided it might be their equally hard-driving approach to their careers. "God help my nearest and dearest," Postlethwaite says about reaching that conclusion.

Complicating things was the fact that Hakeswill's nastiest scenes often were played against actor Sean Bean, an old friend and frequent colleague. They kept the tension going by playing practical jokes and generally needling each other. "We've worked together quite a lot and know each other very well, so there's a great deal of trust," says Postlethwaite. "We're constantly winding each other up. There were jibes of all kinds going on."

Postlethwaite prepared to play Hakeswill first by reading the series of Sharpe novels, then "soaking up" as much as he could about the British campaign against the French on the Iberian Peninsula. He found the key to understanding Hakeswill was finding the genesis of his bad character. "He was hanged at the age of nine and didn't die," says Postlethwaite. "That's where he got the scar and the terrible twitch."

In one of the novels, Postlethwaite recalls, the lowborn Sharpe says he and Hakeswill are very much alike in terms of background and ambition, but they have "just chosen different paths." Postlethwaite seized upon that line to create a pathetically vulnerable side for Hakeswill. To round out the character, Postlethwaite explored Hakeswill's slightly ridiculous aspects, including his soliloquies spoken into his military cap and, of course, those unexpected twitches.

"Fortunately, with that kind of character, there's always the relief of comedy," he says. "We played games with him. I would always try to confuse the director and cameraman as to when the twitch would occur."

While filming, the actor's greatest worry was that he might be playing Hakeswill a mite too broadly. "You just hope these things work, don't you?" he says. "There were times when I went to sleep at night thinking I must have really gone over the top that time by taking it to the extreme and trying to get away with it. But we had a good director, Tom Clegg, who's pretty good at spotting that sort of thing."

Postlethwaite's *Sharpe* episodes were filmed on extremely remote locations in southern Ukraine, near the Black Sea port of Yalta. Most of the battle scenes used Ukrainian soldiers in costume, and the cast and crew were multinational, with French, Spanish, and Russian spoken as often as English.

"It was like being on the real Wellington campaign, miles away from everywhere, completely alienated and disoriented," Postlethwaite explains. "It was a very punishing, tough schedule."

Martin Chuzzlewit

Sharpe

The Dressmaker

When it came time to film Hakeswill's execution, some debate ensued over the wisdom of filming an alternate ending that might leave his demise in doubt. By then, it was clear to most that Hakeswill was going to be a big hit with viewers. Even author Cornwell, who visited the set, argued for keeping the character's fate open, but the decision finally was to let him die, so Sharpe would have his victory over evil.

Now there's talk of filming a prequel to the *Sharpe* saga, set in India, where Hakeswill had Sharpe flogged for a crime he didn't commit, making them lifelong enemies. Postlethwaite is eager to play the role again.

Since Postlethwaite quit teaching drama to become an actor in 1970, that sort of outrageous character has been his stock in trade in films and television, though he frequently gets to play more decent chaps on the English stage, where he does most of his work.

"What's the point of playing regular guys?" asks Postlethwaite, who's happy just being one in real life in the Shropshire hills, where he lives with his wife and son. He'd much rather create a full-bodied character like Hakeswill or Montague Tigg, the notorious con man and trickster in Dickens' *Martin Chuzzlewit* (1994), another Masterpiece Theatre production.

"Tigg was a wonderful, broad, Dickensian, Johnsonian, Rabelesian kind of character," Postlethwaite says. "I didn't do anything with him that isn't there in the text, although I guess they applied a little bit of makeup at one point." Postlethwaite's approach to Tigg was to resolutely refuse to play him with tongue-in-cheek. "I have to take it very, very seriously. Otherwise, it's an insult to the audience." he says.

"There's nothing worse than seeing even very fine actors winking at the audience," he says. "Even if you're very good at hiding it, it will come through. It's like telling them not to be fooled by this character because you're not. They have to believe he means it, that he's serious,

whether he's twitching like mad or poncing about like Liberace. After all, he couldn't have convinced all those people to give him their money to build up the Anglo-Bengalee Disinterested Life & Loan Assurance Co. by being a wally."

Though Postlethwaite's services have been in much greater demand since his Academy Award nomination, he still can't imagine himself as any sort of star, but rather just as a member of a team. He thinks that sense of team consciousness comes from the tradition of the English theater, something he remembers experiencing during his first Masterpiece Theatre drama, *The Dressmaker* (1990), in which he co-starred with two English stage veterans, Joan Plowright and Billie Whitelaw.

"There was a different sort of overall approach," he says. "We haven't had the excessive, hierarchical star system that Hollywood has seen. Their attitude was for us all to get on with it together and make it as good as we can."

Still, Postlethwaite's big international films, such as *The Usual Suspects,* and his many appearances on English TV talk shows, finally have made him a recognizable face that people are matching with the name. He's pretty relaxed about it.

"Before, I could wander about and nobody would know who the hell I was," he says. "Now they might think they went to school with me or maybe shared a cell with me in prison."

Acting Credits

Theater credits include: *Coriolanus, Henry V, Macbeth, A Midsummer Night's Dream, The Good Person of Sichuan,* and *The Rise and Fall of Little Voice.*

Television credits include: *Thuwm, They Never Slept, The Bill, The Dressmaker, Sharpe's Company, Sharpe's Enemy,* and *Martin Chuzzlewit.*

Film credits include: *A Private Function, Alien[3], Waterland, In the Name of the Father, A Pint of Bitter, Crimetime,* and *The Usual Suspects.*

Cherie Lunghi

CHERIE LUNGHI finally found a role she says fit her "like Cinderella's proverbial slipper" when she played Laura Testvalley in Edith Wharton's *The Buccaneers* (1995), the opening attraction of the Silver Anniversary season of Masterpiece Theatre.

The Buccaneers

Miss Testvalley is the English governess who becomes the catalyst for an "invasion" of upper-class British society by four beautiful American debutantes. She watches each of them marry into lofty levels of the aristocracy, then suffers with them when their marriages sour and her own star-crossed romance with a widowed English gentleman turns into her personal heartbreak.

It was a pivotal role in one of the most ambitious serial dramas in the history of Masterpiece Theatre. More important to Lunghi, though, was the fact that she found herself inhabiting the character of a woman who might have been herself 100 years ago.

"It's lovely when a role fits you like a glove," says Lunghi. "You can put a great deal of truth into playing it because you understand what the woman is feeling. You really mean the lines you say."

Laura Testvalley certainly seems a perfect fit for Lunghi. They're about the same age, both are half Italian, and both started earning their own living in their teens—Miss Testvalley as a governess at 17, Lunghi as radio's Alice in Wonderland at 13.

Like Laura, Lunghi has led an unorthodox life. She grew up in what she calls an "unconventional" matriarchal household. Her Italian father and English mother separated when she was a child, and she was raised by her mother, grandmother, and aunt, becoming an early recruit to feminism.

In *The Buccaneers,* Laura becomes a passionate advocate of love over duty, encouraging a romance between the unhappily married Annabelle, Duchess of Trevenick (Carla Gugino),

and Guy Thwaite (Greg Wise), the son of Laura's wealthy suitor (Michael Kitchen), but her willingness to help them break society's rules costs Laura her own chance to marry into the aristocracy.

Lunghi, too, has broken or bent her share of rules. She and former consort Roland Joffe, the director of *The Killing Fields* and *The Mission,* had a daughter but never married. "We're still very good friends," she says. She remains a fiercely independent woman in a society she believes is largely unchanged from Laura's time because it's still dominated by men.

"I can understand Laura's disappointment," she says. "She had to compromise herself in order to have a relationship—or pay the price of being alone. It's very disappointing when you come up against it. It's discouraging to find that men still are limited and unimaginative about their expectations for a woman and about their own role in a relationship."

Lunghi's long road to *The Buccaneers* has included roles with The Royal Shakespeare Company, parts in feature films—from *Excalibur* (1981) through Mary Shelley's *Frankenstein* (1994)—and appearances on American television *(Ellis Island, Master of the Game,* both 1984). But she's mainly known in America through her British television dramas, including *Much Ado About Nothing* (1984), presented on PBS' The Shakespeare Plays; *Praying Mantis* (1985), seen on PBS' Mystery!; and three earlier appearances on Masterpiece Theatre in *Kean* (1979), *Edward and Mrs. Simpson* (1981), and *Strangers and Brothers* (1985).

Lunghi remembers *Kean,* based on the play by Jean-Paul Sartre, mostly for the chance it gave her to work with Anthony Hopkins, Robert Stephens, and "a fabulous cast, most of them with a very strong theatrical background."

In *Edward and Mrs. Simpson,* she had the small, but crucial, role of Lady Thelma Furness, who introduces Edward VIII (Edward Fox) to Wallis Simpson (Cynthia Harris) with the immortal line, "Take care of the little prince while I'm away."

Ironically, Thelma Furness was one of two American sisters, society girls, who came to

Strangers and Brothers

Kean

England and worked their way into the aristocracy, "not unlike the 'buccaneers' of another generation," says Lunghi. "I suppose the first 'buccaneers' started a tradition, and these girls followed on the next wave."

Lunghi particularly enjoyed the part of Lady Thelma because it let her show her flair for comedy. "You know, she was not a terribly bright woman," says Lunghi. "She adored society, partying, and money. She was a bit of a snob. I had a bit of fun with all that."

Lunghi considers her role in *Strangers and Brothers*—a wronged wife who eventually reunites with her husband after extended melodrama—much less memorable and dismisses the program as "one of those terribly complicated, typically British emotional scenes."

But Lunghi found herself fascinated by Wharton's novel about Laura and her four American girls in *The Buccaneers,* not only for what it had to say about the rigidity of 19th-century British society, but for what it still tells us about the differences between Americans and the English.

"I love the fact that Americans don't have a sense of shame about where they came from or how they sound," she explains. "Here in England there are such subtle labels put on one's place in society. I'm half-Italian, so I don't feel typically English. I welcome any escape from the English way of doing things."

That attitude held true through the lengthy filming of *The Buccaneers* with a cast in which American actors played all the American parts.

"I welcomed the approach of the American style of acting," she recalls. "They're ready to throw things around a bit and try new things."

The only hints of friction, she says, came at the end of long, grueling days when the American actors often tried to help resolve problems with certain scenes by chipping in their own ideas.

"I could tell the American attachment to democracy was a little bit disconcerting on an English set, where there's a more rigid, traditional hierarchy," she says.

Her favorite scene was the one in which Laura slips into bed with young Annabelle,

before she marries the Duke of Trevenick, and they read poetry together.

"That's where we really start to establish a close, warm, fun relationship," says Lunghi. "We realize we have a similar level of romanticism. That's when our spirits recognize each other. One is the younger version of the other."

Lunghi also enjoyed her flirtatious scenes with Michael Kitchen's wealthy widower, a courtly womanizer who tries to sweep Laura off her feet without being too crass about it.

"Michael is the kind of actor who doesn't like to rehearse or prepare too much," she says. "That worked for me because that's the kind of man Laura was dealing with—an Englishman who doesn't give up much. She's having to do the emotional work trying to open him up, making allowances for his natural reserve and restraint, which women often have to do in this country."

Adding to the joy of playing a great role in a handsome production was the location filming in some of England's most opulent country estates, which Lunghi describes as "like stepping into a painting." She didn't even mind lacing herself into the tight corsets Laura wears because "they're a sort of symbol of the repression of women, like foot-binding in ancient China."

Lunghi feels she's now at a stage in her career where the roles are more complex and meaningful. "I've always had fabulous roles that suited me for the phase of life I was going through," she says. "But now I'm being offered much more profound roles like Laura Testvalley—women with depth, wisdom, and a past."

Acting Credits

Theater credits include: *Arcadia, The Three Sisters, The Caucasian Chalk Circle, Holiday, As You Like It,* and *Twelfth Night.*

Television credits include: *The Buccaneers, The Canterville Ghost, The Manageress, Strangers and Brothers, Kean, Praying Mantis, Ellis Island,* and *Edward and Mrs. Simpson.*

Film credits include: *Mary Shelley's Frankenstein, Jack and Sarah, To Kill a Priest, The Mission, King David,* and *Excalibur.*

Other Players

MASTERPIECE THEATRE can be considered a very large repertory company of actors who have begun their careers, made their careers, or advanced their careers here. Some of these actors may not be readily associated with Masterpiece Theatre, others may be unrecognizable in well-disguised roles. As in any repertory company, friendships have been forged, marriages made, and professional relationships established among the many players of this distinguished group.

Helen Mirren's acclaimed portrayal of Jane Tennison in *Prime Suspect* made the leap from Mystery! to Masterpiece Theatre during the 25th-anniversary season, but this was not Mirren's first (or even her second) appearance on Masterpiece Theatre: She was seen in *Cousin Bette* during the second season, and more recently in *Where Angels Fear to Tread* ... Her antagonistic colleague on *Prime Suspect*, **Tom Bell**, played a pair of patriarchs in *Sons and Lovers* and *The Cinder Path* ... **Stuart Wilson**, introduced to the *Prime Suspect* series as a psychologist and love interest for Jane Tennison when the show moved to Masterpiece Theatre, made a splash in his brief but memorable role as Silius, purportedly the handsomest man in Rome in *I, Claudius*, and continued to ply his wily way with the ladies as Vronsky in *Anna Karenina* and Major Jimmy Clark, the smarmy seducer of Sarah Layton in *The Jewel in the Crown* ...

Legendary film and theater actor **Sir Laurence Olivier**, well remembered by public television audiences as Lord Marchmain in *Brideshead Revisited* (for which he won an Emmy Award for Supporting Actor), was seen as Harry Burrard in the adaptation of J. P. Priestley's *Lost Empires* ... **Anthony Andrews**, who played Olivier's wayward son Sebastian in *Brideshead*,

led the daring forces of *Danger UXB* and, as Lord Stockbridge, was lucky enough to marry the lovely Georgina toward the conclusion of *Upstairs, Downstairs* ... Lady Olivier, better known as **Joan Plowright**, is a veteran of Masterpiece Theatre productions *The Dressmaker*, *And a Nightingale Sang*, and *All for Love*. While she and *All for Love* co-star **Alec McCowen** were researching their waiter and waitress roles at a Manchester hotel, they were stopped repeatedly by patrons—not for autographs, but for more coffee or clean towels! ...

The Six Wives of Henry VIII star **Keith Michell** was discovered in his native Australia by Olivier, who brought him to Britain and the Old Vic company; Michell's first London stage role was as another king, Charles II ... **Elvi Hale**, who portrayed Anne of Cleves, Henry VIII's third wife, was also discovered by Olivier, who rescued Hale from her secretarial job in the BBC music department ... **Patrick Troughton**, featured in *Henry VIII* as the Duke of Norfolk and in another political role as Clement Attlee in *Edward and Mrs. Simpson*, is perhaps best known to international television audiences as one of the portrayers of science fiction hero *Dr. Who* ...

Alan Rickman and **Nigel Hawthorne**, each of whom has made two appearances on Masterpiece Theatre, have both gone on to worldwide acclaim in such feature film productions as, respectively, *Die Hard* and *The Madness of King George* ... **Sharon Mughan**, who portrayed one of the English settlers on a Kenyan coffee plantation in *The Flame Trees of Thika* (and one of the lead figures in *By the Sword Divided*), has achieved widespread recognition as the star of a popular series of television commercials for—that's right—coffee ... The late **Ralph Bates**, bad guy George Warleggan in *Poldark*, was in fact descended from a true-life hero: He was the great-grandnephew of Louis Pasteur ... It may sound like **Christopher Cazanove**, who played the dashing Charlie Tyrrell on *The Duchess of Duke Street*, should be descended from famed lover Casanova; he isn't, but there is some renown attached to the family name. In New York the small city of Casenovia is named for a distant ancestor …

The producers of *Tom Brown's Schooldays* interviewed nearly 300 young actors for the title role and then decided to go for the "real thing," turning their attention to students, and finding their Tom Brown—young **Anthony Murphy** … As part of her preparation to play the passionate *Thérèse Raquin*, **Kate Nelligan**, who envisioned her character as lush and voluptuous, willingly put on 15 pounds (in part by eating six avocados a day!) …

The late **Georgia Brown**, whose real name was Lillian Klot, got her stage name from a song she was to sing one night early in her career; the announcer drew a blank and introduced her as "Sweet Georgia Brown"—and the name stuck. While well-known for her portraits of social activists on Masterpiece Theatre—as Marie Lloyd in *The Edwardians*, who helped organize British music hall artists into a union, and suffragette Annie Kenney in *Shoulder to Shoulder* (which she co-created)—Brown achieved her greatest fame (and a Broadway Tony award) for her portrayal of the victimized Nancy in the musical *Oliver!* … Another of *The Edwardians* cast, **Anthony Hopkins**, played David Lloyd George in that series and in the feature film *Young Winston* and also was seen as Edmund Kean in *Kean* and as Gwyn Thomas in *Selected Exits*. Hopkins' penchant for historical figures is apparent in his Emmy Award–winning portrayals of Adolf Hitler and Bruno Hauptmann (and his starring role in Oliver Stone's film about Richard Nixon)—but he won his Academy Award as the fictional (but no less monstrous) figure of Hannibal Lecter in *The Silence of the Lambs* …

Nicola Pagett followed in Vivien Leigh's shoes by starring as *Anna Karenina*, whom Leigh had portrayed in a 1948 feature film; Pagett, who trained at the Royal Academy of Dramatic Arts, appeared with the legendary actress in Ms. Leigh's last stage play, *La Contessa* … **Eric Porter** followed up his role as cuckolded Soames in the celebrated *The Forsyte Saga* with the equally betrayed Karenin in *Anna Karenina*. The esteemed actor, who died in May 1995, also appeared as Count Bronowski in *The Jewel in the Crown*—but there he wasn't even in the running for any female attention …

Patricia Hodge, who, as Lady Diana Cooper in *Edward and Mrs. Simpson* played the good friend of the famous couple, introduced Nigel Nicolson to producers at the BBC and convinced him to sell the dramatic rights to his memoir of his parents' unconventional marriage, *Portrait of a Marriage* … **David Haig** and **Janet McTeer**'s performances in *Portrait of a Marriage* marked the third time they appeared as a married couple, having previously performed together in a Royal Shakespeare Company production and also in Shakespeare's *A Midsummer Night's Dream*. **Cathryn Harrison**, McTeer's scandalous love interest in *Portrait of a Marriage*, is the granddaughter of famed actor Sir Rex Harrison; she followed her characterization of Violet Keppel by playing another unconventional role, that of a brothel madam in *Clarissa* …

When **Francesca Annis** and **Denis Lill** portrayed illicit lovers in *Madame Bovary* they were shown in bed together; not so when the two were reunited as another pair of trysters in *Lillie*: Lill was the Prince of Wales, and the royal affair was handled more decorously, showing the couple only before or after bedtime … Both *A Town Like Alice* and *The Shiralee* featured Australian leading man **Bryan Brown**—and both had earlier been produced as feature films starring the late Peter Finch …

At the same time **Derek Jacobi** was seen on American television stuttering through his lines in *I, Claudius*, he was starring in *Hamlet* at London's Old Vic, imploring his fellow players to "speak the speech trippingly on the tongue." Hamlet had also been Jacobi's first male role while attending an all-boys grammar school as a youth; prior to that he had been seen as Anne Boleyn and Lady Macbeth (wouldn't Grandma Livia be proud!). Jacobi received three awards in Britain for his portrayal of Claudius: BAFTA (British Academy of Film and Television Arts), Variety Club, and Broadcasting Press Guild ... **Sian Phillips** won two awards, from BAFTA and the Royal Television Society, for her portrayal of the fiendish Livia in *I, Claudius;* her characterization was so vivid that some felt the program should be retitled *The Godmother* ...

Two-time Academy Award–winning actress **Glenda Jackson** won a matching pair of Emmy Awards for her portrayal of *Elizabeth R.* Jackson reprised her role of Elizabeth in the feature film *Mary, Queen of Scots*, and later on Masterpiece Theatre she was seen as an espionage colleague of George Smiley's in *A Murder of Quality*—but Jackson gave up portraying powerful women for the real thing: in 1992 she was elected a Member of Parliament; having played Elizabeth I, she sits in the House of Commons while Elizabeth II sits on the throne. But Jackson has not entirely given up performing, recently doing books-on-tape recitals of Jane Austen's *Persuasion* and *Pride and Prejudice* ...

Elizabeth Garvie made her television debut as Elizabeth Bennet in *Pride and Prejudice*, and she returned to Masterpiece Theatre as Nancy in *The Good Soldier* ... **Denholm Elliott**, acclaimed as John Jarndyce in *Bleak House*, Salter in *Scoop*, and George Smiley in *A Murder of Quality*, was expelled after one term from England's Royal Academy of Dramatic Arts because, according to Elliott, his instructors decided he had no talent

whatsoever! Elliott proved them very wrong by going on to a distinguished stage, screen, and television career before his death in 1992 ...

Academy Award–winner **Emma Thompson** wrote the first all-woman revue at Cambridge University in 1981, and accomplished something else extraordinary before completing her degree: She introduced **Stephen Fry** to **Hugh Laurie**. The three co-wrote and appeared together in the *Cambridge Footlights Revue* (of which Laurie was president and producer) and later also appeared together in a British television comedy series, *Alfresco*. Fry and Laurie's television program, *A Bit of Fry and Laurie*, aired in the U.S. on cable television, and the two have also appeared together in the comedy program *Blackadder*. The on-camera camaraderie apparent between the two in *Jeeves and Wooster* carries on in real life as well: Fry introduced Laurie to his future wife, was best man at Laurie's wedding, and is godfather to his son ... When still-single Emma Thompson and **Kenneth Branagh** played a married couple in *Fortunes of War*, they each told interviewers they were too busy and content as solo players to have an interest in marriage, but their fortunes changed quickly and the two have been dubbed Britain's prime acting couple ... Their *Fortunes of War* co-stars, **Charles Kay** and **Ronald Pickup**, appeared together years before in an all-male production of *As You Like It*—with Kay as Cecilia, and Pickup assaying the role of Rosalind. Kay was also seen on Masterpiece Theatre in *To Serve Them All My Days*, and Pickup in *A Murder of Quality* and *The Rector's Wife* ...

Samantha Bond of *The Ginger Tree* starred on London's West End as Beatrice to Kenneth Branagh's Benedick in Shakespeare's *Much Ado About Nothing;* in the Masterpiece Theatre presentation, however, Emma Thompson played Branagh's amour. The *Much Ado*–Masterpiece Theatre connection took a new twist when **Jean**

Marsh, the unforgettable Rose in *Upstairs, Downstairs*, made her Broadway debut in a production of the play directed by **Sir John Gielgud**, who won a Best Actor Emmy for his portrayal of Haverford Downs in *Summer's Lease* … **John Mortimer**, who wrote *Summer's Lease*, had worked with several of the program's actors before, Gielgud on *Brideshead Revisited*, **Annette Crosbie** on *Paradise Postponed*, and **Rosemary Leach** on Mystery!'s *Rumpole of the Bailey* …

Nearly everyone knows that in addition to starring as Rose, **Jean Marsh** was also one of the creators of *Upstairs, Downstairs*. What might be less well known is that co-creator **Eileen Atkins** starred as Virginia Woolf in Masterpiece Theatre's presentation of *A Room of One's Own* (which premiered on London's West End) and as Gertrude Morel in *Sons and Lovers* … It would surprise most to learn that **Gordon Jackson**, the unflappable Hudson from *Upstairs, Downstairs* and conventional solicitor Noel Strachan in *A Town Like Alice*, worried chronically about learning his lines for each part. The much-loved character actor lamented that he hadn't "gotten the girl" but once in nearly 30 years of steady acting work—but he did a good job of it that time: the lady he landed in *Floodtide* was Rona Anderson, who soon became Mrs. Gordon Jackson …

When **David Rintoul** needed to do research for his role in *Doctor Finlay* he didn't have to go far: His father, Dr. Leslie Wilson, was a World War II major in the Royal Army Medical Corps, just like Rintoul's television character … **Julia Ormond** has made a striking impact with film audiences as the beautiful romantic heroine in such feature films as *Legends of the Fall* and *First Knight*, quite a contrast to the role she played as a desperate drug addict in *Traffik* … Although she portrayed an Olympic swimmer in *Traffik*, **Lindsay Duncan** did not know how to swim and a double was used for most swimming sequences; Duncan also appeared in *On Approval* and is

remembered as well as one of the mistresses of Mystery!'s *Reilly: Ace of Spies* …

She's Been Away was the last film made by **Dame Peggy Ashcroft** before her death at age 83; the production gave her the opportunity to be reunited with two of her co-stars from *The Jewel in the Crown*, **Geraldine James** and **Rachel Kempson**. James had already reappeared with *Jewel* co-star **Tim Pigott-Smith** in *I Remember Nelson* …

Martin Chuzzlewit marked the first time two veteran Academy Award–winning actors worked together: **John Mills** (who won as Best Supporting Actor for *Ryan's Daughter* in 1971) and **Paul Scofield** (who was honored with a Best Actor Oscar in 1966 for his performance as Sir Thomas More in *A Man for All Seasons*) … While Scofield played dual roles as old Martin Chuzzlewit and his younger brother Anthony, **Philip Franks** did double Dickens duty as selfless Tom Pinch in *Martin Chuzzlewit* (for which he had his head shaved every day for the five months of production) and as Richard Carstone in *Bleak House* … **Keith Allen**, who starred as the cruel and scheming and murderous Jonas Chuzzlewit, and as seedy journalist Thompson in *A Very British Coup*, started his performing career as a stand-up comic …

Rufus Sewell, one of a new pack of British heartthrobs, seemed aptly cast as romantic Will Ladislaw in *Middlemarch;* Sewell attended London's Central School of Speech and Drama just two years ahead of *Middlemarch* co-star **Juliet Aubrey**, whose pre-acting life included a college degree in archeology … **Mira Sorvino** may have played a somewhat empty-headed American heiress in *The Buccaneers,* but her résumé lists a degree from Harvard in Chinese studies; she's also the daughter of actor Paul Sorvino … **Jenny Agutter** must have felt right at home in the posh settings in *The Buccaneers;* her husband, hotelier Johan Tham, purchased Cliveden, formerly the home of the 2nd Duke of Buckingham and Nancy Astor, and turned it into a highly-rated hotel (where Agutter has been known to host monthly soirées) … While training for his role as the latest James Bond, perhaps **Pierce Brosnan** prepared in part by looking back on his portrayal of millionaire playboy Robert Gould Shaw in *Nancy Astor.*

THE MASTERPIECE THEATRE FAMILY TREE

Husband and wife **John Alderton** and **Pauline Collins** appeared together in *Upstairs, Downstairs,* leaving the program when their characters, opportunistic chauffeur Watkins and saucy, ambitious maid Sarah, got married … The wry and ironic narrator in *The Golden Bowl,* **Cyril Cusack**, might well have given daughter **Sinead Cusack** advice on how her character in *Notorious Woman* should handle her on-again, off-again romance with (not-yet husband) **Jeremy Irons** … **Donald Pleasence** and his daughter **Angela Pleasence** appeared together in *Barchester Chronicles;* on her own Angela was featured as Catherine Howard, fifth of *The Six Wives of Henry VIII* and the ill-fated Molly in *Silas Marner* … In *Winston Churchill—The Wilderness Years,* **Sam Wanamaker** played Jewish statesman Bernard Baruch; in *The Countess Alice,* his daughter, **Zoe Wanamaker**, played the daughter of a World War II–era German countess …

In another piece of father-daughter co-casting, **Karen Dotrice** appeared as Maria Beadnell, the first great love of *Dickens of London,* which starred her father, **Roy Dotrice**, as the novelist—but the young Dickens who wooed Maria was portrayed by Gene Foad. Karen also appeared as Lily in the final season of *Upstairs, Downstairs* … As Edward VII, **Lockwood West** was a "Guest of

Honour" in *Upstairs, Downstairs;* his son **Timothy West** was of a very different allegiance as Russian Porfiry Petrovich in *Crime and Punishment* … **Daniel Massey** and his sister **Anna Massey** appeared on opposite sides of the adultery coin: Daniel as the philandering Prince Amerigo in *The Golden Bowl,* and Anna as the betrayed Lady Nelson in *I Remember Nelson* … **Peter Firth** hung out at *Northanger Abbey* and involved himself in *Country Matters,* while brother **Colin Firth** wandered through *Lost Empires* … When **James Fox** starred as Anthony Blount in *A Question of Attribution,* he was featured opposite Queen Elizabeth II (the first time a sitting monarch was ever dramatically depicted, by the way)—the niece of Edward VIII, who had been portrayed by his brother **Edward Fox** in *Edward and Mrs. Simpson* … **John Mills** was featured in adaptations of two classic novels, *A Tale of Two Cities* and *Martin Chuzzlewit,* and daughter **Hayley Mills** was seen in Elspeth Huxley's autobiographical *The Flame Trees of Thika* …

Although **Christopher Cazonove** was one of the regular stars of *The Duchess of Duke Street,* when his wife **Angharad Rees** (of *Poldark* fame) was featured in one episode they did not appear together … The formidable Redgrave clan has been represented across three generations: **Rachel Kempson** in *Country Matters, Love for Lydia, The Jewel in the Crown,* and *She's Been Away;* son **Corin Redgrave** in *The Gambler;* daughter **Lynn Redgrave** in *Vienna 1900* and *Calling the Shots,* which also featured Lynn's daughter **Kelly Clark** (as her daughter in the program); and Corin's daughter **Jemma Redgrave** in *The Real Charlotte* … When **Emma Thompson** appeared as Marie in *The Blue Boy,* the actress who played Marie's mother was Emma's mother, **Phylidda Law.**

MULTIPLE MASTERPIECE THEATRE ROLES

Over the years, a number of actors have made repeat appearances on Masterpiece Theatre. Those who have been in five or more programs include:

Peggy Ashcroft—*Edward and Mrs. Simpson, The Jewel in the Crown, A Perfect Spy, The Heat of the Day, She's Been Away*

Ian Carmichael—*Clouds of Witness, The Unpleasantness at the Bellona Club, Murder Must Advertise, The Nine Tailors, Five Red Herrings, The Great Kandinsky*

Anna Cropper—*Père Goriot, The Moonstone, The Unpleasantness at the Bellona Club, Country Matters, Memento Mori*

Annette Crosbie—*The Six Wives of Henry VIII, The Edwardians, Lillie, Paradise Postponed, Summer's Lease, Doctor Finlay*

Rosalie Crutchley—*The Six Wives of Henry VIII, Elizabeth R, The Possessed, Cold Comfort Farm, Country Matters, Testament of Youth, By the Sword Divided*

James Fox—*Nancy Astor, She's Been Away, A Perfect Hero, A Question of Attribution, The Choir*

Robert Hardy—*Elizabeth R, Upstairs, Downstairs, Winston Churchill—The Wilderness Years, The Death of the Heart, Northanger Abbey, Middlemarch*

Nigel Havers—*Winston Churchill—The Wilderness Years, Nancy Astor, Strangers and Brothers, Star Quality, The Death of the Heart, The Charmer, Sleepers, A Perfect Hero*

Michael Hordern—*Cakes and Ale, The Tale of Beatrix Potter, Paradise Postponed, Scoop, Memento Mori, Middlemarch*

Rachel Kempson—*Elizabeth R, Country Matters, Love for Lydia, The Jewel in the Crown, She's Been Away*

Judy Parfitt—*Shoulder to Shoulder, The Jewel in the Crown, Pride and Prejudice, Star Quality, The Charmer, The Blackheath Poisonings*

Sian Phillips—*How Green Was My Valley, Shoulder to Shoulder, I, Claudius, Crime and Punishment, Winston Churchill—The Wilderness Years*

Emma Thompson—*Fortunes of War, Henry V, Much Ado About Nothing, Impromptu, The Blue Boy*

Dorothy Tutin—*The Six Wives of Henry VIII, Vienna 1900, The Yellow Wallpaper, Body and Soul, The Great Kandinsky*

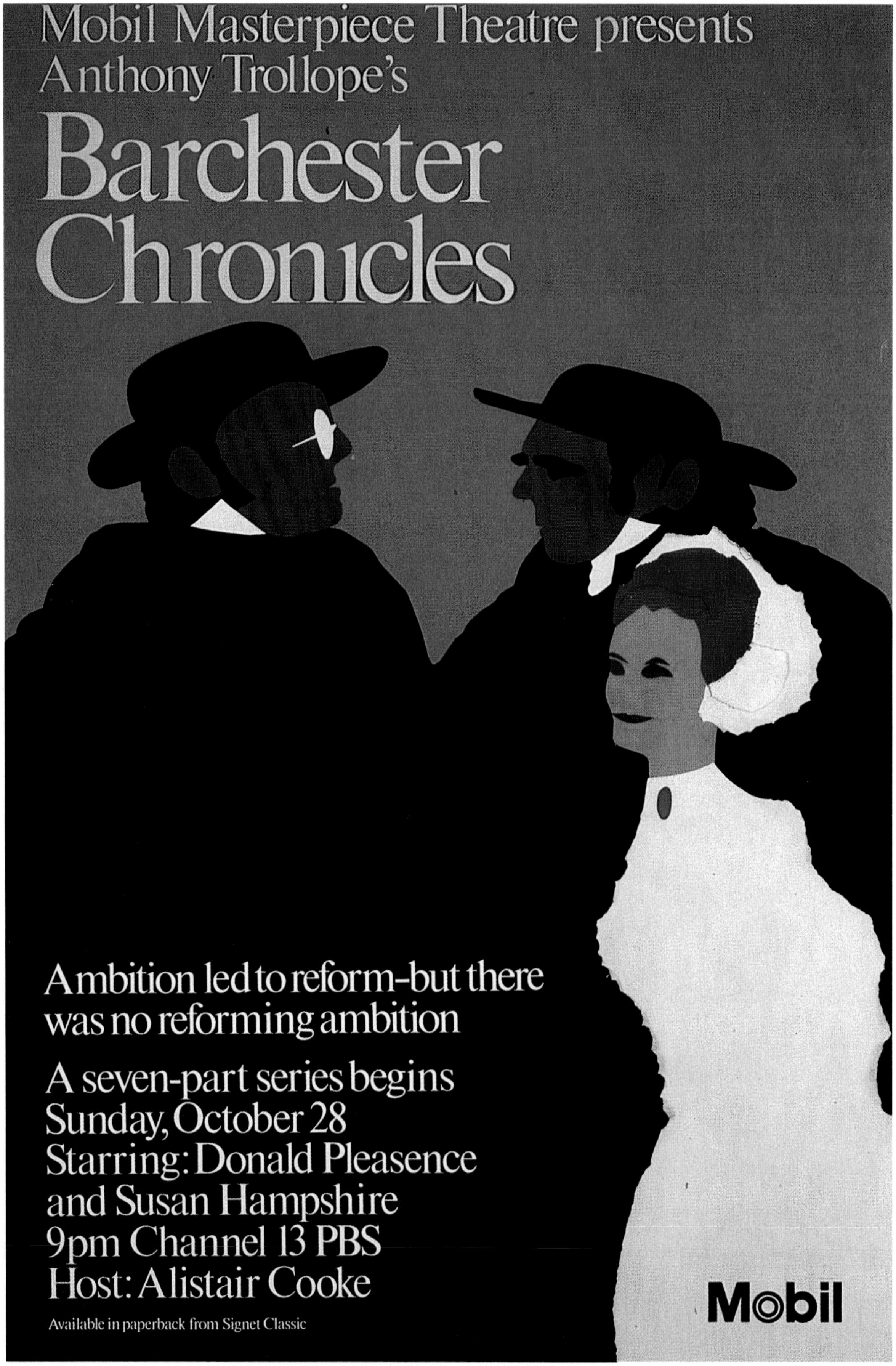
Mobil Masterpiece Theatre presents
Anthony Trollope's
Barchester Chronicles
Ambition led to reform–but there was no reforming ambition
A seven-part series begins
Sunday, October 28
Starring: Donald Pleasence and Susan Hampshire
9pm Channel 13 PBS
Host: Alistair Cooke
Available in paperback from Signet Classic
Mobil

Masterpiece Theatre

Quiz

Scoring

90–100 correct answers

Clearly you're devoted to Masterpiece Theatre body and soul; you deserve the jewel in the crown

80–89 correct answers

Pretty sharpe; you're head and shoulder (to shoulder) above the rest

70–79 correct answers

Not quite heaven on earth, but clearly you had the best intentions

Less than 70 correct answers

Bet you thought it would be a piece of cake

Questions

1. How many of Charles Dickens' novels have been adapted for Masterpiece Theatre?

   a. 3   b. 6   c. 9

   Bonus question: Name the novels.

2. Which Masterpiece Theatre series is based on the life and loves of novelist Vita Sackville-West?

3. Sean Bean, who portrays the honorable romantic hero in the *Sharpe* series (and plays the dishonorable rake in *Clarissa)*, is perhaps best known to American audiences as the villain of what popular action film?

   a. *Die Hard*
   b. *True Lies*
   c. *Patriot Games*

   Bonus question: What other Masterpiece Theatre player also appears in the film?

4. In *I, Claudius,* whom does Livia not kill?

   a. her husband
   b. her son
   c. her grandson

5. What does the "UXB" in *Danger UXB* stand for?

6. What is Middlemarch?

   a. an estate
   b. an aristocratic family
   c. a town in northern England

7. Which non-royal British family is the subject of two Masterpiece Theatre series?

8. Who plays the title role in *The Mayor of Casterbridge?*

   a. Alan Bates
   b. Jeremy Irons
   c. Richard Harris

9. Which Masterpiece Theatre heroine is not portrayed by Susan Hampshire?

   a. Becky Sharp
   b. Elizabeth Bennet
   c. Sarah Churchill

   Bonus question: Susan Hampshire won an Emmy Award for each role she played. True or False?

10. In *Upstairs, Downstairs,* what is Mr. Hudson's first name?

    a. Charles
    b. Ernest
    c. Angus

    Bonus question: What is Rose's last name?

11. In which other Masterpiece Theatre production is David Rintoul, star of *Doctor Finlay,* also featured?

12. Who wrote the Lord Peter Wimsey mystery novels?

   a. P. D. James
   b. Dorothy L. Sayers
   c. Ruth Rendell

13. The life story of writer George Sand has been dramatized for Masterpiece Theatre. True or False?

14. Which of the following are based on a true story?

   a. *The Flame Trees of Thika*
   b. *Testament of Youth*
   c. *Christabel*
   d. *The Last Place on Earth*

15. *Day After the Fair* is based on which story by Thomas Hardy?

16. In *The Jewel in the Crown,* whose ill-fated love affair provokes much of the subsequent plot?

   a. Sarah Layton and Ronald Merrick
   b. Daphne Manners and Hari Kumar
   c. Barbie Batchelor and Guy Perron

17. Who is Louisa's great love in *The Duchess of Duke Street?*

   a. Charlie Tyrrell
   b. Mr. Starr
   c. Major Smith-Barton

18. Which Victorian novelist is purportedly the model for the character Edward Driffield in *Cakes and Ale?*

19. Nicola Pagett, who plays Elizabeth Bellamy in *Upstairs, Downstairs,* also plays the title role in

   a. *Thérèse Raquin*
   b. *Madame Bovary*
   c. *Anna Karenina*
Bonus question: In which other Masterpiece Theatre production does she also appear?

20. *Love in a Cold Climate* is loosely based on writer Nancy Mitford's own life. True or False?

21. Which actress plays the same historical character in both *The Six Wives of Henry VIII* and *Elizabeth R?*

22. In *The Golden Bowl,* what happens to the bowl?

23. Which Masterpiece Theatre character is played by Nigel Havers?

   a. Roy Calvert
   b. Bobbie Shaw
   c. Hugh Fleming
Bonus question: Name the programs in which each character is featured.

24. John Mortimer adapted the teleplay *Paradise Postponed* from his novel of the same name. True or False?

25. *Sons and Lovers* is set in Nottingham, *Poldark* in Cornwall, and *How Green Was My Valley* in South Wales. What do these three series have in common?

26. Which of the following characters portrayed by Francesca Annis is not based on a real person?

   a. Kitty O'Shea
   b. Emma Bovary
   c. Lillie Langtry

27. What was the first non-British program to air on Masterpiece Theatre?

Bonus question: What was the first non-English language presentation?

28. What becomes of the rector in *The Rector's Wife?*

   a. He gets a promotion.
   b. He leaves his wife.
   c. He dies.

29. Who portrays Oscar Wilde in *Lillie?*

30. What is the name of Lord Peter Wimsey's valet?

   a. Bunter
   b. Bailey
   c. Bridges

31. Which male performer has appeared in the most Masterpiece Theatre productions?

Bonus question: Name the programs.

32. In a classic episode of *Upstairs, Downstairs,* fact meets fiction when the Bellamy family is visited by

   a. King Edward VII
   b. Lillie Langtry
   c. Randolph Churchill

33. Name the Masterpiece Theatre presentations in which married actors Kenneth Branagh and Emma Thompson appear together.

Bonus question: In which other Masterpiece Theatre programs has Emma Thompson appeared?

34. In *Titmuss Regained,* Kristin Scott Thomas portrays the widow of an Oxford don and the love interest of Leslie Titmuss. What kind of character does she play in *Body and Soul?*

a. a doctor
b. a model
c. a nun

35. *After the War* takes place after which war?

36. The lead character in *To Serve Them All My Days* is dedicated to what profession?

a. veterinary medicine
b. waiting tables
c. teaching

37. With whom does David Copperfield live happily ever after?

a. Dora
b. Betsey Trotwood
c. Agnes Wickfield

38. Match the program and the century in which it is set.

a. *By the Sword Divided*   f. 16th
b. *Elizabeth R*   g. 17th
c. *The Real Charlotte*   h. 18th
d. *The Cinder Path*   i. 19th
e. *Poldark*   j. 20th

39. In *Goodbye, Mr. Chips,* what is the revered schoolmaster's last name?

40. *The Edwardians* is based on Vita Sackville-West's novel of the same name. True or False?

41. What juvenile performer is featured prominently in two Masterpiece Theatre presentations?

42. Nancy Astor was the first woman to

a. fly a plane across the English Channel
b. become a physician in Great Britain
c. have a seat in the British Parliament

43. The game being played for very high stakes in *The Gambler* is

a. gin rummy
b. roulette
c. baccarat

44. Which actress portrays a Queen (Mary), a Cousin (Bette), and Claudius' mother (Antonia)?

45. Which political figure has not been the subject of a Masterpiece Theatre program?

a. Lloyd George
b. Disraeli
c. Neville Chamberlain
d. Charles Parnell

46. *Flickers* is about the development of electricity in Great Britain. True or False?

47. Name the four characters who succumb to Lydia in *Love for Lydia.*

Bonus question: Name the Academy Award–winning actor who portrayed one of Lydia's suitors.

48. In *Our Mutual Friend,* John Rokesmith is revealed to be

a. the heir to the Harmon fortune
b. Mr. Boffin's illegitimate son
c. the killer of John Harmon

49. *Shoulder to Shoulder* chronicles what political struggle?

50. At the end of *Martin Chuzzlewit,* Jonas Chuzzlewit is reconciled with his uncle Martin. True or False?

51. What mother, daughter, and granddaughters have performed on Masterpiece Theatre?

52. What happens to Dr. Niel in *Doctor Finlay?*

a. He loses his medical license.
b. He moves to Glasgow.
c. He takes over Finlay's medical practice.

53. Barchester is the name of the protagonist in *Barchester Chronicles.* True or False?

54. What happens to Mattie Storin at the end of *House of Cards?*

a. She kills Francis Urquhart.
b. Francis Urquhart kills her.
c. She becomes a member of Parliament.

55. Who is Helen in *Traffik?*

    a. a drug smuggler's wife
    b. Jack Lithgow's drug-addicted daughter
    c. a DEA agent

56. Academy Award–winning actor Ben Kingsley plays the title role in *Kean.* True or False?

57. The family in *The Bretts* is involved in

    a. the theater
    b. the military
    c. politics

58. Under what circumstances do the lead characters in *A Town Like Alice* meet?

59. Where is *A Foreign Field* set?

60. What famed literary spy uncovers a killer in *A Murder of Quality?*

61. What 1960s rock-and-roller appears in *By the Sword Divided?*

62. Match the actor with his title role.

a. Robin Ellis	f. *Disraeli*
b. Ben Kingsley	g. *Adam Bede*
c. Roy Dotrice	h. *Silas Marner*
d. Ian McShane	i. *Poldark*
e. Iain Glen	j. *Dickens of London*

63. Match the actress with her title role.

a. Glenda Jackson	f. *Thérèse Raquin*
b. Lisa Harrow	g. *Elizabeth R*
c. Kate Nelligan	h. *Clarissa*
d. Saskia Wickham	i. *Christabel*
e. Elizabeth Hurley	j. *Nancy Astor*

64. What is the name of the title character of *The Last of the Mohicans?*

    a. Magua
    b. Chingachgook
    c. Hawkeye

65. On whose short stories is *Star Quality* based?

66. How many Masterpiece Theatre presentations are based on the works of A. J. Cronin?

67. In *The Moonstone,* what kind of object is the moonstone?

    a. a souvenir of the first landing on the moon
    b. a gypsy's talisman
    c. a diamond

68. Who plays the title role in *The Dressmaker?*

69. In how many Masterpiece Theatre programs has Winston Churchill appeared as a character?

    Bonus question: Name the programs and the actors who have portrayed Churchill.

70. Which of these Jane Austen novels has not been presented on Masterpiece Theatre?

    a. *Emma*
    b. *Pride and Prejudice*
    c. *Northanger Abbey*

71. What famed British writer, known for his very original teleplays, wrote the script for *Christabel?*

72. *The Dressmaker, And the Nightingale Sang, The Death of the Heart,* and *The Heat of the Day* all take place in England during World War II. True or False?

73. What is the nickname for the troop of soldiers led by Sharpe?

74. *The Best Intentions* is based on Ingmar Bergman's own life. True or False?

75. What is used to kill pesky weeds (and people) in *Dandelion Dead?*

76. What surprising action does Becky Sharp take at the end of *Vanity Fair?*

77. Which character does James Fox play in *A Perfect Hero?*

    a. Tim Holland
    b. Julian Masters
    c. Angus Meikle
    Bonus question: What is the character's profession?

78. Match the couples in *Pride and Prejudice.*

a. Lydia Bennet	e. Mr. Bingley
b. Charlotte Lucas	f. Mr. Collins
c. Jane Bennet	g. Mr. Darcy
d. Elizabeth Bennet	h. Mr. Wickham

79. *Sunset Song* is set in what country?

80. George Eliot's novel *The Mill on the Floss* has been produced for Masterpiece Theatre. True or False?

81. Who is Philip Quarles?

82. Who torments young Tom in *Tom Brown's Schooldays?*

    a. Gerald Flashman
    b. Dr. Arnold
    c. Ned East

83. What is the ultimate fate of Thérèse Raquin?

84. What is the name of the family whose saga is dramatized in *How Green Was My Valley?*

    a. Miller
    b. Morton
    c. Morgan

85. How many roles does Roy Dotrice play in *Dickens of London?*

86. How many Lord Peter Wimsey mysteries have been presented on Masterpiece Theatre?

87. *Glory Enough for All* is about the discovery of

    a. the Shroud of Turin
    b. a dinosaur skeleton
    c. insulin

88. John Hurt dies in both of his Masterpiece Theatre appearances. True or False?

    Bonus question: Which other performer has a role in both of those productions?

89. In *Testament of Youth,* why does Vera Brittain cut short her studies at Oxford?

90. Do the title characters of *Edward and Mrs. Simpson* marry while Edward is king?

91. What former child star plays a leading adult role in *The Flame Trees of Thika?*

92. Which autobiographical novel by D. H. Lawrence has been adapted for Masterpiece Theatre?

    a. *The Rainbow*
    b. *Sons and Lovers*
    c. *Women in Love*

93. *Jeeves and Wooster* is based on a comedy routine Stephen Fry and Hugh Laurie developed while they were students at Cambridge. True or False?

94. What is the goal of the figures in *The Last Place on Earth?*

    Bonus question: Who succeeds?

95. Who is revealed as Esther's mother in *Bleak House?*

    a. Ada Clare
    b. Lady Dedlock
    c. Miss Barbary

96. What happens to the son in *Sorrell and Son?*

97. Annette Crosbie portrays housekeeper Janet MacPherson in *Summer's Lease.* True or False?

    Bonus question: In what other Masterpiece Theatre programs has she appeared?

98. Who portrays the title role in the Masterpiece Theatre production of Ibsen's *Hedda Gabler?*

    a. Fiona Shaw
    b. Juliet Stevenson
    c. Diana Rigg

99. *Precious Bane* is about

    a. the Prince of Wales' ambivalence about ascending to the throne
    b. a greedy 19th-century farmer
    c. a famous kidnapping case

100. Who is the composer of the theme music for Masterpiece Theatre?

Answers

1. b.
Bonus question: *Our Mutual Friend, David Copperfield, A Tale of Two Cities, Bleak House, Hard Times, Martin Chuzzlewit.*

2. *Portrait of a Marriage.*

3. c.
Bonus question: James Fox.

4. b.

5. Unexploded bomb.

6. c.

7. The Churchills.

8. a.

9. b.
Bonus question: True.

10. c.

Bonus question: Buck.

11. He plays Mr. Darcy in *Pride and Prejudice*.

12. b.

13. True. George Sand (real name Aurore Dupin) is profiled in *Notorious Woman* and is also featured in *Impromptu*.

14. a, b, c, and d.

15. "On the Western Circuit."

16. b.

17. a.

18. Thomas Hardy.

19. c.

Bonus question: Scoop.

20. True. The character of Uncle Matthew is based on Mitford's father, the second Baron Redesdale.

21. Rosalie Crutchley (as Catherine Parr).

22. It is smashed by Fanny Assingham.

23. a, b, and c.

Bonus question: *Strangers and Brothers, Nancy Astor, A Perfect Hero*.

24. False. *Paradise Postponed* was originally conceived for television, and Mortimer concurrently wrote the novel of the same name.

25. Each tells the story of a family involved in mining.

26. b.

27. *A Town Like Alice,* which was produced in Australia.

Bonus question: *The Best Intentions,* by filmmaker Ingmar Bergman, which is in Swedish.

28. c.

29. Peter Egan.

30. a.

31. Nigel Havers, in 8 programs.

Bonus question: *Winston Churchill—The Wilderness Years, Nancy Astor, Strangers and Brothers, Star Quality, The Death of the Heart, The Charmer, Sleepers, A Perfect Hero.* He also appeared in one episode of the final season of *Upstairs, Downstairs*.

32. a.

33. *Fortunes of War, Henry V, Much Ado About Nothing.*

Bonus question: *Impromptu, The Blue Boy.*

34. c.

35. World War II.

36. c.

37. c.

38. a-g, b-f, c-i, d-j, e-h.

39. Chipping.

40. False. *The Edwardians* is based on the real-life stories of four individuals during the early 1900s, not on Sackville-West's novel. (*All Passion Spent* is based on a novel by Sackville-West.)

41. Holly Aird, in *The Flame Trees of Thika* and *The Tale of Beatrix Potter*.

42. c.

43. b.

44. Margaret Tyzack.

45. c.

46. False. *Flickers* is about the early years of the motion picture industry.

47. Edward Richardson, Alex Sanderson, Tom Holland, Blackie Johnson.

Bonus question: Jeremy Irons.

48. a.

49. The fight for women's suffrage in Great Britain.

50. False. At the end of *Martin Chuzzlewit,* Jonas Chuzzlewit is dead by his own hand; however, young Martin Chuzzlewit is reconciled with his grandfather, for whom he is named.

51. Rachel Kempson (*The Jewel in the Crown, Love for Lydia, She's Been Away*); Lynn Redgrave (*Vienna 1900, Calling the Shots*); Corin's daughter Jemma Redgrave (*The Real Charlotte*); Lynn's daughter Kelly Clark (*Calling the Shots*).

52. b.

53. False. Barchester is the city in which the story is set.

54. b.

55. a.

56. False. The role is played by Academy Award–winning actor Anthony Hopkins. (Kingsley performed a one-man stage show about Edmund Kean in London's West End and on Broadway in New York.)

57. a.

58. They meet while they are held as prisoners of war by the Japanese during World War II.

59. Normandy, France.

60. George Smiley.

61. Jeremy Clyde (of Chad and Jeremy) as King Charles I.

62. a-i, b-h, c-j, d-f, e-g.

63. a-g, b-j, c-f, d-h, e-i.

64. b.

65. Noel Coward.

66. 2, *The Citadel* and *Doctor Finlay.*

67. c.

68. Joan Plowright.

69. 3.
Bonus question: *Edward and Mrs. Simpson* (Wensley Pithey); *Winston Churchill— The Wilderness Years* (Robert Hardy); *Lord Mountbatten–The Last Viceroy* (Malcolm Terris).

70. a.

71. Dennis Potter.

72. False. *The Death of the Heart* takes place in the late 1930s, just before the war began.

73. "The chosen men."

74. False. It is based on the lives of his parents in the early years of their marriage, before he was born.

75. Arsenic.

76. She performs perhaps the first unselfish act of her life, bringing about the happy union of Amelia Osborne and Captain Dobbin.

77. c.
Bonus question: Meikle is a plastic surgeon.

78. a-h, b-f, c-e, d-g.

79. Scotland.

80. False. Three of her other novels have been presented on Masterpiece Theatre: *Silas Marner, Adam Bede,* and *Middlemarch.*

81. Quarles is the writer-protagonist of *Point Counterpoint.*

82. a.

83. She and her lover commit suicide.

84. c.

85. 3: Charles Dickens, his father John Dickens, and Daniel Quilp, a character in *The Old Curiosity Shop.*

86. 5: *Clouds of Witness, The Unpleasantness at the Bellona Club, Murder Must Advertise, The Nine Tailors, Five Red Herrings.*

87. c.

88. False. He dies as Caligula in *I, Claudius,* but as Raskolnikov in *Crime and Punishment* he is banished to Siberia.
Bonus question: Sian Phillips.

89. To become a nurse during World War I.

90. No; Wallis Simpson's divorce did not become final until May 1937, after Edward had abdicated the throne.

91. Hayley Mills.

92. b.

93. False. The series is based on the stories of P. G. Wodehouse (but Fry and Laurie did meet while undergraduates at Cambridge).

94. To be the first to reach the South Pole.
Bonus question: Roald Amundsen, of Norway

95. b.

96. He becomes a successful surgeon.

97. False. She portrays Janet MacPherson in *Doctor Finlay* and in *Summer's Lease* she is Connie Tapscott.
Bonus question: *The Six Wives of Henry VIII, The Edwardians, Lillie, Paradise Postponed.*

98. a.

99. b.

100. Jean-Jacques Mouret. The piece is his "Rondeau" from *Symphonies and Fanfares for the King's Supper.*

CONTRIBUTORS

Terrence O'Flaherty is among the best-known television critics in America. During his 36-year association with the *San Francisco Chronicle* he was nominated for a Pulitzer Prize and became the only television critic to be honored with an Emmy. The Terrence O'Flaherty Collection, a unique compilation of more than 75,000 photographs, 300 books, and many boxes of program materials (including lots on Masterpiece Theatre), all representing the medium's first four decades, is preserved in UCLA's Theater Arts Library, a major research center for scholars and historians. O'Flaherty is a resident of San Francisco, where he is working on his next book.

Ron Miller is the nationally syndicated television columnist of the *San Jose Mercury News* and Knight Ridder Newspapers. He's a former national president of the Television Critics Association, national judge for the Cableace awards, convention panelist for the National Association of Television Program Executives and other TV industry organizations, and was a 1994 National Headline Award winner for his columns.

Karen Sharpe has been an editor and writer for more than 25 years, working for and contributing to a variety of publications and organizations including the National Endowment for the Arts, Jossey-Bass, Peachpit Press, and the *San Francisco Chronicle.* Before becoming project editor at KQED Books (where she seems to have the British beat—the last book she worked on was *Are You Being Served?),* she was publisher of Vanstar Books, a line of computer titles. She lives in Berkeley, California.

Ellen Baskin is a writer living in Santa Monica, California. She has been a creative executive in the motion picture and television industries and is the author of *Filmed Books and Plays* (Ashgate, 1993) and *Serials on British Television* (Ashgate, 1995), from which some of the filmography material for this book was taken.

Support Your Local Public Broadcasting Station!

Every community across America is reached by one of the 346 member stations of the Public Broadcasting Service. These stations provide information, entertainment, and insight for the whole family.

Think about the programs you enjoy and remember most:

Masterpiece Theatre...Mystery!...Nova...Nature...Sesame Street... Ghostwriter...Reading Rainbow...Baseball...The Civil War... MacNeil/Lehrer News Hour...Great Performances... Washington Week in Review ... and so many more.

On your local PBS station, you'll also find fascinating adult education courses, provocative documentaries, great cooking and do-it-yourself programs, and thoughtful local analysis.

Many public television series—like Masterpiece Theatre—are underwritten by generous corporate citizens like Mobil. But more than half of all public television budgets come from individual member support.

For less than the cost of a night at the movies, less than a couple of months of a daily paper, less than a month of your cable TV bill, you can help make possible all the quality programming you enjoy.

Become a member of your public broadcasting station and do your part.

Public Television. You make it happen!